This is the first book to explore the world of the theatre in Russia after Stalin. Through his work at the Moscow Art Theatre, Anatoly Smeliansky is in a key position to analyse contemporary events on the Russian stage and he combines this first-hand knowledge with valuable archival material, some published here for the first time, to tell a fascinating and important story. Smeliansky chronicles developments from 1953 and the rise of a new Soviet theatre, and moves through the next four decades, highlighting the social and political events which shaped Russian drama and performance. The book also focuses on major directors and practitioners, including Yury Lyubimov, Oleg Yefremov and Lev Dodin, and contains a chronology, glossary of names, and informative illustrations.

ANATOLY SMELIANSKY is Associate Head of the Moscow Art Theatre and Professor of the Institute for Advanced Theatre Training at the American Repertory Theatre. He is the author of numerous books and articles on Russian theatre and is editor-in-chief of *The Collected Works of Konstantin Stanislavsky*.

Volumes for Cambridge Studies in Modern Theatre explore the political, social and cultural functions of theatre while also paying careful attention to detailed performance analysis. The focus of the series is on political approaches to the modern theatre with attention also being paid to theatres of earlier periods and their influence on contemporary drama. Topics in the series are chosen to investigate this relationship and include both playwrights (their aims and intentions set against the effects of their work) and process (with emphasis on rehearsal and production methods, the political structure within theatre companies, and their choice of audiences or performance venues). Further topics will include devised theatre agitprop, community theatre, para-theatre and performance art. In all cases the series will be alive to the special cultural and political factors operating in the theatres they examine.

The Russian theatre
after Stalin

Anatoly Smeliansky

translated by
Patrick Miles

PUBLISHED BY THE PRESS SYNDICATE OF THE UNIVERSITY OF CAMBRIDGE
The Pitt Building, Trumpington Street, Cambridge CB2 1RP, United Kingdom

CAMBRIDGE UNIVERSITY PRESS
The Edinburgh Building, Cambridge, CB2 2RU, UK http://www.cup.cam.ac.uk
40 West 20th Street, New York, NY 10011–4211, USA http://www.cup.org
10 Stamford Road, Oakleigh, Melbourne 3166, Australia

First published in English by Cambridge University Press 1999

Printed in the United Kingdom at the University Press, Cambridge

Typeset in 9.25/14 pt Trump Medieval   [GC]

A catalogue record for this book is available from the British Library

ISBN 0521 58235 0 hardback
ISBN 0521 58794 8 paperback

Contents

Contents

Plates

List of plates

All photographs reproduced by courtesy of the Moscow Art Theatre

Foreword

LAURENCE SENELICK
Tufts University

The short-sightedness of politicians is proverbial. When Mikhail Gorbachev injected *glasnost* into official policy, in the hope that a few basic reforms could rejuvenate an arteriosclerotic Soviet Union without the abandonment of Communism, he failed to foresee its long-term effects. He did not conceive that, by loosening traditional information control, he was sowing seeds for the destruction of a system which could not exist without such control. The most forceful grass-roots movement fostered by the new openness was Memorial. Founded in 1987 with the intent of recovering and rehabilitating the names of the millions who perished in Soviet prisons and labour camps, it bent its strenuous efforts to exhume suppressed information of past evil with a purpose that went beyond honouring the dead, however belatedly. Memorial wanted its discovery of the truth to serve as prophylaxis, to prevent such things occurring in the future.

An historian might ask, with Pilate, 'What is truth?' Activists in the Soviet underground during Gorbachev's regime would have no patience with such philosophic hair-splitting. They knew that ever since the Bolshevik seizure of power in 1917, 'truth' – plain facts, the record of everyday events – had been deliberately and regularly suppressed, distorted and perverted. Rewriting the past was a growth industry in the USSR, and historiography often seemed to be the application of factional interests to a scholarly practice. Facility in manipulating facts and disrespect for the document were sometimes carried to improbable extremes. The Soviet past had been so thoroughly refashioned that it had to be recovered before any kind of normal future could be expected. In those occasional cases when the powers-to-be had acknowledged their excesses or the extremes of terror, they had done so in an attempt at damage limitation, to stop up leaks and put a reasonable face on irrational behaviour. Deeply traumatized by torture, show trials, mass deportations, slave labour and countless betrayals, Soviet society was not eager to learn the ugly truth about itself. It preferred to trust the bromides of the Party and idolize its executioners rather than confront reality. Memorial's sense of mission, its moral imperative, required that, once the truth was unearthed, it had to be exhibited to the eyes of fellow Russians, whatever feelings of shame, outrage, denial or shock might ensue. A brow-beaten and often reluctant populace had to be compelled to face unwelcome truths.

In its early attempts at uncovering the facts about repression, Memorial had to rely heavily on oral testimony. Simply gathering the memories of those who had lived through the worst that Soviet life had to offer was itself a political act: at this stage, compiling data was more urgent than analyzing its veracity. Later, as the Soviet Union toppled and fell, corroborative official and archival material surfaced. Memorial established a Scientific Information Centre to process the recently accumulated documentation on repression.

Where does the theatre come into this? As with every other aspect of life in the USSR, the theatre cannot be extricated from political imperatives and influences. Historically, the Russian theatre was always expected to implement the progress of civilization. Even before the nineteenth-century critic Belinsky prescribed a social role for the theatre, it had been tasked to carry out education, uplift and propaganda for Enlightenment ideals in a benighted cultural landscape. This function of the theatre was a deeply held tenet of belief of the pre-revolutionary intelligentsia, and was explicit in the mandate of the Moscow Art Theatre when it was launched in 1898. Stanislavsky's claim that the theatre was a temple assured a middle-class, cultivated public that it would be edified as well as entertained, and that the theatre's aesthetics served to promote social betterment. After the Revolution the vocabulary changed but the aim remained the same: theatre was seen as a tool to train the proletariat in Socialist ideals and to serve a cause larger than itself. Mere amusement was distrusted by the authorities, as was experimentation for experimentation's sake.

Government-imposed restrictions worked hand in glove with self-censorship. If the Russian Revolution recalls Goya's ogreish painting of Saturn devouring his children, we should bear in mind that those children were themselves initially bent on parricidal cannibalism. The artistic far left, spearheaded by Meyerhold and Mayakovsky, called for the extermination of all existing Russian theatres, including the Moscow Art, the Maly and the Aleksandrinsky, as outworn remnants of a disposable past. When, a generation later, Meyerhold and Mayakovsky became themselves disposable, they were set up for annihilation by journalistic denunciations of their irrelevance, their being 'out of step' with the progress to the future. Totalitarianism always wants to begin at point zero, to obliterate memories of its precursors and competitors: sow the fields of Carthage with salt, or ask the subscribers to the *Great Soviet Encyclopedia* to slice out the page about the liquidated secret police chief Beria and replace it with a newly supplied entry on the Bering Straits. Thus, a lavish anniversary volume on Meyerhold's production of *Masquerade* could be published without his name being mentioned anywhere in the abundant text.

It would be a mistake to think that matters altered in any substantial way after Khrushchev's denunciation of Stalin and the short-lived Thaw. Rehabilitation took place off-handedly, to minimalize the original abuse. The English specialist Nick Worrall recalls poring over documents on the rehabilitated Meyerhold in the Moscow archives, totally unaware that a collection of his writings had been published until he saw a man hawking them on an underground platform. Russian historians could still run afoul of the authorities by misreading shifts in the cultural climate. During the Thaw, one scholar decided to print, in a scholarly journal, an acrimonious correspondence between Stanislavsky and Nemirovich-Danchenko, making public an animosity well known to the experts but carefully concealed in the hagiography of the Moscow Art Theatre. He was severely rebuked and his career was blighted for years. Only now are the archives disgorging the materials they had so carefully preserved.

An imperative similar to that of Memorial informs a recent volume of documents and essays of twentieth-century theatre history edited by Vladislav Ivanov. Tellingly, Ivanov calls his garner *Mnemozina* (Mnemosyne) after the goddess of memory and, not coincidentally, mother of the Muses. This is no rhetorical flourish. It proclaims the need to retrieve a mutilated or stifled history in order to establish a basis of truth on which to build a future. 'A new history of the Russian theatre of the past century is irrelevant without the creation of a new documentary, factological basis,' Ivanov writes. 'On this foundation we may be able to build the widest aesthetic conception.'[1] In his mission statement, Ivanov explicitly states his aim of filling in the 'blank spaces' and 'black holes' of the bygone Russian theatre.

He is not alone. Over the past seven years or so, the leading Russian theatre journals, *Theatre, Theatrical Life* and the *Moscow Observer* have devoted a large number of pages to documents and retrospective articles about individuals, plays and theatres whose names had gone unspoken for nearly fifty years. New publishing houses issue memoirs, rehearsal protocols and previously censored materials of all kinds. There is an avid readership for such things. While post-structuralism in the West has the luxury of questioning the objective reality of any statement, Russians, long fed on lies, still endorse Ranke's injunction to historians to find out 'how it actually was'.

The Moscow Art Theatre, the Russian troupe best known in the West, was particularly subject to political makeover once Stalin had determined that it would be the model for all other theatres in the Soviet Union. Its pre-eminent position was poised over a pit: the honours and privileges showered on the theatre were bought at the cost of a slavish endorsement of government policy and the stunting of its artistic development. The Art Theatre's early links with symbolism and art nouveau, Stanislavsky's fascination with yoga and spiritual forces, and similar deviations from socialist realism were obliterated when the theatre was renamed the Gorky Academic Art Theatre in 1932. A theatre whose insignia was the Jugendstil seagull associated with Chekhov was now expected to promulgate the Soviet aesthetic of sugar-coated propaganda, poster-like stances, and 'conflictlessness'.

This metamorphosis has its graphic representation in a photograph: the famous picture of Chekhov reading *The Seagull* to the Art Theatre troupe in 1898. (The event itself was a fiction, since the picture was taken in Yalta in 1899 after the production had opened.) When Meyerhold was arrested in 1938, he became a non-person both in life and in art. His figure disappeared from its prominent place in the foreground, even though he had created the role of Treplev. Adjustments were made to prevent these absences from marring the composition.[2] Soviet proficiency in retouching enabled pictures to lie even more persuasively than words.

Expunging a person's image was a totemic way of expunging that person entirely from MKhAT's record. The company had split during the Civil War, with part of the troupe performing in Europe, first as the Kachalov Group, then as the Prague Group of the Moscow Art Theatre. During the American tour of 1923/4, other actors defected or chose to remain in the United States. Until emigration was made all but impossible in 1929, there was a steady seepage of talent to the West. Some of these individuals, such as Richard Boleslavsky, managed to make successful careers as directors in their adopted countries. Others, chiefly actors, carried on in the commercial theatre and film, but were most significant as teachers: Michael Chekhov, Vera Soloviova, Maria Ouspenskaya, among them. Their fates and fortunes were virtually unknown back home. The historian Inna Solovyova relates that in the card file of the Moscow Art Theatre Archive the dates on which actors failed to return to Russia often stood in as death dates. They went West in both senses.

The actual deaths of Stanislavsky in 1938 and Nemirovich in 1943 and their subsequent canonization by the Soviet establishment laid a spell on the Art Theatre: it became Sleeping Beauty's castle, once the site of glory but now a cobweb-filled wax museum full of moribund dignitaries. The Prince Charming selected to awake Beauty from her artistic doze was Oleg Yefremov. He had been the artistic director of the Sovremennik (Contemporary) Theatre, which during the Thaw had been regarded as the harbinger of spring, the voice of youth and hope. Typically, as the Thaw recongealed, the Sovremennik too fell prey to internecine dissension, freeing Yefremov to accept the position as artistic director of the Moscow Art Theatre. The symbolic nature of this transfer is obvious. Yefremov was moving from what had been a promising nursery of talent and new ideas to a theatrical morgue. His fate there and the work of the theatre itself fibrillated to every change in the political mood, and, even when its productions were lacklustre compared with the brilliant experiments of Tovstonogov, Efros and Lyubimov, MKhAT's peculiar relationship to the Soviet government made every one of its policy decisions fraught with significance. Its position as the flagship of the theatrical armada was particularly burdensome, often preventing it from taking the chances lighter craft could venture.

By the late 1960s and 1970s, Soviet audiences were coming to the theatre to hear 'truths' unavailable in the press or other media. The metaphoric *mise-en-scène*, Aesopic dialogue and actors' asides were avidly sought and caught by an alert public. The gap widened between what was really going on and what was officially acknowledged to be going on: the caustic songs of the *chansonnier* Vladimir Vysotsky, a leading actor at Lyubimov's theatre, went unpublished and unrecorded, yet most of the populace knew them by heart, learning them from *magnitizdat*, boot-leg tape recordings. Ironically, with the introduction of *glasnost* and a relatively liberated press, theatre abruptly lost its special function. It had too many competitors for the role of Prometheus, bringer of light.

The cut-throat capitalism that followed the eventual collapse of the Soviet system also put the Russian theatre in jeopardy. Its new freedom was intoxicating, but at the same time there was a tremendous amount of catching up to do. Not only had Russia been bypassed by major contemporary movements in theatre and drama (Theatre of Cruelty, Theatre of the Absurd, Grotowski and imagistic *mise-en-scène*), it had to rediscover its own lost traditions – the symbolist and decadent drama of the Silver Age, the Leningrad absurdist movement the OBERIU, satires of the New Economic Policy period, and the influential work of those who had fled the country. In the first blush of openness, the repertories of Moscow and St Petersburg became glutted with the long-proscribed plays of Bulgakov and Erdman, which were in turn replaced by the more exotic and remote dramas of Andreyev. Attracted by his hazy mysticism, organizations devoted themselves to reviving the teachings of Michael Chekhov, while others reconstructed the biomechanical exercises of Meyerhold and Eisenstein. There was a gorging on once forbidden fruits, but it was a necessary phase of the reclamation process.

Throughout all these upheavals, Anatoly Smeliansky, serving both as a leading Moscow critic and as the literary manager of the Art Theatre during Yefremov's tenure, was in an ideal position to observe both backstage manoeuvrings and front-of-house responses. His account of the Russian theatre after Stalin is part of the process of recovery and re-evaluation begun by Memorial. This book is not so much a history as a testimony offered by someone who was a close witness to events, even as he had a hand in shaping them.

Smeliansky is adept at shifting focus. Now he is the participant, passionately engaged in tussles with the bureaucracy and arguments with playwrights. Now he is the observer, shrewdly following the career paths of directors and actors, assaying and appraising the value of their work with remarkable objectivity. Always he is the writer, finding the telling simile or vivid adjective to pin the ephemeral experience of the performance in the reader's memory. Never, however, is he uncommitted or disengaged. Smeliansky shares the moral vision of the Russian theatrical tradition. Artistic results are judged primarily by their effect on the human spirit, as it works itself out under the special circumstances of Soviet and post-Soviet life. In some sense, his personal chronicle of the last fifty years of Russian theatre can be read as a Pilgrim's Progress, with no clear end, certainly no Heavenly City, in sight. Smeliansky offers no easy explanations or glib predictions; for he is that rare thing, a theatre critic with a conscience.

Preface

The idea for this book came to me in the summer of 1991, when I was in East Berlin. Several times in the past I had gone up to the Brandenburg Gate from the eastern side and peered over 'there', beyond the Wall. I would recall the extraordinary tales of people who had tried to cross it using home-made gliders or microlights. One could imagine thousands of ways of getting round, flying over, or outwitting the Wall. The only scenario one could not imagine was that one day the Wall would come down.

Now I could stroll freely from East Berlin into West Berlin. By the ruins of the Wall some Turks and gypsies were selling Soviet army belts, medals and officers' hats, plonked unceremoniously on the bare earth. Trade was slow. Evidently Russia was already going out of fashion.

When I saw this flea market I experienced a variety of emotions. First, joy that there had been a happy ending. The fifth act of the tragedy was over and in Pasternak's words 'the survivors have done the washing-up and no one remembers anything'. But this was immediately followed by a much stronger sensation: one of speechless awe. Were these stale props all that remained of a performance that had lasted seven decades? Was the great Utopia, its Gulag, and all the suffering they caused, merely to end up on the rubbish-heap of history? And was this also to be the fate of the art that had been born from it and sealed with the blood of millions?

Sometimes film-makers have to rush out to capture a particular seasonal landscape before it vanishes. This book is about the vanishing landscape of the Soviet theatre, which is fading into oblivion before our eyes. It is not a conventional history of the Russian theatre since Stalin, because it is written by someone who had a stake in the subject and is undoubtedly biased. The 'vanishing landscape' was not someone else's life, it was my own.

For many years I not only wrote books and worked on editions of Stanislavsky, I headed the literary section of the Moscow Art Theatre (MKhAT), which was the showcase theatre of the state. I saw from the inside how the careers of major artists were made and broken and the repertoire chosen. The problem of 'the artist and power', which may now seem utterly academic, was a real one: literally, it was a question of whether theatre in Russia would survive as an art. This is why the resistance that the theatre put up was so strong and the place that it occupied in the country's spiritual life was disproportionately large.

In a way, the theatre's place had been assured it by the very nature of Bolshevik ideology. The revolutionary leaders saw theatre as a kind of spiritual surrogate to replace a suppressed Church. The place where the latter had been was not to be left empty. For decades – right up to the collapse of the Soviet Union – this model of the theatre–church more or less prevailed. Sacrilegious though it was, it proved remarkably resilient. But then it had fallen on well-prepared ground. In Tsarist times, Alexander Herzen had compared the theatre to the parliament Russia did not have. In Soviet Russia the theatre took the place of both the sham parliament and the half-strangled Church. Generations of directors, actors and theatregoers developed a conditioned reflex: they went to the theatre not just to be entertained, but to take communion. The theatre became virtually the only place where people could have free, live contact with one another. Directors and actors became as it were the priests of a theatrical religion. The audience expected a production–sermon that would change their lives. So the phenomenon of the Soviet super-theatre evolved: a theatre powered by the 'energy of self-delusion'.[1]

At the time of the collapse of the USSR there were about 600 state-subsidized theatres, with permanent companies of between 25 and 160 actors. In most towns the theatre was situated next to the regional party headquarters or the 'House of Party Political Enlightenment'. Even topographically, then, the regime emphasized the importance of the theatre as a tool for controlling its 'flock'. The overwhelming majority of theatres obediently performed this function. Some, however, succeeded in modifying it. Oleg Yefremov, Georgy Tovstonogov, Yury Lyubimov and Anatoly Efros, who are the heroes of the first two chapters of this book, not only embodied the main directions that the Russian stage took, they also perpetuated Stanislavsky's idea of a theatre-family that would work together not for five weeks of rehearsals but for many years. This is a vital element of what was understood in Russia by theatre and still is – just.

Theatre in Russia is a shared home and shared activity for life. It presupposes a particular way of going about things, particular aesthetics, and a particular ethical outlook. The title of Stanislavsky's *My Life in Art* sums up one aspect of it. The view in Russia was that there could be no genuine theatre without this lifelong commitment. People in the USSR did not just go to plays and productions, they went to particular theatrical 'homes', to see particular people, who became 'shapers of minds'. This will be one of the themes of this book.

The history of the theatre has never been just the history of plays, but this is particularly so in our case.[2] Plays in Russia had to pass a literary censor and a theatrical censor.[3] This is probably why the swarm of post-Stalinist playwrights produced only a few writers who actually offered new theatrical ideas. The two most gifted – Aleksandr Vampilov and Lyudmila Petrushevskaya – became outcasts; their ideas were not wanted and it was horrendously difficult for their plays to reach the stage.

The main problems raised in the Russian theatre in the second half of the century were raised by *directors*. The best of them saw themselves as inheriting the mantle of the greatest Russian exponents of the director's art. They saw their work as a mission and regarded their predecessors in the art as martyrs who had entrusted them with their unfinished business. The name of one of these martyrs – Vsevolod Meyerhold – could not even be uttered in public until the mid-fifties. He had changed the face of twentieth-century world theatre in many ways, but he had been tortured, executed, and his body flung in a pit. Fresh in people's memories as well was the destruction of the Kamerny Theatre in the late forties, after which its creator Aleksandr Tairov wandered Moscow half-demented looking for posters advertising it. Even Stanislavsky's fate had been tragic. He had died in his bed, but been canonized as a Soviet saint in his own lifetime and killed off that way. For the last four years of his life he never set foot inside his own theatre. Shortly before his death, however, he did something almost unique for the times: he invited Meyerhold, his prodigal son, to work in the Stanislavsky Musical Theatre.

All this history had entered the genes of post-Stalin theatre directors and ensured that their profession enjoyed an exceptionally high status.

In Russia theatrical art is very closely linked to events in the sociopolitical sphere personified by a particular ruler. This book therefore consists of three sections corresponding to the main periods in our recent history: the short Khrushchev 'Thaw', which ended in August 1968 when Soviet tanks rolled into Prague; almost two decades of Brezhnevian stagnation; and the first ten years of freedom unleashed by Gorbachev, for which there is as yet no universally accepted name.

A massive tectonic shift occurred in Russia in the mid-1980s. What collapsed during the August 1991 putsch was not *perestroika* but a whole country shaped over centuries. The ordeal of freedom turned out to be no less painful for our theatre than the ordeal of slavery. Our directors had once again to shoulder the burden of choice. The main figures in this new theatrical period are Anatoly Vasilyev, Lev Dodin, Kama Ginkas, Mark Zakharov and Pyotr Fomenko. They had been educated under the previous theatrical system, but now had to use their art to express a time of troubles. The final chapter suggests that the theatrical 'pulpit' may be about to be engulfed by 'entertainment' and the whole model of the Russian theatre changed. Only time will tell.

Anatoly Smeliansky

Chronology

Political and social events		Theatrical events
1953		
March	Death of Stalin	Akimov's and Diky's
September	Nikita Khrushchev	productions of Saltykov-
	made First Secretary	Shchedrin's *Shadows*
1956		
February	Khrushchev denounces	Ravenskikh's production of
	crimes of the Stalin	Tolstoy's *The Power of*
	regime	*darkness*
September	Hungarian uprising	
	crushed with Soviet	
	tanks	
1957		
	Furore over publication	Tovstonogov's production of
	of *Doctor Zhivago*	*The Idiot*
	in the West	
1958		
December	Andrey Sakharov calls	Efros directs Eduardo de
	for an end to Soviet	Filippo at the Sovremennik
	testing of the hydrogen	
	bomb	
1960		
May	Death of Boris	The Sovremennik performs
	Pasternak	Shvarts's *The Naked King*
	American U-2 spyplane	
	shot down	

Chronology

1961

| April | Gagarin is first man in space | Okhlopkov's production of Euripides' *Medea* |
| August | Berlin Wall built | |

1962

| October | Cuban missile crisis | Tovstonogov's production of *Woe from Wit* |
| November | Solzhenitsyn's *One Day in the Life of Ivan Denisovich* published | |

1964

| October | Khrushchev removed, Brezhnev becomes General Secretary | Lyubimov's production of *The Good Person of Setzuan* |

1966

| February | Trial of the writers Sinyavsky and Daniel | Volchek directs Goncharov's *A Common Story* at the Sovremennik |

1967

| | | Efros's production of *Three Sisters* |

1968

| August | Soviet invasion of Czechoslovakia | Key theatre productions banned |

1969

| | Andrey Amalrik's *Will the Soviet Union Survive Until 1984?* published in the West | |

1970

| April | Centenary of Lenin's birth | Yefremov appointed Artistic Director of the Moscow Art Theatre |
| October | Solzhenitsyn awarded Nobel Prize for Literature | |

1971

| September | Death of Khrushchev | Lyubimov's production of *Hamlet* |

1974		
February	Solzhenitsyn expelled from USSR	
1975		
August	Signature of Final Act of Helsinki Conference	Efros's production of Gogol's *The Marriage*
December	Andrey Sakharov awarded Nobel Peace Prize	Tovstonogov's production of *The Story of a Horse*
1976		Yefremov's production of *Ivanov*
1977	International condemnation of Soviet political use of psychiatry	Lyubimov's production of *The Master and Margarita*
1978		
May	Trial of dissidents monitoring observance of Helsinki Final Act	Vasilyev's production of first version of *Vassa Zheleznova*
1979		
December	USSR invades Afghanistan	Lyubimov's production of *Crime and Punishment*
1980		
January	Sakharov exiled to Gorky	Efros's production *The Road* (*Dead Souls*)
July	Olympic Games held in Moscow	
1982		
November	Death of Brezhnev, Yury Andropov becomes General Secretary	Lyubimov's production of *Boris Godunov* banned
1983		
September	Korean airliner shot down by Soviet fighter over Sakhalin	Lyubimov forced into emigration

Chronology

1984		
February	Death of Andropov, Konstantin Chernenko made General Secretary	Dodin's production of *The Golovlyovs*
1985		
March	Death of Chernenko, Mikhail Gorbachev becomes General Secretary	Zakharov's production of *Three Girls in Blue*
April	Gorbachev declares programme of *perestroika* and *glasnost*	Dodin's production of *Brothers and Sisters*
1986		
April	Sakharov returns from exile Chernobyl power station disaster	Free 'Unions of Theatre-Workers' formed
1987		
October	Party plenum at which Boris Yeltsin criticizes Gorbachev's policies	Death of Efros Splitting of the Moscow Art Theatre Yanovskaya's production of *Heart of a Dog*
1988		
June	Withdrawal of Soviet troops from Afghanistan begins	Lyubimov returns to Russia
1989		
April	Demonstrations suppressed in Tbilisi, nineteen dead	Death of Tovstonogov Lyubimov revives his 1968 production of *Alive*
November	Destruction of the Berlin Wall	
1990		
January	Gorbachev made President of the USSR	Commemoration of the 50th anniversary of Meyerhold's murder

1991		
June	Boris Yeltsin elected President of Russia	Ginkas's production of *We Play 'The Crime'*
August	Attempted *coup d'état* by Communist faction	During the attempted coup, Soviet television broadcasts the whole of *Swan Lake* twice
December	Collapse of USSR, formation of CIS	
1992		
	Yegor Gaydar's government begins privatization	Dodin's production of *The Devils*
1993		
October	Parliament building in Moscow stormed by government troops	Fomenko's production of *More Sinned Against Than Sinning*
1994		
	Solzhenitsyn returns to Russia	Dodin's *Claustrophobia*
1995		
January– December	War in Chechnya	Ginkas's production of *The Execution of the Decembrists*
December	Communists win parliamentary elections	
1996		
	Boris Yeltsin re-elected President	Vasilyev's production of *The Lamentations of Jeremiah*
1997		
	Celebrations for the 850th anniversary of the founding of Moscow	Yefremov's *Three Sisters* Slavyansky Bazar conference

Biographical notes

AKIMOV, Nikolay Pavlovich (1901–1968). Director and designer. His 1932 production of *Hamlet* was condemned as 'Formalist' and he was in constant trouble with the authorities. He made a comeback to the Leningrad Comedy Theatre in 1955.

BALIYEV, Nikita Fyodorovich (1877–1936). Moscow Art Theatre actor. Created 'The Bat' cabaret theatre in 1908, with which he emigrated to America.

BARKHIN, Sergey Mikhaylovich (b. 1938). Architect and designer. Worked with Yefremov and Lyubimov. Since 1995, chief designer at the Bolshoi Theatre.

BASILASHVILI, Oleg Valerianovich (b. 1934). Actor. Graduated from the Moscow Art Theatre studio school, but since 1959 has worked at the Bolshoy Drama Theatre.

BOROVSKY, David Lvovich (b. 1934). Designer. Became chief designer at the Taganka in 1969; also designed for Efros, Kheyfets, Yefremov. Left the Taganka in 1984, but returned with Lyubimov in 1988.

BRONEVOY, Leonid Sergeyevich (b. 1928). Actor. Played major roles in Efros's productions; joined the Lenkom in the mid-eighties.

CHURIKOVA, Inna Mikhaylovna (b. 1938). Actress. Graduated from Shchepkin drama school. Performed at the Young People's Theatre from 1965 to 1968. Since 1973, star actress of the Lenkom.

DEMIDOVA, Alla Sergeyevna (b. 1936). Actress. Joined the Taganka Theatre in 1964. Lead actress in Shakespeare, Chekhov, and Sophocles.

DODIN, Lev Abramovich (b. 1944). Director. Graduated from the Leningrad Theatre Institute in 1965 under Boris Zon. Started as director at the Leningrad Young People's Theatre. From 1981 to 1984 directed at the Bolshoy Drama Theatre and the Moscow Art Theatre. In 1982 became artistic director of the Maly Drama Theatre, Leningrad, with which has staged *Brothers and Sisters*, *Lord of the Flies*, *The Devils*, *Claustrophobia*, *Play Without a Title*, and others. The company has toured worldwide since 1985.

DORONINA, Tatyana Vasilyevna (b. 1933). Actress and director. Graduated from the Moscow Art Theatre studio-school 1956. Acted leads for Tovstonogov from 1959 to 1966, worked in the Moscow Art Theatre from 1967 to 1971, and at the Mayakovsky Theatre from 1971 to 1983, then returned to the Moscow Art Theatre and led the anti-Yefremov group. Since 1987, artistic director of the Gorky Moscow Art Theatre.

DUROV, Lev Konstantinovich (b. 1931). Actor and director. Worked continuously with Efros at the Lenkom and the Malaya Bronnaya.

EFROS, Anatoly Vasilyevich [Isayevich] (1925–87). Director. Born in Kharkov, graduated as director from the State Institute of Theatre Art in 1950. At first worked in Ryazan, and in 1954 joined the Central Children's Theatre, Moscow. In 1964 was appointed artistic director of the Moscow Lenkom. Sacked in 1967 and moved with his actors to the Malaya Bronnaya Theatre. Also directed for the Moscow Art Theatre, for television and abroad. Taught at the State Institute of Theatre Art. In 1984 was appointed to replace Lyubimov at the Taganka.

FOKIN, Valery Vladimirovich (b. 1946). Director. Graduated from the Shchukin theatre school. First production, *Valentin and Valentina* at the Sovremennik, 1971. Stayed at the Sovremennik until 1985, where he directed Vampilov and Edward Albee. In 1986 he became artistic director of the Yermolova Theatre, Moscow. After this theatre split, he became head of the newly recreated Meyerhold Centre.

FOMENKO, Pyotr Naumovich (b. 1932). Director and teacher. Graduated from State Institute of Theatre Art. Directed *Tarelkins's Death* at the Mayakovsky Theatre in 1966, but the production was banned. Became peripatetic director. Directed Chekhov, Dostoyevsky, Molière, Arbuzov and others at the Leningrad Comedy Theatre from 1972 to 1981. In 1993 he directed *More Sinned Against Than Sinning* at the Vakhtangov Theatre, Moscow, and opened his own theatre, called Fomenko's Workshop.

GAFT, Valentin Iosifovich (b. 1935). Actor. Worked at the Lenkom and Malaya Bronnaya. Since 1969 has been lead actor at the Sovremennik.

GALIN, Aleksandr Mikhaylovich (b. 1947). Playwright, director and actor. Plays staged by the Sovremennik, the Lenkom, the Moscow Art Theatre and Dodin's Maly Drama Theatre (*Stars in the Morning Sky*, 1986).

GELMAN, Aleksandr Isaakovich (b. 1933). Playwright. *A Meeting of the Party Committee* was successfully staged by the Moscow Art Theatre in 1975 and led to a long collaboration. A founder of Soviet 'production drama'.

GINKAS, Kama Mironovich (b. 1941). Director. Born at Kaunas (Lithuania), graduated from the Leningrad Theatre Institute under Tovstonogov. Began at the Krasnoyarsk Young People's Theatre and directed Mark Twain in the Siberian Far East. In the 1970s he worked in Leningrad, where he staged his own play, *Pushkin and Nathalie*. From 1980s onwards he has directed in Moscow at the Mossoviet Theatre, Moscow Art Theatre and Young People's Theatre. He has worked and taught for several years in Finland.

GONCHAROV, Andrey Aleksandrovich (b. 1918). Director. Graduated from State Institute of Theatre Art in 1941. Began at the Moscow Satire Theatre, moved in 1951 to the Yermolova Theatre, and since 1967 has been artistic director of the Mayakovsky Theatre. He has staged Arthur Miller, Edvard Radzinsky, Ostrovsky, Bulgakov, Babel and Tennessee Williams.

GORIN, Grigory Izrailevich (b. 1940). Popular comic playwright. House dramatist at the Moscow Satire Theatre and the Lenkom.

GUBENKO, Nikolay Nikolayevich (b. 1941). Actor. Worked at the Taganka, obtained return of Lyubimov in 1988, and became Minister of Culture in 1989. In 1993 he headed the breakaway part of the Taganka.

GVOZDITSKY, Viktor Vasilyevich (b. 1952). Actor. Worked in Young People's Theatre Riga under Adolf Shapiro. Since 1995 he has been a member of the Moscow Art Theatre. Played Tuzenbakh in the 1997 Yefremov production of *Three Sisters*.

ILINSKY, Igor Vladimirovich (1901–87). Actor and director. Worked with Komisarjevsky and Meyerhold (*A Buffo Mystery Play*, 1921; *The Magnanimous Cuckold*, 1922). Joined the Maly in 1938, where he played in Gogol, Griboyedov, Dostoyevsky and Ostrovsky. Supreme acting achievement, Akim in *The Power of Darkness* (1956).

KALYAGIN, Aleksandr Aleksandrovich (b. 1942). Actor. Graduated from the Shchukin drama school in 1965. Classical actor, but played roles from Charley's Aunt to Lenin. Worked with Lyubimov, Yefremov, Efros and Ginkas. In 1993 he founded his own theatre, Et Caetera.

KARACHENTSEV, Nikolay Nikolayevich (b. 1944). Actor. Graduated from Moscow Art Theatre studio school; joined the Lenkom in 1967. A lead actor in Zakharov's productions.

KEDROV, Mikhail Nikolayevich (1893–1972). Actor, director and teacher. Joined Moscow Art Theatre in 1924. Worked with Stanislavsky in latter's 'Opera and Drama Studio'; headed it from 1938 to 1948. From late 1940s to 1970, one of the heads of the Moscow Art Theatre. Responsible for repertoire combining classics with political ephemera.

KHEYFETS, Leonid Yefimovich (b. 1934). Director. Graduated from State Institute of Theatre Art under Popov and Knebel. Moved to the Maly in 1971, where he directed Hauptmann, Arbuzov, Gorky and others. Artistic director from 1989 to 1995 of the Central Theatre of the Soviet Army, where in 1989 he staged Merezhkovsky's *Paul I* for first time since the Revolution.

KNEBEL, Mariya Osipovna (1898–1985). Actress, director, teacher. Trained in Michael Chekhov's studio in 1918. Member of Moscow Art Theatre's company from 1924 to 1950. Moved to Central Children's Theatre in 1950 and became its artistic director in 1955. Taught at State Institute of Theatre Art from 1948. Author of books on Stanislavsky's methods.

KOCHERGIN, Eduard Stepanovich (b. 1937). Designer. Has worked mainly in Petersburg. His long collaboration with Tovstonogov began in 1966 with Steinbeck's *Of Mice and Men*. Co-designed Bolshoy Drama Theatre's *Story of a Horse* (1975). Also designed for Dodin at the Moscow Art Theatre and the Maly Drama Theatre. Designs in Petersburg tradition of Golovin and Dmitriyev.

KOPELYAN, Yefim Zakharovich (1912–75). Actor. Graduated from the Bolshoy Drama Theatre studio in 1935 and played leads in Tovstonogov's productions.

KOZAKOV, Mikhail Mikhaylovich (b. 1934). Actor. Worked with Yefremov at the Sovremennik and Efros at the Malaya Bronnaya.

LAVROV, Kirill Yuryevich (b. 1925). Actor. Joined the Bolshoy Drama Theatre in 1955 and played important roles in Tovstonogov's productions. Took over as head of the theatre after Tovstonogov's death.

LAVROVA, Tatyana Yevgenyevna (b. 1938). Actress. Graduated from the Moscow Art Theatre studio school 1959. Worked at the Sovremennik from 1961 to 1978. Since 1978 has acted for the Moscow Art Theatre in Chekhov, Gelman and Petrushevskaya.

LEBEDEV, Yevgeny Alekseyevich (1917–97). Actor. Shared the Stalin Prize 1949 with Tovstonogov for the latter's production of *From a Spark*, in which Lebedev played the young Stalin. From 1956, played completely different roles at the Bolshoy Drama Theatre, culminating in Strider (*The Story of a Horse*, 1975).

LEONOV, Yevgeny Pavlovich (1926–94). Actor. Worked at the Stanislavsky and Mayakovsky Theatres; joined the Lenkom in 1972.

LEVENTAL, Valery Yakovlevich (b. 1938). Designer. Worked at the Bolshoy Drama Theatre. Designed all Chekhov productions at Moscow Art Theatre from 1980 to 1997.

LUSPEKAYEV, Pavel Borisovich (1927–70). Actor. Graduated from the Shchepkin drama school in 1950 and worked in the Bolshoy Drama Theatre from 1959 to 1964.

LVOV-ANOKHIN, Boris Aleksandrovich (b. 1926). Director and critic. Graduated from the Leningrad Theatre Institute in 1950. Became artistic director of the Stanislavsky Theatre, where he staged Volodin and other new playwrights. Was sacked at the end of the 'Thaw'. Directed at the Moscow Maly; since 1989 has headed the Moscow New Drama Theatre.

LYUBIMOV, Yury Petrovich (b. 1917). Actor and director. Started as an actor at the Vakhtangov Theatre, Moscow. Acted in NKVD ensemble. Began teaching at the Shchukin drama school and in 1963 staged *The Good Person of Setzuan* with students. With these young actors he created the Taganka Theatre. Deprived of Soviet citizenship in 1984, whilst abroad. Returned to Russia in 1988. In 1994 the Taganka split; Lyubimov heads one half.

MIRONOV, Andrey Aleksandrovich (1941–87). Actor and director. Graduated from the Shchukin drama school and joined the Moscow Satire Theatre in 1962, for which played lead roles.

OKHLOPKOV, Nikolay Pavlovich (1900–67). Actor and director. Trained in 1923 in Meyerhold's experimental studio. In 1930 became head of the Realistic Theatre, for which staged monumental productions on revolutionary subjects. This theatre was liquidated in the campaign against 'Formalism'. From 1938 he acted and directed in the Vakhtangov Theatre.

PETRUSHEVSKAYA, Lyudmila Stefanovna (b. 1938). Playwright. Graduate of Moscow University. Her first play, *Music Lessons* (1973), was banned by the censor but was very popular with amateur groups. *Three Girls in Blue* was banned in Zakharov's production. All her plays have been staged and published since *glasnost*.

PLUCHEK, Valentin Nikolayevich (b. 1905). Director. Began as an actor with Meyerhold. Founded his own studio with Arbuzov in 1940. Artistic director of the Satire Theatre from 1957.

POPOV, Aleksey Dmitriyevich (1892–1961). Director and teacher. From 1912 worked with the Moscow Art Theatre, during the Revolution ran his own provincial theatre, and in 1925 directed Bulgakov's *Zoya's Apartment* at Moscow's Vakhtangov Theatre. Set up and ran the Central Theatre of the Red Army from 1938 to 1958.

POPOV, Andrey Alekseyevich (1918–83). Actor. Son of preceding. Moscow Art Theatre actor from 1974 to 1983, artistic director of the Stanislavsky Theatre, Moscow, 1977 to 1979.

RADZINSKY, Edvard Stanislavovich (b. 1936). Playwright. First plays staged by Efros and Tovstonogov. Now writes non-fiction.

RAVENSKIKH, Boris Ivanovich (1914–80). Director. Worked as assistant to Meyerhold. Directed at the Stanislavsky Drama Theatre, Moscow, from 1941 to 1950; at the Maly Theatre from 1952 to 1960 and from 1970 to 1976.

ROSHCHIN, Mikhail Mikhaylovich (b. 1933). Playwright. Worked on the magazine *Novy mir*; began writing plays in late 1950s. First plays banned for Aesopic references. Worked with Sovremennik (*Valentin and Valentina*, 1971), then with Yefremov at the Moscow Art Theatre.

ROZOV, Viktor Sergeyevich (b. 1913). Playwright. Started as an actor. First success with *Her Friends* (1949). From the 1960s to the 1980s his middle-brow plays were immensely popular throughout the USSR. Also adapted Goncharov's *A Common Story* (Sovremennik, 1966).

ROZOVSKY, Mark Grigoryevich (b. 1937). Playwright and director. In 1958 he set up the Moscow University student theatre company 'Our House', which was axed by the authorities in 1969. Author of *Story of a Horse*, which he co-directed with Tovstonogov. Has directed for the Moscow Art Theatre .

SHAPIRO, Adolf Yakovlevich (b. 1939). Director. Appointed head of the Young People's Theatre in Riga in 1961 and made it into one of the USSR's best repertory companies. Staged Brecht, Vampilov, Kleist and Brodsky. The theatre was closed after Latvian independence and Shapiro now lives and works in Moscow.

SHATROV (real name MARSHAK), Mikhail Filippovich (b. 1932). Playwright. Famous for historical plays *The Bolsheviks* (1973), *Dictatorship of Conscience* (1986), and many others. His plays lost popularity in the nineties and he became a businessman.

SHEYNTSIS, Oleg Aronovich (b. 1949). Designer. Graduated from the Moscow Art Theatre studio school, then became principal designer at the Lenkom. Has worked with Mark Zakharov on all his major productions.

SHVARTS, Yevgeny Lvovich (1897–1958). Playwright. Wrote classic stage versions of fairytales, which for many years were banned from performance. The best interpreter of his plays was Nikolay Akimov at the Leningrad Comedy Theatre, which first staged *The Dragon*. Yefremov directed his *The Naked King* in 1959.

SLAVINA, Zinaida Anatolyevna (b. 1941). Actress. Graduated from the Shchukin theatre school and has worked with Lyubimov since the foundation of the Taganka Theatre in 1964.

SMEKHOV, Veniamin Borisovich (b. 1940). Actor. Graduated from the Shchukin theatre school. Has played leads in Lyubimov's productions and written memoirs of the Taganka Theatre (1986).

SMOKTUNOVSKY, Innokenty Mikhaylovich (1925–94). Actor. From a peasant family, served in the army, trained at the theatre studio in Krasnoyarsk, and acted for ten years in the provinces. Prince Myshkin in Tovstonogov's production of *The Idiot* (1957). After 1960 he was mainly a film actor. In 1976 he joined the Moscow Art Theatre, for whom played Ivanov (1976), Dorn in *The Seagull* (1980), Serebryakov in *Uncle Vanya* (1985), Louis XIV in *Molière* (1988), and others.

TABAKOV, Oleg Pavlovich (b. 1935). Actor. Graduated from the Moscow Art Theatre studio school and became the leading actor in Yefremov's Sovremennik. Moved to the Moscow Art Theatre in 1983. In 1987 he became Rector of the Moscow Art Theatre studio school and founded his own studio theatre.

TOPORKOV, Vasily Osipovich (1889–1970). Actor and teacher. Graduated from Petersburg Imperial Academy in 1909 and joined the Moscow Art Theatre in 1927. Personification of Stanislavsky's 'school'.

TOVSTONOGOV, Georgy Aleksandrovich (1915–89). Director and teacher. Boy actor in the Tbilisi Young People's Theatre. Graduated from the State Institute of Theatre Art under Andrey Lobanov and Aleksey Popov in 1938. Directed at the Griboyedov Russian Theatre, Tbilisi, from 1938 to 1946, then worked in Moscow theatres. In 1950 he was appointed artistic director of the Leningrad Leninsky Komsomol Theatre. From 1956 he was head of the Bolshoy Drama Theatre, Leningrad.

VAMPILOV, Aleksandr Valentinovich (1937–73). Playwright. After graduating from Irkutsk University, worked as a journalist. Main plays *Twenty Minutes with an Angel* (1962), *The Elder Son* (1967), *Duck-Hunting* (1970) and *Last Summer in Chulimsk* (1972). Plays not accepted at the time, but have had great influence since.

VASILYEV, Anatoly Aleksandrovich (b. 1942). Director. Graduated from the State Institute of Theatre Art under Mariya Knebel. Worked with Yefremov at the Moscow Art Theatre in 1974 on *Solo for a Chiming Clock*. Moved to the Stanislavsky Theatre, Moscow, where he staged the first version of Gorky's *Vassa Zheleznova*. In 1985 he directed Slavkin's *Hoopla* at the Taganka. In 1987 he founded his own theatre, the School of Dramatic Art, in Moscow. In 1993 he directed Lermontov's *Masquerade* for the Comédie Française.

VERTINSKAYA, Anastasiya Aleksandrovna (b. 1944). Actress. Worked with Yefremov at the Sovremennik and Moscow Art Theatre .

VIKTYUK, Roman Grigoryevich (b. 1936). Director. After *glasnost* he directed a sensational production of Genet's *The Maids* and in 1991 founded his own theatre in which he staged David Hwang's *M. Butterfly*.

VOLCHEK, Galina Borisovna (b. 1933). Actress and director. Founding member of the Sovremennik, who acted in many Yefremov productions there. Artistic director of the Sovremennik since 1970.

VOLKOV, Nikolay Nikolayevich (b. 1934). Actor. Played leads for Efros at the Malaya Bronnaya. Since 1984 at the Mayakovsky Theatre.

VOLODIN, Aleksandr Moiseyevich (b. 1919). Playwright. Made his début in the 'Thaw' with *Factory Girl* (1956). Plays staged by Lvov-Anokhin, Efros, Yefremov and Tovstonogov throughout the fifties and sixties.

VYSOTSKY, Vladimir Semyonovich (1938–80). Actor, poet and singer. Graduated from the Moscow Art Theatre studio school. Played leads in *The Life of Galileo*, *Hamlet*, *Crime and Punishment* and other productions by Lyubimov at the Taganka Theatre.

YAKOVLEVA, Olga Mikhaylovna (b. 1941). Actress. Graduated from the Shchukin drama school in 1962. Acted leads in almost all of Efros's productions after 1964 at the Lenkom, the Malaya Bronnaya and the Taganka. Abandoned stage for many years after Efros's death.

YANKOVSKY, Oleg Ivanovich (b. 1944). Actor. Began at the Saratov Drama Theatre and moved to the Lenkom in 1973. Played Hamlet in Panfilov's production there, and Trigorin in Zakharov's *Seagull*.

YANOVSKAYA, Genriyetta Naumovna (b. 1940). Director. Graduated from the Leningrad Institute of Theatre, Music and Film in 1967. Worked with her husband Kama Ginkas in Krasnoyarsk, then founded the Blue Bridge Theatre in Leningrad. In Moscow worked at the Mossoviet and the Mayakovsky. Appointed head of the Young People's Theatre in 1986, for which directed *Heart of a Dog* (1986), *Goodbye, America!!!* (1989), *Ivanov and Others* (1993), and Ostrovsky's *The Storm* (1997).

YEFREMOV, Oleg Nikolayevich (b. 1927). Actor and director. Graduated from the Moscow Art Theatre studio school in 1949 and began teaching there. Acted at the Central Children's Theatre, Moscow. In 1956 he founded the group 'Studio of Young Actors', which later became the Sovremennik Theatre. Appointed artistic director of the Moscow Art Theatre in 1970. At his suggestion, in 1987 the theatre split into two companies; Yefremov became head of the 'Chekhov Moscow Art Theatre'.

YERYOMIN, Yury Ivanovich (b. 1944). Actor and director. Started as a director in Rostov-on-Don. Artistic director of the Central Theatre of the Soviet Army from 1981 to 1987. Since 1987 has been artistic director of the Pushkin Theatre.

YEVSTIGNEYEV, Yevgeny Aleksandrovich (1926–92). Actor. Key performer in Yefremov's Sovremennik, and moved with him to the Moscow Art Theatre.

YURSKY, Sergey Yuryevich (b. 1935). Actor and director. Worked with Tovstonogov at the Bolshoy Drama Theatre from 1957 to 1979, since when he has been at the Mossoviet Theatre, Moscow. Main roles at the Bolshoy Drama Theatre were Chatsky, Tuzenbakh, Osip (*The Government Inspector*) and Molière in *The Cabal of Hypocrites*. Has directed Ionesco, Ostrovsky and others.

ZAKHAROV, Mark Anatolyevich (b. 1933). Actor and director. Graduated as an actor from the State Institute of Theatre Art. Began as a director in the Moscow University theatre. In 1965 joined the Satire Theatre in Moscow, but had his early productions banned. In 1969 he directed Fadeyev's *The Rout* at the Mayakovsky Theatre in Moscow. In 1974 appointed artistic director of the Moscow Lenkom, where he created the Soviet musical. Since 1991 he has been a member of the Presidential Council. He teaches at the State Institute of Theatre Art.

ZAVADSKY, Yury Aleksandrovich (1894–1977). Actor and director. Played Prince Calaf in Vakhtangov's 1922 *Turandot*. At the Moscow Art Theatre from 1924 to 1936. Was head of the Mossoviet Theatre from 1940.

ZORIN, Leonid Genrikhovich (b. 1924). Playwright. Versatile author constantly plagued by censorship. Wrote the famous two-hander *Warsaw Melody*, which was staged at the Vakhtangov Theatre in 1967.

Translator's note

Russian words have been transliterated in this book using a simplified form of the BGN/PCGN system. Where there are already accepted English versions of names (e.g. Alexander Herzen, Michael Chekhov, Mikhail Gorbachev) these have been used.

Some essentially Russian concepts (e.g. *balagan*, *narod*, *tusovka*) have been kept in transliterated form, but approximate English equivalents are given in brackets the first time they occur in the text, and occasionally afterwards as reminders.

The following abbreviations occur throughout:

BDT	Bolshoy Drama Theatre (Leningrad/Petersburg)
GITIS	State Institute of Theatre Art (Moscow)
Lenkom	Leninsky Komsomol Theatre (Moscow)
MDT	Maly Drama Theatre (Leningrad/Petersburg)
MKhAT	Moscow Art Theatre since 1920
MKhT	Moscow Art Theatre until 1919, and occasionally for the post-1986 Chekhov MKhAT
MTDK	Moscow Theatre of Drama and Comedy
TYuZ	Young People's Theatre (Moscow or Leningrad).

The Moscow Maly Theatre is referred to as 'the Maly Theatre' or 'the Maly'. 'The Bolshoi Theatre' or 'Bolshoi' refers to the Moscow theatre usually known in English by that spelling.

For consultation concerning the translation I am extremely grateful to Arkady Ostrovsky and, of course, Anatoly Smeliansky.

Patrick Miles

1 The Thaw (1953–1968)

The mythology of socialist realism

Before introducing the main heroes of this book, I shall attempt to sketch the historical background preceding the death of Stalin. This is necessary in order to understand the minds of the first theatrical generation that grew out of the scorched earth Stalin left behind him.

In 1953 Nikolay Akimov staged Saltykov-Shchedrin's play *Shadows* in Leningrad. It had been written almost a hundred years earlier, on the eve of the abolition of serfdom in Russia. As a prologue to the action, a silhouette of the famous equestrian statue of Nicholas I was projected onto a drape on-stage. Occasionally the drape rippled and the 'shadow' of the autocrat seemed to come to life. It was clamouring for new sacrifices. It suggested to the critic Naum Berkovsky that the late Boss was still 'tending his sheep' even from another world.[1]

Josef Stalin died on 5 March 1953, but his shadow continued to strike fear into the country for many years to come. The Stalinist cancer was not just a political phenomenon, it was an aesthetic one. It is crucial to understand the deeper intentions behind Stalinist painting, theatre, literature and architecture. Why, for instance, was it so important to erect the seven famous skyscrapers above Moscow after the Second World War? Seen from the ground, they suggested the watch-towers of the Gulag. But from the Boss's vantage point they were supposed to suggest that there was 'one above you all' who saw everything and knew everything that 'you at ground level' could not. From the street, one cannot see that the Theatre of the Soviet Army has been built as a five-pointed star; but from above one can. The idea, then, was that life should not be viewed in such a pedestrian manner, as it might appear to the man in the street or at his trough in a prison camp, but from a 'higher' position. This belief, which was reflected in the phallic architecture of the one Father, Son and Soviet Holy Ghost, found its expression in all the arts, and was called 'socialist realism'.[2]

In Russia today it is fashionable among liberals to claim that socialist realism never existed, any more than 'Soviet literature' did.[3] This is a serious mistake. Socialist realism, which was proclaimed as the heir to world culture, must be studied like any other style that evolved and burned itself out over several decades in the USSR. In the theatre, it was the result of setting in concrete the tradition of Russian realism; its declared enemy was 'formalism', which was to be exterminated at all costs. Gradually a style developed whose main features were rationalism, didacticism, clarity and simplicity. It was everywhere: in the typology of the heroes, the voices of the actors, the sets, and the choreography of the major scenes, which were staged diagonally or front-on depending on the position of the special box in which He might appear at any moment.

Socialist 'royalism', as the sixties dissident Arkady Belinkov called it, used the techniques of naturalism without the nature. Artists went to extraordinary lengths to depict situations, characters and conflicts that never existed. The method was therefore more akin to black magic: things that never were had to be conjured into being by artists meticulously reproducing the void. Aleksandr Laktionov, for instance, one of the most popular socialist realist painters, could paint with extreme fidelity to detail a group portrait entitled *Happy Old Age*, in a country where people were dying of starvation, and the photographic perfection of these well-groomed old people, of a neatly cut lemon and some pretzels, seemed to assure you that the whole of Soviet life was as good as these irresistible details.

Neither the revolution nor life under Soviet power could be mythologized with a cold heart. Very often the leading artists agreed with one part of the great Utopia and attempted to dress it up in biblical clothes. Drawing such exalted parallels was a way of surviving aesthetically, of coming to terms with a blood-soaked reality in which one had to find a hidden purpose. In the 1930s, however, both the 'positive' and the 'negative' use of a Christian gloss on Soviet subjects became dangerous. The new ideology no longer needed biblical sanction. A symbolic break with the past was the blowing up of the Cathedral of Christ the Saviour in Moscow in 1931 (it has now been rebuilt). Its destruction was not only an act of barbarism, it was meant to symbolize the triumph of the new culture.[4] The same thing happened in the other arts. Meyerhold's attempt in 1937, shortly before his own destruction, to dramatize Nikolay Ostrovsky's memoir *How the Steel Was Tempered* as a biblical parable about a 'Red' martyr in the Civil War was firmly rejected by the authorities. Sergey Eisenstein's film *Bezhin Meadow*, which was to deal with the popular theme of Pavlik Morozov, a boy who denounced his 'kulak' family to the new masters and paid for it with his life, also came unstuck. The Soviet propaganda subject was seen through biblical eyes. The boy's murder by bearded, beast-like kulaks was presented by Eisenstein as a tale of sacrifice. The new world was an Isaac-figure that had to be sacrificed to the old. The fact that the film was banned shows what a huge difference there was between the twenties and the thirties. Complex or merely rented biblical imagery that had been commonplace in post-revolutionary art became in the 1930s politically suspect: it obscured and distorted the issue of 'class struggle'.

Some Russian theatre directors attempted to take another course, by adapting their previous techniques to the new political imperatives. Aleksandr Tairov's favourite bas-relief techniques were applied to Soviet plays in order to give the new reality some aesthetic legitimacy. Kulaks and fifth columnists moved along the footlights like figures on Egyptian wall paintings. MKhAT used all its incomparable powers of psychological portrayal to breath life into the class message of Gorky's *Enemies*, to make it humanly convincing. The 75-year-old Nemirovich-Danchenko ensured that this was done with supreme technical skill.

After the Second World War, however, it became impossible to deceive oneself either with mythology or technique. The theatrical 'churches' were turned into bazaars. Yet actually strangling the theatre was not easy. It had experienced all the repressions and aesthetic pogroms of the twenties and thirties – and survived. *Othello* with Ostuzhev at the Maly, or *King Lear* with Mikhoels at the Jewish Theatre, *Romeo and Juliet* with Mariya Babanova, *The Queen of Spades* in Meyerhold's original staging, Nemirovich-Danchenko's *Three Sisters*, or Aleksandr Tairov's *Madame Bovary* at the Kamerny, were pre-war productions which, despite all their links with the new ideology, were major achievements of theatrical art. The methods and techniques they used retained some autonomy – the theatrical language itself held out against the vulgarization and mediocritization going on all around it. But after the war a devastating blow was dealt to culture generally, to the very methods and language of the theatre, to its very roots. Party decrees such as 'On Theatre Repertoire' and 'On the Magazines *Zvezda* and *Leningrad*'; the campaign in the late forties against 'cosmopolitanism', which led to the persecution and murder of Jewish theatre people; and the notorious theory of 'conflictlessness', according to which the only conflict there could be in a Soviet play was between good and better – all these meant that the theatre ceased to exist as an art that fulfilled an inner need and felt a responsibility towards its audiences.

The wave of repression that hit the Soviet theatre after the Second World War was deliberate. Stalin's ideologues set out to destroy any possible spin-off from the victory over Nazism. The proud, independent spirit of the liberators of Europe, their ability to think, and even the ability to enjoy themselves, had to be eradicated immediately. The victor was not allowed for one second to relax, return to his family, or become absorbed in his private life. Consequently, not only major writers like Akhmatova, Zoschenko and Platonov were roughed up in the press, even works of light entertainment came under fire. The operetta *Mam'zelle Nitouche* had opened at the Vakhtangov Theatre in 1944 and been a source of innocent delight, but after the war it was classified as a harmful insect that had to be exterminated.

The sanity of artists was severely tested. My older friends at the Moscow Arts tell me that at rehearsals of Aleksandr Surov's *Green Street*, one of the most untalented pieces of counterfeit staged by MKhAT in 1948, Boris Livanov (a fine actor and a friend of Pasternak) had hardly started rehearsing in the morning before he was showing the director, Mikhail Kedrov, a clock-face drawn on his hand with the hands set at noon, and pronouncing the hallowed words: 'It's time, Misha!' This meant that the café opposite MKhAT was open and they should go straight over there for their alcoholic 'dose'.

The whole of Soviet theatre was drug-dependent. In many of the major houses, especially MKhAT, the drinking reached heroic proportions. It became a way of life. It was not just a social phenomenon, it was an aesthetic one. To take up a life in the theatre and survive in it one had to be in a state of permanent optimism.

It was in just such a state that Mikhail Romanov, a major Russian actor at the Lesya Ukrainka Theatre in Kiev, occasionally took his curtain calls after 'conflictless' performances. He accompanied each bow to the audience with the fairly audible words 'I'm sorry.' This was the only way left for a Russian artist to resist the throttling of his theatre.

Genuine humour that penetrated forbidden areas was as ruthlessly purged as sentimentality. Any sign of life was pounced upon. Inna Solovyova, now an eminent theatre historian, worked at that time in the censorship. She attacked Viktor Rozov because she found his play *Her Friends*, about a blind girl whom everyone tries to help, 'impossibly sentimental'. According to the criteria of 1949, the play should have been banned, but Rozov, who had been a front-line soldier, had suffered shellshock and been wounded, returned her fire with: 'Yes, I am terribly sentimental, and I'm going to carrying on being.'

The oases of theatrical culture that had survived from the twenties and thirties were now virtually swallowed up by the desert of officially approved plays. It was insidious, for instance, to have Chekhov and Surov next to each other in MKhAT's repertoire. The fungus got to everyone; it penetrated to their creative marrow. In 1949 Yury Zavadsky, who had been an unforgettable Prince Calaf in Vakhtangov's *Turandot*, staged Konstantin Simonov's anti-American Cold War pot-boiler *The Russian Question*. Aleksey Popov, who had once shone in Shakespeare productions, perfected the bombastic style of the 'battle drama' on the enormous firing range of a stage at the Theatre of the Red Army. Nikolay Okhlopkov, a disciple of Meyerhold, poured all his mastery into banner-waving shows like *The Young Guard*, which were held up as an example to others.

The outward appearance of productions – their use of space – changed beyond recognition. Whereas in the 1920s there were genuinely original designers who led the world, now there were dreary copyists of an imaginary reality who could only turn out dusty pseudo-realistic box-sets.

The artistic flame, the flame of the old techniques and living speech, was kept alive in various theatrical 'catacombs'. After being sacked from MKhAT, Mariya Knebel went to ground in the Central Children's Theatre. This is actually where, immediately after the death of Stalin, the revival of the Russian stage would begin. Knebel's and Aleksey Popov's pupil Anatoly Efros would come to this theatre, as would the playwright Viktor Rozov and the young actor Oleg Yefremov – the future creator of the Sovremennik Theatre.

At the relatively safe Vakhtangov Theatre, among a handful of first-class actors and actresses got together by Ruben Simonov, Yury Lyubimov's talent was coming to maturity. He played everything from Oleg Koshevoy in Fadeyev's *The Young Guard* to Mozart in Pushkin's *Mozart and Salieri*. But the *jeune premier* of the Vakhtangov stage was destined for a different historical role: a few years later he gave Moscow Brecht's *The Good Person of Setzuan*, and with it the Taganka Theatre, of which more below.

Even the older generation of directors, which appeared to have been completely discredited and squeezed dry in the Stalin years, came to life. They suddenly spoke again with their own voices and revealed their carefully concealed theatrical pasts. In the early fifties Nikolay Akimov staged brilliant productions of Russian classics such as Shchedrin's *Shadows* and Sukhovo-Kobylin's *The Case*, in which the Stalinist state could be seen as a metamorphosis of Russia's primeval bureaucratic system bent on crushing the individual. In 1954 Mariya Knebel turned to Chekhov's *Ivanov* in an attempt to understand what had happened to the Russian intellectual in the twentieth century. Valentin Pluchek, who had begun his theatrical career in 1926 by jumping out of a large hatbox in Meyerhold's *The Government Inspector*, now directed *The Bathhouse* (1953) and *The Bedbug* (1955) and brought back to life not only Mayakovsky's satire, but the spirit of Meyerhold's own poetics secreted in these plays. Thus, although Meyerhold himself had not been rehabilitated, he already existed in the air of the new stage.[5]

In 1954 Nikolay Okhlopkov directed the first post-war production of *Hamlet* (Stalin, for obvious reasons, intensely disliked the play and banned it at MKhAT after it had been in rehearsal for a long time in Pasternak's translation). The production was in an overblown style, as the times still demanded, but it struck a completely new, unnerving chord. Hamlet's discovery of the truth had a quite special effect on Soviet audiences. He was very reminiscent of the young men in Rozov's plays at the Central Children's Theatre. Hamlet was tackling the problems of Soviet young men, or rather Soviet youths were beginning to

tackle Hamletesque problems. In both cases a blood-soaked world built
on lies was being thrown open, a young man discovering that there was
'something rotten in the state of Denmark'. The massive wrought-iron
gates of the Castle/Prison and the youth in black who appeared from
them and began to question a world that was 'out of joint', remained in
one's memory as the simplest and clearest indication that the wheel of
history had turned and something was about to happen in our lives.[6]

Quite soon after the death of Stalin the first western visitors
began to trickle through. The Comédie Française came, followed by the
Théâtre National Populaire with Gérard Philipe and Maria Casarès.
The Berliner Ensemble was invited over for the first time, shortly after
the death of Bertolt Brecht. Italian neo-realistic films progressed triumphantly across our screens and had a seminal influence on the new
theatrical generation. In December 1955 the 30-year-old Peter Brook
and the 33-year-old Paul Scofield stunned Moscow's theatre world with
their *Hamlet*. This was one of those productions that made an indelible
impression on all who were to decide the course of Russian theatre for
decades to come.

What amazed the critic Iosif Yuzovsky about Brook's *Hamlet*
was its relaxed approach to the tradition, its new, utterly unrealistic
use of space, the director's and actors' sense of freedom, and their complete contempt for stage clichés: 'instead of a singing Ophelia with pale
blue eyes and hair down to her ankles, there is this frightening little
fury with spiky, close-cropped hair, in a crumpled black dress and with
a harsh voice designed, it seems, to set the nerves on edge of anyone
who was hoping at this point to wallow in emotion.'[7] However, the
critic stopped at the line separating the Soviet consciousness from the
European consciousness, as it were. He took exception to Brook's statement that Hamlet's tragedy was that it was impossible for him to do
what he was being asked to do ('Hamlet is tragically mistaken in thinking that you can commit a murder without yourself being changed by it;
the true Hamlet knows that he will not be able to go on living once he
has been stained' was how Yuzovsky paraphrased Brook's programme
note). In response to this, the brilliant, 'stained' critic, who had been a
victim of the 'anti-cosmopolitan' campaign of the late forties and could
have thought of plenty of examples of what Brook was saying from
his own moral experience, forced himself to write: 'Er . . . How to put

it tactfully? A bit wet, isn't it?!' He then quoted chapter and verse to prove that 'if a foe doesn't surrender, you destroy him'. To the Soviet consciousness, brought up on this famous saying of Gorky's, and in a country where millions of lives had been destroyed in the name of a Utopian idea, Yuzovsky's arguments seemed irrefutable.

A few months after Brook's *Hamlet*, the subversive almanack *Literaturnaya Moskva* published Boris Pasternak's 'Notes on some translations of Shakespeare'. The poet had worked on these translations for several decades. They were not only a source of income for him, they were a way of surviving spiritually. In these notes he offered a completely new level of thought about Shakespeare and ourselves. What he said would be absorbed by all who were beginning to revive the Russian stage. He wrote of Hamlet as an 'odd man out', a dissident chosen by chance to judge his time and be the servant of a more remote one. 'When it is discovered that appearances do not match reality, that there is a chasm between them, it does not matter that this has been revealed supernaturally and that the ghost demands vengeance from Hamlet.'[8] In *Othello*, Pasternak examines the colour symbolism and shows that the black Othello is a man living in history, a Christian, whereas the white Iago is an 'unconverted animal still'. And having come through Stalinism, the poet can see that in *King Lear* 'duty' and 'honour' are merely concepts juggled by criminals and everything decent is either strangely silent or expresses itself in nonsense. 'The positive heroes in the tragedy are fools and madmen, people who are defeated or heading for disaster. The work is written in the language of the Old Testament prophets and set in a legendary age of pre-Christian barbarism.'[9]

A few years later, when Pasternak was already dead, a stocky young man in a black jumper would detach himself from a wall on the stage of the Taganka Theatre, amble down to the footlights with a guitar in his hand, and in a hoarse, fearless voice – as though his throat were gripped by an invisible hand – hurl at the audience words from Doctor Zhivago's poem about Hamlet:

> The buzz subsides. I come out on the boards.
> Leaning against the door-frame,
> I try to get an inkling from afar
> Of what will happen in my time.

The actor was Vladimir Vysotsky, whose underground songs were then all the rage.

The gap between the boy Hamlet before whom the earth has just opened up, and Hamlet the grown man and soldier, who knows everything in advance, was actually the distance that this generation had to travel spiritually. It was a bitter and relentless process of growing up.

The Russian theatre had experienced its own period of pre-Christian barbarism. Yet its spirit had not been consumed entirely. Somehow the 'flight paths' of human thought, as Pasternak called them, had survived and been passed on. New life had begun to sprout through the ashes. People were queuing to see Italian films about bicycle thieves, everyone was listening to the songs of Aleksandr Vertinsky, a pre-revolutionary cabaret artist who had returned to the USSR after years in emigration, and the young generation was acquiring its own poetic voice in the verse of Yevgeny Yevtushenko and Andrey Voznesensky. In autumn 1957 the first sputnik was launched and people thronged the streets and rooftops to get a glimpse of it and of 'other worlds'. In the same year, Eldar Ryazanov made *Carnival Night*, a film in which the famous Meyerhold actor Igor Ilinsky created a stupendous image of the Soviet Fool – a bureaucrat in a tightly buttoned field jacket who attempts to deliver an ideological speech at a New Year's party and is made fun of like Malvolio in *Twelfth Night*.

The death of the 'Father of Nations' became a massive, unexpected turning-point in Russian history. Viktor Rozov, the principal dramatist of the period, was to say later that in March 1953 he believed only death could solve the problem of Stalin; so he was prepared to pray for it.[10] 'Death came to him along the Kremlin's corridors without showing any pass',[11] and the steel fist of the regime slightly relaxed its grip on the strangled throat. The sight and smell of this new life were summed up in the word *Thaw*, which tripped from the pen of writer Ilya Ehrenburg.[12] The Soviet theatre and its 'high priests' did not miss the opportunity that history was offering them.

Tolstoy and Dostoyevsky initiate a new Soviet theatre

As always, the first on the scene were the opportunists. Plays like Aleksandr Korneychuk's *Wings* and Aleksandr Shteyn's *Personal File* were hastily thrown together and flooded the stage in the mid-fifties. In them a strictly controlled amount of debunking of Stalin's 'cult of personality' was combined with a glorification of the basic tenets of Soviet ideology. The latter was not subjected to any doubt: it was portrayed as the immortal truth that no cult of personality could ever shake. A more profound approach to reality was discovered through the classics. The Soviet Renaissance called 'the Thaw' was begun by Lev Tolstoy and Fyodor Dostoyevsky.

In 1956 Boris Ravenskikh staged at the Maly 'court theatre' Tolstoy's peasant tragedy *The Power of Darkness*. Ravenskikh had trained as a director under Meyerhold – a fact that was not advertised after the Master's death. For the main role of Akim he chose Igor Ilinsky, another Meyerholdian. The play had hardly been performed since the Revolution. The reason was not so much its unrelieved gloom as its inherent 'Tolstoyism', which had to be exposed as deeply fallacious. According to Tolstoy, the 'power of darkness', or plain evil, is born in the soul of the individual and resolved there and nowhere else. The peasant world and way of life are presented in the play as things that are absolutely fixed and unchanging; it is only the souls of people that ebb and flow. For Tolstoy, the most important thing in life was for the individual to act according to his conscience, thus retaining the image of God within him. Clearly, Ravenskikh and Ilinsky were playing with dynamite.

Soon after the triumphant first night, Ilinsky explained what had happened in an article in *Literaturnaya gazeta* significantly entitled 'Believe Tolstoy!' Here, and in his memoirs, he described how a split occurred in the consciousness of an artist who had been a prisoner of ideological orthodoxy: 'To be honest, I was afraid that Tolstoy's ideas in this play might be regarded as not quite modern. I couldn't betray Lev Tolstoy, nor could I betray contemporary Soviet ideology. At one point I was so torn between the two that I turned the part down.'[13]

Ilinsky's personal drama produced a shift in the public consciousness. People began to look inside themselves, to discover themselves, and to judge themselves. Ravenskikh had refused to curry favour by showing how awful life was before the Revolution. Paradoxically, he revealed a festive, luminous side to this atrabilious play. Into its claustrophobic world of murder, jealousy, and the terror in an old woman's dark soul, he brought the white light of tragedy. The power of darkness was transmogrified into the 'power of light'. The moral unease, boredom and heartache of Nikita, the play's hero, culminated in a biblical scene of repentance before the people, repentance in the bright light of day merging with a powerful, triumphant musical dimension.

Innokenty Annensky, a turn of the century Russian poet and critic, once compared Tolstoy's play with Nietzsche's *The Birth of Tragedy from the Spirit of Music*, which was written at the same time. He insisted that there were no two more opposite works in world culture; that if ever there was anything contrary to the 'spirit of music' it was Tolstoy's play. The latter, he wrote, contained 'reality, but an impossible reality, because it is merely reality, reality *tout court*, and not the mixture that we accept every day under this name'.[14]

In fact, Ravenskikh seemed to have musically orchestrated the whole text. It was not straightforward musical accompaniment; rather, a certain 'spirit of music' informed the whole production. This music expressed the theme of reckless abandon, the rhythm of work, and the resurrection of the soul, but also the dark, ironic, hostile force contending with these. The murder of the baby was planned to the sounds of a drunken orgy and the howling voices of the marriage brokers from behind the door to the peasant hut, which kept being opened and closed. As Boris Zingerman commented at the time: 'The people singing drunken songs and dancing wildly behind the door or outside the gates, and those front of stage planning to bury the child, could easily change places. In this production the very concept of *narodnost* (peasant virtue) is fragmented. It is shown in all its contradictoriness: in its true form and in its distorted, sordid, tavern aspect.'[15]

The critic added cautiously that the director did not always draw a clear line between these two versions of *narodnost*. This was prophetic: shortly afterwards Ravenskikh was to become one of the mainstays of post-Stalin official theatre, with its saccharin idealization of 'the people'. However, in 1956 Ravenskikh was still able to produce a powerful, integrated effect and with it a sense of what people called then 'the fresh wind of change'.

As I have said, the play was achieved by director and actor together. Akim, a miserable cesspool cleaner, is presented by the playwright as the secret bearer of Tolstoy's own ideas. In this role, Ilinsky, who was an actor of the eccentric school, discovered himself as an actor of tragic proportions. A rare fusion occurred: the painfully inarticulate *t-yeh . . . t-yeh* sounds that Akim made as he tried to start a sentence, and his dumb gestures, somehow conveyed the music of a pure soul. Ilinsky may have been ideologically sterile, but he had put his trust in what Tolstoy himself trusted – his instinct and his sense of truth. Akim did not embody an argument about whether it was right or wrong to believe in God's judgement and resist or not resist evil. He was not a philosopher. He was a Russian peasant for whom God was his conscience and the absence of God was darkness. And for this specific peasant brushing the snow off his bast shoes in front of his hut, rather than for mankind in the abstract, it was vitally important that this God exist. It was an unforgettable personal experience, therefore, to see this illiterate peasant hand back the 10-rouble note, folded into a tiny square, that he had been given by his murderer-son. He walked out of the hut unable to bear the drunken revelry, into the freezing darkness; only to return a moment later, open the door, and shout at his son something that had been forgotten in Russia for five decades: 'Wake up, Nikita. You must have soul!'

Where soul was concerned, of course, Tolstoyism and the new ideology did not see eye to eye. But all the power of which theatre is capable was used to show how impossible and terrible the actual 'power of darkness' was, that is to say a life unsanctified by any moral beliefs, in which 'everything was permitted'. Akim's peasant God could save people from the mire – including the bloody mire that was revealed to society in the mid-1950s. The ethical idea of repentance and resurrection imbued the whole production. Yet again, the theatre was replacing the Church in a bid to cleanse and revive people's souls.

In their attempt to get to the heart of Tolstoy, the director and his actors had moved into an area of difficult choices. Ravenskikh understood the religious basis of the play, the sublimity of the wandering pilgrim's way of life, and Tolstoy's hatred of property and all forms of outward struggle, and he tried to convey this somehow in his production. To believe Tolstoy in this way was to take an enormous step. Tolstoyism was not a kind of ideological varnish that could be stripped off the way our directors had for decades when 'bringing an author closer to the present day'. Tolstoyism was a definite way of thinking about the world and people. It was the dark language of another culture that was beginning to emerge from oblivion.

A year later, this culture sprang another revelation on us. Georgy Tovstonogov directed a stage adaptation of Dostoyevsky's novel *The Idiot*. It opened on 31 December 1957 and soon became a legend. Untheatrical words like 'miracle', 'pilgrimage', 'revelation' appeared in the reviews. Since this production introduces one of the main heroes of the book, Georgy Tovstonogov, a few biographical details are in order. Like Nemirovich-Danchenko, he came from Tiflis, the capital of Georgia, where he was born in 1915. He trained at GITIS (the State Institute of Theatre Art) in pre-war Moscow under Aleksey Popov and Andrey Lobanov, returned to Georgia, then moved back to Moscow in 1946 and up to the death of Stalin directed in various theatres what everyone else directed in those years. He had to wait two decades for his moment.

Tovstonogov had learned the lessons of Meyerhold and Tairov well, but those of MKhAT even better. He was attracted to staging on a large scale, took what he wanted from all over the place, but still managed to achieve a rich artistic unity. He was excellent at analyzing a play and had a nose for the good actor. He created what was virtually the strongest Russian company of the post-Stalin period. This company was united by a common cause, which Tovstonogov promoted with rare skill, steering brilliantly between the reefs in the Soviet theatrical sea (another thing he had in common with Nemirovich-Danchenko). He was *persona grata* with the Party establishment, had been awarded every prize imaginable, yet (most unusually) his authority among the theatrical profession was unshakable. Several productions that he staged in the mid-fifties, for example Vsevolod Vishnevsky's *An Optimistic Tragedy* and Aleksandr Volodin's *Five Evenings*, immediately defined the salient features of his art. I shall return to these productions later. First we must look at *The Idiot*, which stands at the source of the most interesting line in his evolution, namely his work with the Russian classics.

He had dreamt of putting on Dostoyevsky immediately after the war, which would certainly have been appropriate amidst the un-precedented suffering and degradation of the times. But after the war Dostoyevsky had fallen into disfavour. Following Gorky's lead, the hacks had begun to present him as a 'medieval inquisitor' (Gorky's phrase at the First Congress of Soviet Writers in 1934). *The Devils* was seen as merely a vicious anti-revolutionary pamphlet, and *The Idiot*, which is an apologia for the 'absolutely beautiful person' Prince Myshkin, was strongly suspected of preaching proscribed Christian ideas. Initially Tovstonogov decided to follow the long tradition of staging not so much a production about Myshkin as a hysterical melodrama about the humiliated *femme fatale* Nastasya Fillipovna. He had previously put on plays about 'strong people' such as Lenin, Stalin and Pavel Korchagin, the hero of one of the key works of Soviet literary mythology *How the Steel Was Tempered*. But the times had changed radically, there were now new opportunities, and the director's attention swung to Lev Myshkin, the 'idiot' who had come from a mental hospital in Switzerland to save Russia.

Theatrical sensations are often the result of luck. So it was in this case. Rehearsals began with a good actor as Myshkin, but Tovstonogov felt in his bones that someone else was needed, someone quite different, whom the Soviet stage did not yet know. A performer and person with a different mentality was needed. In the 1920s this actor could have been Michael Chekhov. In the 1950s Tovstonogov found Innokenty Smoktunovsky (who is probably best known in the West for his performance of Hamlet in Kozintsev's famous film).

The appearance of the word *miracle* among the usual hieroglyphics of our theatre criticism signified that Tovstonogov and Smoktunovsky had succeeded in revealing on the Soviet stage an image of the 'absolutely beautiful person', Jesus Christ, who had been spat upon by the new bosses. The theatrical revelation of Christ to the people was not announced in so many words, but that is what was being acted, that is exactly what one experienced, as a kind of revelation overflowing the bounds of theatre. As confirmation of my hypothesis, let me quote Naum Berkovsky at the time:

> Smoktunovsky's voice completes the impression conveyed by his appearance: it is a voice that is not being steered, it has no stresses or italics, it is not imperious or didactic: its intonations jump out of their own accord, 'from the heart', free of any premeditation . . . Every dialogue is a contest. Prince Myshkin's dialogues as performed by Smoktunovsky are paradoxical: there is no contest in them. They are not dialogues, they are

the desire to echo, to find within oneself the person to whom speech is being directed, to respond to him, to be drawn into his inner world.[16]

There is only one person who could be described in this way – the Son of Man.

Many years later, I asked Innokenty Smoktunovsky what sources, so to speak, his Myshkin had drawn on, for it to have had such an effect on recent theatre history. Smoktunovsky recalled his rehearsals with Tovstonogov and various old scores he had to settle with him (he did not look kindly on directors and disliked sharing his fame with them, in which regard he remained a true provincial). He recalled that Tovstonogov had wanted to take him off the part, that the people he was acting with did not like him, that he had hated himself, because he felt he did not understand the 'absolutely beautiful person' and had no experience to help him act him. The turning-point came quite by chance. One day, amidst the usual bustle and muddle of a film set, he suddenly saw something unusual, spellbinding even: a man with a very expressive face and cropped hair was standing by a pillar in the thick of the crowd reading a book. It was a case of unique public solitude: the crowd was flowing round him on all sides, but the man existed entirely on his own. He was so absorbed in his book and his thoughts that he noticed no one. The next day at rehearsals for *The Idiot* Smoktunovsky's fellow-actors and the director were astonished by a kind of sea change in Prince Myshkin. Stanislavsky would have said that the actor had found the 'seed' of his part, its soul and shape. Later Smoktunovsky discovered that the silent man at the film studios had just returned from many years in a prison camp.

The Idiot became a festival of light for our theatre. Its hero was woven from the air of those times, the dust of the camps, and the Arctic nights around the labour camp town of Norilsk where Smoktunovsky had lived. Myshkin was born of the experience of Smoktunovsky the actor and the experience of millions of nameless human beings whom the silent man in the crowd had proffered to the performer's imagination. The Tolstoy and Dostoyevsky productions became a kind of tuning-fork for the first decade after the death of Stalin. The short Thaw had come into its own.

The rise and fall of the Sovremennik Theatre

Recalling the production of Rozov's *Alive Forever* with which the Sovremennik studio theatre opened in 1956, Oleg Yefremov has said that some theatregoers and critics expressed their disappointment thus: 'It's excellent, of course, but all you've done is give us a good version of MKhAT. It's what the "old" MKhAT used to be like.'[17]

Yefremov still regards this as the highest praise. The young actors, who were all graduates from the MKhAT drama school, had in effect created a new Art Theatre studio to polemicize with the 'main house', which was in a state of deep crisis. The polemics proceeded on every front, starting with MKhAT's repertoire. The old theatre, which had begun life with plays like *The Seagull*, had long since lost any notion of quality where repertoire was concerned. Sometimes the plays were so embarrassing that they were taken off after only a few performances. The actors expected to collect their Stalin Prizes anyway, on the principle of Buggins's turn. Plays were chosen and parts shared out with an eye to these prizes (of course, only those who played the 'positive' heroes got them). The name of MKhAT still carried a cachet, but the theatre's art had evaporated – it had lost all connection with people's real lives. Even the dictator's death did not bring MKhAT back to life. It had been blinded by its own academic splendour. Nor had it any faith in its pupils. It was a case of self-betrayal crowned with official laurels.

In its early years, the Art Theatre had sprouted several studios, because it regarded them as necessary if the theatre was to stay alive. The studios were a guarantee against rot. Young blood, new ideas, experimentation, were part and parcel of MKhAT right through to the end of the twenties, that is, the 'time of the great change'. Its studios produced major actors and directors (whole theatres!), who together helped determine the history of the Russian stage in the twentieth century. The last great MKhAT studio was the First Studio set up by Stanislavsky before the Revolution. In 1924 Michael Chekhov used it as the basis for a theatre which he called MKhAT 2. In 1928 Michael Chekhov emigrated, MKhAT 1 was turned into a model theatre of the Stalin empire, and in 1936 MKhAT 2 was annihilated. Nothing was to be left to remind people of MKhAT's pre-Stalinist past.

It took another quarter of a century and the death of 'The Best Friend of All Soviet Performers' before the idea of a studio theatre bore fruit again.

The Sovremennik (which means 'Contemporary') called itself a studio of MKhAT, but its relations with the main house were very peculiar. From MKhAT's point of view, it was illegitimate and all they expected from it was trouble. This MKhAT did not need a studio, because a studio merely exacerbated its own crisis. The Sovremennik was a living reminder of what was wrong in MKhAT itself. As Ibsen, who was so popular with the Art Theatre at the turn of the century, put it: 'youth is retribution'.

In the way it went about things, the Sovremennik tried to revive the image of the old MKhAT 'home', its artistic and ethical ideals. Of course, this was an historical hoax, but all theatrical revolutions need mythological clothes. In a different land and culture they were attempting to put into practice the legendary founding principles of the original Moscow Art Theatre. Recalling that Stanislavsky's theatre was a 'partnership of belief', they drew up special articles of association intended to create a new brotherhood of actors. The Sovremennik began to operate not according to the regulations governing 'theatrical enterprises for public spectacle', as all state theatres in the USSR were then called, but according to laws devised for themselves by themselves. Decisions about whether to stage a play, or whether a production was ready to show to the public, were taken collectively. The whole company also decided whether an actor could stay in the company. When it was the turn of Yefremov, the artistic director of the theatre, to be assessed, he would come out of his office and they would discuss him without mincing their words. They attempted to clear away the layers of tarnish that had been deposited by the realities of the Soviet theatre on Stanislavsky's crowning idea of a theatrical home. They had no actorial dead wood and were not coerced into artificial groups the way that actors in most companies were at that time. The right to stay or to leave was restored with dignity. It was the first Russian theatre for decades that had been created not from above but from below, by the will of the artists themselves rather than by theatrical bureaucrats.

Plate 1 Mayakovsky Square, Moscow, early 1970s, with the remains of the
Sovremennik Theatre in foreground.

Many of their productions were banned. This only encouraged
them: if they were being banned, they must be doing something worth-
while. Rehearsals at the Sovremennik often ended with a Russian-style
party around a table, which might turn into a rehearsal again. However,
there was none of the sheer drinking to forget that was associated with
MKhAT. Their parties provided space for free, familiar contact, which
was in its turn an expression of these young people's new feeling for
life. They understood that good theatres are not created from books
and cardboard morality, but from the air of freedom, levity, badinage
and friendly conviviality, without which no true theatre can live.

A band of young poets, musicians, critics, writers and painters
quickly gathered around the Sovremennik, who would subsequently
be called the 'sixties generation'. Aleksandr Solzhenitsyn, Vasily
Aksyonov, Anatoly Kuznetsov and Aleksandr Galich all brought their
plays here. They and many others who started this theatre would later
become dissidents and leave the country, voluntarily or otherwise. The
fate of this generation was highly dramatic, but its linchpin, its hearth
and home, was the little theatre (now a parking space) stuck on the side
of the Pekin Hotel on Mayakovsky Square.

The Thaw (1953–1968)

This theatre was greatly influenced by the character of its leader, Oleg Yefremov. He was born in Moscow and graduated from the Studio School of MKhAT in 1949, where he was taught by Mikhail Kedrov and Vasily Toporkov, pupils of Stanislavsky himself. After graduating, he became a teacher at the MKhAT school, from whose graduates he formed the Sovremennik. Simultaneously, he began his own acting career at the Central Children's Theatre, and soon became the idol of Moscow's youth.

Yefremov's attitude to Stanislavsky bordered on the religious. When he was a student at the MKhAT school, he and some friends swore an oath to remain true to Stanislavsky's teaching, and signed it with their own blood. This may sound grotesque, but it is true, and it explains a lot about this generation. In the summer of 1952, Yefremov and a friend set off on a journey through Russia to study life, just as Stanislavsky and Russian literature said they should. They went down the Volga from Yaroslavl as far as the Volga-Don canal, at the entrance to which stood a 70-metre-high figure of Stalin. This symbolic journey shaped Yefremov's views about the Soviet form of serfdom that the country was suffering from.

The Sovremennik acquired a leader who knew what he believed in and what he hated. The theatre's social programme was, in a word, anti-Stalinist. Its aesthetic ideas were much vaguer and for want of a terminology of their own were summed up in Stanislavsky's phrase 'the life of the human spirit'. This formula they attempted to pack with high explosive. They wanted to return to the natural human being on the stage, to the passionate search for truth, to the actor's ability to re-embody himself. They sought those penetrating methods of reaching an audience that had been practised by the Art Theatre, especially its First Studio, with its 'spiritual realism', its greatly reduced gap between actor and audience, and its ability to draw the latter into its energy field. They were the first to risk acting 'confessionally' (one of the keywords of this generation), meaning that the role should be illumined by the performer's own human 'theme' and his personal fate, if he had one.

The style of delivery at the Sovremennik was the diametric opposite of the ululating of the Stalinist pseudo-heroes. The Sovremennik's enemies immediately christened this style 'whispering realism', but it launched a massive theatrical reform. The language of the street, of life that was really alive, burst on to this stage and produced not only a new type of speech, but a new performer whom people called 'a blender', someone who even in terms of appearance could have walked in off the street. The typical actor of the 1940s as lauded by the critics was something quite unique. One looked up at him from very far below. He was the epitome of a craggy man of the people. A fifties critic quipped that when you saw such a performer coming along the street you could not decide whether he was an actor or a head waiter.[18] The actors at the Sovremennik were bringing back to the stage the forgotten taste of truth.

At first the Sovremennik's programme was built on contrasts. Basically, the theatre was fond of 'two colours', as one of the studio's first productions was called.[19] It had to look for a long time before it found a play with which to open, and eventually chose Viktor Rozov's *Alive Forever*. This was a play in which the recent war with Nazism was not only the setting for the action, but a time when everyone had to make moral choices. In telling a story about the war, the studio actors succeeded in telling one about the fate of their generation.

Yefremov both directed the production and played the part of Boris Borozdin, a young man who had volunteered for the front line. He had left behind him a girl who did not wait for him, and friends who betrayed him. Each had chosen his own path. The strict moral standards that the theatre was putting forward were applied, of course, not so much to the war as to the whole way of life that the nation had grown used to. Here is a portrait of the young Yefremov as Boris early in the opening run:

> Boris/Yefremov appeared in only two short scenes but carried the lyrical theme of the play with him. One felt infinitely sorry for this tall, lanky, boy-like Boris, with his shy perseverance, his elegant hands that would turn themselves to any piece of work . . . his purity and his grown-up sense of responsibility. And one thought how much poorer life was for having lost the best people of this generation . . . They were too young to have fallen beneath the terrible scythe of 1937, but they were too grown-up and 1917, the year of their birth, was too firmly imprinted on their souls, for them to be hypnotized by the universal paranoia and euphoria – to lose their individual conscience and their sense of personal responsibility.[20]

It was precisely Boris/Yefremov who uttered the famous line that entered the theatrical language of the time: 'I must do it, if I am honest.'

At the Sovremennik, a theatre of the living human image was cultivated; but this image included all the tricks of the theatre. One of the most sparkling instances of this was *The Naked King*, performed in 1959. The author, Yevgeny Shvarts, was a brilliant playwright who stitched his own patterns on the canvas of classical fairytales. His improvisation on themes from Hans Christian Andersen's *The Emperor's New Clothes* was extremely opportune in the post-Stalin period.

The Sovremennik performed it in the spirit of the famous MKhT *kapustniki* ('cabbage pie shows'). These were started by Nikita Baliyev at the turn of the century during Lent, when people ate only cabbage pies. Public performances were forbidden, so the company put on entertainments for itself on subjects to do with MKhT. Many leading actors, including Stanislavsky, took part. They laughed at themselves, at MKhT's conventions, and those of modern art generally. The *kapustniki* became a kind of in-house carnival. Echoes of this carnival would survive in Russia even in the darkest times, when the actors' *kapustniki* would be almost the only corner that Big Brother's eye could not see into.

The Sovremennik performed its first *kapustnik* with the daring of a tightrope-walker crossing an abyss. The fairytale setting did not prevent the actors from conveying certain resemblances between the ministers, kings, official bards and courtiers in the fairytale and their far from fairytale counterparts in Russian reality. The show had people rolling in the aisles. When Igor Kvasha, playing the prime minister, 'told the King straight' what a genius he, the King, was, it was received as something more than a hint at the customs of the Russian Communist Party court: the actor had taken off to a tee the upwardly mobile Soviet sycophant whom everyone knew.

This theatrical fairytale produced an image of a state that was mad and personified by a 'King with no clothes'. The show became a kind of litmus test of Soviet mugwumps' loyalty to the regime. Yefremov told me that whenever someone big fell from office the first thing they did in their new life was to go and see *The Naked King*. Nikita Khrushchev himself (after October 1964, of course) was a regular attender and would roar with laughter at the system that he had once tried to reform.

Like all Russian art in this period, the Sovremennik developed in a complex historical and political space. The very term *Thaw* conveys its transitional, changeable nature: it was neither winter nor spring. Life carried on in the style of the old Russian choral game 'We sow millet', in which one chorus dances and sings 'We sow millet', demonstrating how they 'sow' it, and another replies 'But we will stamp it, stamp it out' (also demonstrating). The whole of our Thaw enacted this extra-ordinary game. As soon as anything was initiated and 'millet' was sown in the form of a new book, production or film, the ideological bovver boys would descend on it and with whoops of glee dance their ritual 'We will stamp it out'. In 1957 they 'stamped out' Pasternak's novel *Doctor Zhivago* and brought him to his grave, then they turned to Dudintsev's novel *Not By Bread Alone*, and after that they turned on the abstract painters, using bulldozers to wipe their works from the face of the earth.

At the Sovremennik they were well aware of the change in the weather. Yefremov was invited to Khrushchev's meeting with intel-lectuals in March 1963 and saw writers and painters baying for the blood of other writers and painters. Yefremov has told me more than once that it was one of the most depressing experiences of his life. He had to exercise courage and a special brand of resourcefulness in order both to preserve the spirit of the studio in these circumstances and develop his art further.

The studio began to move from the 'truth of life' to the 'truth of the theatre'; they simply learned new ways of getting at the truth. When Anatoly Efros directed Eduardo de Filippo's *De Pretore Vincenzo* at the Sovremennik, with Yefremov as the thief Vincenzo, the author turned up to a rehearsal. The flamboyant Italian showed them on the spot what really expressive, unpredictable human gestures are, and what theatricality is, which they were extremely wary of at the Sovremennik. The experience of staging *De Pretore Vincenzo* and *The Naked King* was invigorating. It was taken further in various productions, but espe-cially in Vasily Aksyonov's play *Always Available*. Here the soul of the modern hero was split into two parts: the elegant cynic, scoundrel and journalist Yevgeny Kistochkin, and the naive dreamer Treugolnikov. The stage presented a section through a block of Moscow flats. In each small room life was in full swing. Top right a young mother was ironing baby clothes, bottom left a red-faced pensioner was exercising with a chest expander, and there was a girl doing the hula-hoop. The old people were telling ancient jokes, the young ones 'getting off with the birds'. Yefremov produced a kind of X-ray of the house and attempted with the author and actors to understand where this house/country was going and what was in store for it.

Both the director and the writer had personal experience of the Soviet *kommunalka* ('communal flat'), crammed with all kinds of lodgers. As an adolescent Yefremov had lived in a *kommunalka* on Moscow's Arbat, where the 'clean' rubbed shoulders with the 'unclean', Trotskyists with secret policemen, and religious dissenters with fanatical Communists. He still regards this 'Noah's Ark' as the main source of impressions in his youth. During the war, Yefremov's father was drafted as a book-keeper to one of the countless camps in the far north at Vorkuta, and Yefremov went with him. This experience helped mould his talent; it gave him an acute social sense, a knowledge of Soviet life from the inside that nourished him for many years. Aksyonov, who collaborated on the production of *Always Available*, had his own score to settle with the regime: his father had been arrested in 1937, and his mother Yevgeniya Ginzburg, the future author of the famous book *Into the Whirlwind*, had spent almost twenty years in a camp.

Life on the brink of death called for new theatrical forms that would go beyond realism and the recognizable. The production of *Always Available* tried to 'make strange' modern reality, to submit it to moral judgement and mockery. The actors did not 'live themselves into' the characters or seek the audience's sympathy. In a way, it was the first attempt to inject Brecht's experience into Russian art (he was just beginning to become known in Moscow). At the time, grafting Brecht on to Stanislavsky produced nothing startling. But it led to other discoveries, such as Oleg Tabakov's talent for the grotesque. He played several parts in Aksyonov's play, but his portrayal of Zina, a fast Russian barmaid ready for anything, so to speak, was particularly juicy. Clearly, the young theatre had talents that were not being used to the full in modern realistic plays (i.e. by Viktor Rozov and Aleksandr Volodin; Aksyonov did not count, as his début in the theatre was not followed up).

In 1964 the Sovremennik stopped being a studio and became a normal Soviet theatre. The actors' endurance was tested by new historical forces, which they themselves anticipated in their art. In 1966 the theatre staged a production of Goncharov's novel *A Common Story*, which in many ways was prophetic. It was directed by Galina Volchek, an actress at the theatre, and the novel, first published in 1847, was adapted for the stage by Viktor Rozov. The central theme of the play became the transformation of a person into a lackey of the regime. The theatre was less interested in the circumstances that shape a personality than in the flexibility, the molten quality, of the human being himself, whom society inexorably pours into the mould already prepared for him.

The duet between Pyotr Aduyev, a melancholy cynic and respectable civil servant of the time of Nicholas I, and his nephew Aleksandr Aduyev, a keen provincial youth who had arrived to conquer the capital, was gripping. In the hands of the actors Mikhail Kozakov and Oleg Tabakov it became about the turning of a face into a mask. The fact that the young man who was to undergo this operation was played by Oleg Tabakov gave it a special edge, because the happy, dimpled Tabakov had already played a series of young Rozov characters and other favourites of the new generation. It was Tabakov who in Rozov's *In Search of Joy* (1957) had pulled his grandfather's Civil War sabre off the wall and hacked up the accursed three-piece suite which was regarded at the time as the symbol of the petty bourgeoisie. Now we saw a completely different side to this boy, who had been the lyrical hero of his time. Not afraid of self-parody, the Sovremennik showed how the hero's life might have developed differently. With surgical precision, Tabakov exposed in the starry-eyed young man a phenomenal talent for time-serving. Uncle Aduyev, as Mikhail Kozakov played him, was a cynic of the old school. His scepticism was mildly attractive, since it was based on long experience. His nephew, however, was 'transformed' in a jiffy: he did not survive his first brush with life. The moment when instead of the enthusiastic youth with dimples and blazing eyes a well-fed hog with sleeked-down hair came on-stage, and the mask could be seen growing through the face, was terrifying. It was an uncanny glimpse of the future, which few at the time foresaw.

In 1967 the theatre decided to do something quite different: to stage a trilogy about the Russian revolutionary movement from the Decembrists to the Bolsheviks. The moment was opportune, as the country was about to celebrate the fiftieth anniversary of the October revolution. However, the idea behind this legendary trilogy needs some explanation. The last thing the Sovremennik was setting out to do was attack the then regime or question its origins. On the contrary, they wanted to defend those origins, to refurbish the idea of Revolution. This, in fact, was all that the ideology of the sixties liberals came down to. Bulat Okudzhava, the favourite poet of this generation and of the Thaw generally, still believed in the Revolution despite the fact that his revolutionary father had been shot in 1937 and his mother put in a camp. The father of Aleksandr Svobodin, author of the second play in the trilogy, *Narodovoltsy* (The People's Will Party), belonged to the same revolutionary clan, was active in the Comintern, had been killed in Germany during the Ruhr uprising, and his wife had been rewarded for her involvement in the Revolution with many years in a labour camp. Mikhail Shatrov, the author of *The Bolsheviks*, which concluded the trilogy, had a similar background. He was related to the shot Chairman of the Council of People's Commissars, Aleksey Rykov, a Bolshevik of the Lenin generation; his own parents had been purged; and yet he became the principal writer of plays about Lenin in the post-Stalin period, taking over from Nikolay Pogodin.[21] His plays were banned and mangled, but not because Shatrov was somehow trying to get his own back on Lenin. On the contrary, he used every means at his command to try to prove that the wellsprings of the Revolution were crystal clear and it was only Stalin and his satraps who had muddied them and brought Lenin's ideas into disrepute. This was a very persistent liberal myth, which the Sovremennik also subscribed to.

The Sovremennik's trilogy was propelled by the belief in a 'pure' Revolution. The main ethical theme of the plays, however, was that of revolution and morality – a subject that occupied people's minds at that time more than any other. Created at white-hot heat (the company literally worked on them day and night), the productions of *The Decembrists*, *The Narodovoltsy* and *The Bolsheviks* presented Russian history as a single space, an endless chain of connections and cross-connections. Any action, whether of heroism or treachery, affected the whole chain. The theatre was trying to understand where the terror of 1937 had come from and why the Great Revolution they believed in so fervently had turned into such a catastrophe for the country.

Yefremov set out to investigate a single question: the relation of ends to means in the struggle for liberation, when unjust 'means' distorted the lofty 'end' to the point where it was unrecognizable and no one could remember whether a purpose had ever existed at all.

In Leonid Zorin's *The Decembrists*, both as director and actor (he played Nicholas I) Yefremov dug into the ethical mystery of the Decembrist movement. People of whom Alexander Herzen had spoken as doughty knights very quickly crumbled when interrogated in their cells or face to face with the tsar. They failed the test. The production tried to find some justification for this. They had been brought up in the aristocratic code of honour, and proved defenceless when confronted in the person of the dissembling tsar with the logic of pure political expediency. Yefremov was portraying the actor Nicholas I and his particular talent for theatrical direction for the first time on the Russian stage. The first generation of Russian noblemen-revolutionaries found themselves transported from the world of dreams and starry-eyed illusions to a *grand guignol* set in a torture chamber. They did not know the rules of such a game. They realized for the first time what an infernal machine they were dealing with.

The production showed that the problem of the ends and the means came down to a choice between apolitical morality and amoral politics. There was no third way. The theatre focused on this aspect with all the artistic integrity then available to it. But they found no way out of this dilemma, either within the Decembrists' consciousness or their own.

In Aleksandr Svobodin's *Narodovoltsy* the problem of ends and means acquired a new twist. Zhelyabov, one of the heroes of the People's Will Party, and his comrades are hunting down Alexander II. Eight times their assassination attempts on the tsar-emancipator fail, but finally they run him to ground like an animal. Martyrs to their idea, the *narodovoltsy* expunged all personal feelings from themselves except hatred. The human in them was consumed by the idea. 'We have terrorized ourselves', Zhelyabov/Yefremov said with grim humour (again Yefremov took on the most difficult role himself).

Yefremov used all the resources of the stage to show the inherent tragedy of the People's Will movement. The 'people' in whose name they claimed to act were not only indifferent, they were hostile to the revolutionaries. The Sovremennik's best actors performed the sort of 'people scene' for which MKhT was once famous. They needed to create a kind of collective portrait of the 'people' through vignettes of city dwellers, peasants and traders. The 'people' ranted, bought and sold, drank and sang. The theme of the liberation of the people began to look somewhat ironic, rather as in *The Cherry Orchard* Firs describes the emancipation of the serfs as 'the calamity'.

The intellectuals wanted to make people happy through terror – to give freedom to those who did not want it. Blood cried out for blood and yet more blood. The five nooses slung above the stage at the end of *The Decembrists* were a prelude to the ghastly scene of the execution in *Narodovoltsy*. The mob hooted and jeered at the terrorist-liberators. But only up to a point. Actually seeing the savage reprisal carried out literally turned the mob round. At the very moment of the execution, the entire ragbag of half-drunk folk who had been standing with their backs to the auditorium turned sharply towards the audience, who felt as though they were standing around the scaffold themselves. The face of the mob was transformed (remember that these parts were being played by the best actors in the company). Fear, horror and compassion had awoken in these individuals. For a short moment the mob became the people. 'My conscience is clear' – with these words the heroes of the People's Will Party went to their deaths, having thoroughly prepared the ground for those who would call themselves Bolsheviks.

The Bolsheviks completed the trilogy and set its issues in a new historical context. Power, the lever of freedom for all, was now in the Bolsheviks' hands. They saw themselves as the direct heirs of the Decembrists and *narodovoltsy*. The play was set in the days following the attempt on Lenin's life in 1918. The People's Commissars were debating the use of 'Red terror'. Lenin himself did not appear in the production: he was wounded and apparently dying in the next room. A stream of telegrams, requests and orders in Lenin's name issued from the Sovnarkom room, where the meeting was taking place. Every ten minutes the guard was changed (this was totally unrealistic, but it gave the performance a tense rhythm). The commissars argued until they were hoarse about where the terror that they were going to unleash could lead. They recalled the French Revolution, the Convention, the Committee of Public Safety. They remembered how terror had mutated into a blood-bath, and a policy of deterrence had become one of annihilation. Applied to the Russian Revolution, all of these issues were stunningly new to Soviet audiences. Moreover, the play was presented in the style of documentary drama, that is, it had pretensions to historical accuracy. For fifty years it had been impossible even to raise these issues. The Sovremennik *had* raised them, and this was quite enough for the liberal consciousness that presumed Lenin was innocent and right to spill the blood he did.

The Bolsheviks voted on the issue late at night. They raised their hands in favour of Red terror in different ways. No one who saw the way Lunacharsky, the Commissar for Enlightenment (played by Yevgeny Yevstigneyev) voted, would ever forget it. It was one of Yevstigneyev's famous 'turns', which helped make the political subject humanly convincing. Lunacharsky's hand went up slowly, as though he were changing his mind. Then it stuck; it froze at the critical point. And finally it shot straight up: the fatal choice had been made, the decision taken. At the end of the play, the commissars began to sing the Internationale; quietly, in a whisper, so as not to disturb their wounded leader. They drew their chairs close up to one another, there was a sense of fraternity, as though they were uttering the words of the proletarian anthem for the first time. They stared out into the auditorium, seeming to ask it a question. The audience rose from their seats and joined in the anthem. 'The world of violence we will shatter, and then –' The people on-stage did not know their own future. The audience did know what would happen 'then'. This fusion of stage and audience in a single gesture was probably one of the most powerful theatrical experiences of the sixties generation.

Of course, attempts were made to close this 100 per cent Soviet production down. Revisionists do not like being reminded of their past. The central censorship banned the play, but Yefremov managed to drag the Minister of Culture, Yekaterina Furtseva, to see a run through. She took personal responsibility for permitting it, and the production opened on 7 November 1967, the fiftieth anniversary of the Bolshevik revolution. After the performance, she graciously pronounced her verdict: it was the 'best Party meeting' she had ever been to.

Furtseva's description of the play struck no one as odd. The artists were wearing the same ideological blinkers as the government. They might be swimming against the current, but they were in the same river, between the same banks. I have already mentioned Shatrov's background. Oleg Yefremov grew up in the same soil. He joined the Party immediately after the death of Stalin and I can personally vouch that he never questioned the idea of revolution itself (although he had no time for the contemporary version of the Soviet regime, any more than he would accept later the post-Soviet version of a 'democratic regime'). At the end of the sixties a split would occur, when Solzhenitsyn would dare to cast doubt on the idea of revolution itself. But most of the 'sixties people' left this idea intact. Arkady Belinkov, who had spent ten years in a camp, wrote in his book about Tynyanov (1965) that there had not been enough revolutions in Russia. He was sure that only revolutions could keep the blood of history moving.[22] The best of his generation thought the same.

However, the year following the opening of *The Bolsheviks* was a fateful one. In August 1968 the 'Prague Spring' came to an end and the myth of 'socialism with a human face' evaporated. The inhuman face of the regime was no longer hid. Preparations were made to sack the editors of *Novy mir*,[23] and Solzhenitsyn wrote his open letter to the Soviet Writers' Congress. Everyone's position changed. Pensioner Nikita Khrushchev grew tomatoes on his allotment and occasionally came to *The Naked King* for a laugh and to complain to the actors that he had not had time to 'expose Stalin' to the full. The ghost of the recently reburied dictator was roaming Russia again. The historical ground was slipping from beneath the Sovremennik's feet. In the summer of 1970 Yefremov staged his last production in this theatre – *The Seagull*. The play that had once initiated the Moscow Arts, now brought one of its best studios to a close.

All of the resentment, disappointment and disaffection that had built up in the company was poured into Chekhov's text. Yefremov tried to turn Chekhov into a pamphleteer. At that time he disliked Chekhov's intellectual heroes intensely. He disliked the fact that they talk so much and do nothing. He imported into *The Seagull* the intellectual confusion and despair of the late 1960s. People had stopped listening to or even hearing each other. All they did was discuss relationships, dig up worms for bait from the flower-bed set in the centre of the stage by designer Sergey Barkhin, drink, plot, and hate one another.

The Seagull marked the collapse of the Sovremennik from within. It crashed at the same time as the ideology of the Soviet 'sixties people'. The idea of 'refurbishing the Revolution' had exhausted itself. In 1970 Furtseva introduced Oleg Yefremov to the MKhAT company. The state was entrusting the weary rebel with the job of heading a dying theatrical enterprise. Yefremov proposed to the Sovremennik company that they all join MKhAT. Two exhausting days of arguing about it got them nowhere. Most of the Sovremennik people refused to go to the 'Academy': they thought it was dead in the water.

Yury Lyubimov and the birth of the Taganka Theatre

Yury Lyubimov is ten years older than Yefremov; he was born on 30 September 1917. His ancestors were Russian peasants, his grandfather was dispossessed as a 'kulak', and at the end of the twenties his father was imprisoned as a 'nepman' (one of those enterprising peasants who during Lenin's New Economic Policy managed in two years to feed and clothe the whole country). Nevertheless, Lyubimov did not become a pariah of the regime. Quite the opposite: in Russian terms his life could be said to be eminently successful. He swam with the tide, believed in the Utopia, worked almost seven years in the ensemble of the NKVD (secret police), joined the Party on Stalin's death like Yefremov, and performed in hits on the Soviet stage and screen for which, in the early fifties, he was awarded the tyrant's own prize. He was moulded in the depths of the Vakhtangov Theatre, which always had a special relationship with the centre of power. Well-built and with fiery gypsy eyes inherited from his mother's family, he was definitely one of the favoured few. He was married to Lyudmila Tselikovskaya, a Soviet film star, and was the *jeune premier* of the Vakhtangov stage. No one, it seemed, was less likely to lead a theatrical revolt. Yet that is precisely what he did.

Lyubimov was just young enough to have seen Tairov's, Stanislavsky's and Nemirovich-Dancheko's productions and to have sat in on Meyerhold's rehearsals. At his entrance examination for the MKhAT 2 drama school he recited not the standard poem but Yury Olesha's speech to the First Congress of Soviet Writers. The sincerity of this speech had greatly impressed Soviet intellectuals, although at the time few stopped to think what it really meant. At the first Writers' Congress, which had been called to collectivize the writing fraternity

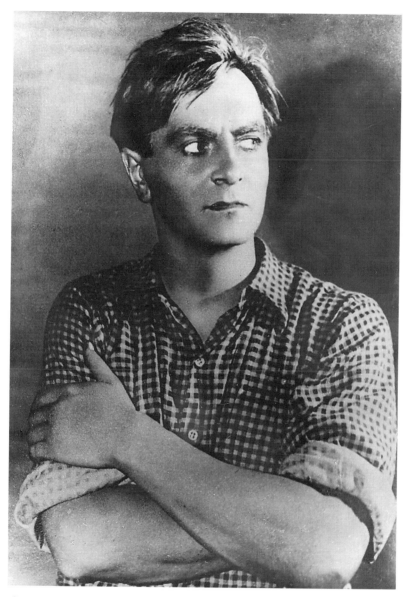

Plate 2   Yury Lyubimov as Oleg Koshevoy in *The Young Guard*, late 1940s.

into a single farm, this brilliant short-story writer and master of the honed metaphor had agreed that it was necessary to be assimilated to the new regime. He spoke of the agony of killing one's own vision and voice. Basically, he was legitimizing this self-murder, trying to justify it aesthetically. Whether the young Lyubimov understood this, I do not know.

Lyubimov took a long time to find his own voice. Occasionally his conscience was pricked, for example on the set of the film *The Kuban Cossacks*, when an old peasant woman, astonished by the sight of tables groaning with requisitioned food in the midst of a famine, asked him: 'Which life is the film based on?' Or whilst making himself up, he would suddenly be disgusted at the idea of a grown man having to paint his face and go around inhaling dust from the realistic back-drops and floor coverings depicting the happy Soviet open spaces.[24] Just as Andrey Sinyavsky would later say that his differences with Soviet power were less political than stylistic, so Lyubimov's were mainly aesthetic. Working in the NKVD ensemble had thrown him together with people as talented as Shostakovich and the playwright Nikolay Erdman. Lyubimov had no great objections to the political system, but he could not stand the stuffy box-sets and boring blazers of Soviet 'realistic' theatre. The interesting thing is how stylistic differences could become crucial, and lead to hard labour in Sinyavsky's case and emigration in Lyubimov's.

It seems that Lyubimov's peasant roots and Vakhtangov training suddenly impelled him to change his life radically. He withdrew into a drama school and at forty-six staged Brecht's *The Good Person of Setzuan* with his third-year students. From this student production sprang not only the Taganka Theatre but a whole period in the life of the Russian theatre after Stalin.

The choice of play can only be explained in the context of the times. Yefremov began the Sovremennik with the plays of Rozov and Volodin. Anatoly Efros also entered the new theatre with Rozov's young male heroes. Anti-theatricality was the slogan of the day; most of the battles with the mendacious official Stalinist art that had appropri-ated Stanislavsky's system were fought under this banner. And despite the fact that there had been one or two productions of Brecht and the Berliner Ensemble had visited Moscow in 1957, Brecht was regarded by both left and right as highly suspect. Some people were embarrassed by his open revolutionary commitment, which did not fit into the author-ized framework. Others were disconcerted by his rationalism. Instead of the familiar 'being the part' – the complete immersion of the actor in his role, as Stanislavsky demanded – 'alienation' was offered, the actor could step out of his part, and even communicate directly with the audience. It was disturbing that Brecht seemed not to respect emotion, that he trusted reason more, relied on it and made great play of it. The German actors amazed Muscovites by explaining that their art was an attempt to 'resist the stream of vague, unconscious, mass emotions and instincts that for many years had been stirred up and exploited by fascism for its own evil ends'.[25]

The latter was one of the secret reasons for Russians' interest in Brecht. The experience of a country that had survived fascism and of an artist who had succeeded in extracting an amazingly powerful theatre from recent German history, pushed Lyubimov towards self-determination. The production mounted by students in the spring of 1963 became the manifesto of the new Muscovite stage.

Photographs of *The Good Person* early in its run show that it was excitingly new. On an empty stage (itself a novelty!) defined by raised walkways round the edges and a light grey canvas backcloth, stood two actors: one with a guitar, the other with an accordion. A third loafed around to one side of them, wearing a cap and jacket. The first two sang a brash, assertive song, and the third, who also had a guitar, announced the aesthetic programme of 'street theatre'. Watching all this from one side was a large portrait of Brecht, with his sunken eyes in their horn-rimmed glasses and a grimace that could have been comic or tragic. After the actor with the cap had finished, he doffed it and bowed to Brecht. This prologue was followed by a very short blackout, then a water-seller, wearing a jumper riddled with holes, ran on with a large bottle and a mug on a string, some passers-by walked up and down the raised gangways, and the spellbinding action was away.

Why was it so spellbinding? Here is Natalya Krymova's response from an article she wrote at the time:

> The water-seller did not bash his head against a wall, he merely pretended he did; a woman looked out not from a window, but from the portrait of Brecht – and she was far too dishevelled for naturalistic purposes; on the pavement sat joke gods; and all these characters were played not by performers from some

Plate 3   Vladimir Vysotsky and Zinaida Slavina in Yury Lyubimov's production of *The Good Person of Setzuan* at the Taganka Theatre, 1964.

popular theatre, but by ordinary drama school students. One felt a catch in one's throat, there's no doubt about it.[26]

The actors had not set out to 'be' inhabitants of Setzuan or the gods who were visiting Earth. They were interested witnesses – exactly as Brecht intended. The actors beautifully demonstrated and narrated what happened, but this acting manner did not detract from the drama of events or reduce the audience's involvement in them. On the contrary, one had the impression that the young actors had punched an enormous hole in the so-called 'fourth wall', erected for so many years by studious disciples of Stanislavsky. The performers began to communicate not just between themselves, but as it were through the auditorium, pulling the audience into their energy field. This, presumably, is what made the critic's throat catch.

Lyubimov began by reforming the technical side of the theatre, but this had wider consequences. Brecht was opening up the opportunity to touch on social paradoxes that the previous theatre could not. The themes of the crowd and the hero, the homeless and the rich, were being rediscovered. The only 'good person' the gods could find in the town was the prostitute Shen Te. Her tobacco shop was inundated by down-and-outs. A blind man was led in from the street, then some more relations of Shen Te's, and they all sat crammed together on a bench like sardines. Scenically it was an experiment in montage, in a new sense of space and its metaphoric possibilities. But it was also an experiment in a new social vision. The crowd of beggars became more and more insolent. They heckled, they rebelled, they all demanded a piece of the cake. Goodness proved incapable of saving the world. Thereupon Shen Te (played by Zinaida Slavina) turned into her nasty male cousin, Shui Ta, which she did simply by putting on a bowler hat and dark glasses. One critic suggested that the heroine's transformation was a metaphor for the dual nature of despotic power: side by side with the kind person (tsar or General Secretary), there is always the villain who does the Boss's dirty work.[27] I do not think Zinaida Slavina was playing this at all. She was remote from politics. She was, so to speak, putting heart into Brecht, that is all. She was not afraid of emotions, any more than the rest of the ensemble. Brecht had awoken slumbering forces. The students were restoring the healthy, direct spirit of plebeian entertainment, buffoonery, and the marketplace to a stage steeped in lies.

The production, which was designed by Boris Blank, had nothing concretely historical about it, nothing Chinese or 'Setzuanese' as was then the form. It was all recognisably Soviet. Only the choreography occasionally suggested oriental theatre. Lyubimov had learned how to blur the historical outlines of a play – a skill that would get him into a lot of trouble in the future.

In this production, the personal initiative of the performer was liberated from the burden of the so-called character whom he was supposed to embody. The character was created by two or three deft strokes, then it was played with like a mask; the actor poked his face round the mask and addressed the audience as himself and in the name of all the other thinking plebs in the gang. Among the new techniques used, the songs were the first to hit you. They had been translated by the poet Boris Slutsky and set to music by the actors themselves. They had been completely Russified. They were not just songs, they were a new way of presenting a dramatic production as a musical structure. They gave the show a definite rhythm, infecting the audience with an energy that freed its thoughts. 'The sheep step into line, the drums beat out', began the song innocently, but then it opened out and everyone took up the mischievous refrain: 'And the sheep themselves supply the drumskins!' The song suddenly hit you between the eyes, the audience were drawn into a stream of devastating paradoxes, and revelled in their own daring.

The country was slowly getting the fascist syndrome out of its soul. The people in the auditorium and those on-stage felt drawn together and recognized their true position. A critique of worn-out theatrical techniques had unexpectedly joined up with a critique of the life in which we were all marching in step, like the sheep. The sheep had unexpectedly straightened up and decided to protest. Handing over one's skin gratis for the regime to make drums from was coming to an end.

Of course, not all of this was said in so many words in 1963. Indeed, Yury Lyubimov attempted to persuade public opinion that the play he had staged was a 'parable about how impossible it is for a person to exist in an unjustly organized class society',[28] but few believed this sort of assurance any longer. People had learned to read between the lines.

When Konstantin Simonov supported the production in *Pravda* and thereby helped ensure that a new theatre would be created in Moscow, no one paid any attention to the arguments he used: 'It is a long time since I saw a production that launched such an uncompromising, frontal – yes, frontal – attack on capitalist ideology and morality, and with so much talent.'[29] I quote this passage to show just what our way of life, which was marvellously exposed in Lyubimov's production by a parable about submissive sheep, was like.

The company was set up in April 1964 in an old, dying theatre on Taganka Square. The building was renovated and portraits of Brecht, Vakhtangov, Meyerhold and Stanislavsky were hung in the foyer (actually, to begin with Stanislavsky was left out, but the district Party committee insisted). However, the portraits were the least of it. Lyubimov really did begin to return the spirit of revolutionary theatre to his stage. He began to feel for his roots, his origins; to claw back his own memory.

As I have said, the Taganka came into being just before the door slammed and the bald Nikita Khrushchev was replaced by the amazingly hirsute Leonid Brezhnev. To begin with, the Taganka was not a political theatre but a poetic one. Lyubimov immediately rejected the so-called Soviet play. In the two decades that he worked in Moscow, he never even staged a *good* Soviet play. He did not stage Rozov, Volodin, Arbuzov, Radzinsky or Zorin – not one of those who determined the repertoire in hundreds of our theatres. After *The Good Person*, he would create *Anti-Worlds* by the poet Andrey Voznesensky, *Ten Days That Shook the World* (after John Reed), then return to Brecht (*The Life of Galileo*) and tackle the classics (Molière's *Tartuffe*). He would open his theatre to the war poets (the production *The Fallen and the Living*), he would create a show about Mayakovsky (*Listen!*), and stage Sergey Yesenin's long poem *Pugachev*. At the end of the sixties he would begin to adapt prose for the theatre himself (Boris Mozhayev's *Alive*, followed by Gorky's *The Mother*). These efforts eventually led to a unique theatre without plays; one capable of turning poetry, prose, telegrams or film scripts into a stage experience.

Necessity is the mother of invention. Because Lyubimov could not stomach the pap of the modern Soviet play, he created an author's theatre in which the absence of 'normal plays' was made up for by exploiting to the full all the other ingredients of theatre. Lighting, music, scenery, using a 'montage of attractions' to unfold a stage composition, treating the stage as a painter's or sculptor's workshop in which everything is to hand yet transformed by art, from the trapdoors and fly bars to the brick wall of the theatre itself – all this spiritualized the stage itself and the stage began to inspire the imaginations of the performers.

Lyubimov discovered the designer David Borovsky and Borovsky created a different Lyubimov. It was like this in everything and with everyone. The director and the theatre built each other up. The actors had much of their leader in them, but he also took much from them: from Vladimir Vysotsky, Valery Zolotukhin, Alla Demidova, Veniamin Smekhov, or Leonid Filatov. I repeat: his actors were not just performers, they were co-authors of the production. Many of them wrote music and poetry, or dramatized prose works. One of them – Vladimir Vysotsky – became famous all over the country for his songs, which originated in the acting circle of the Taganka and were often written for Taganka productions. These songs of protest and humour accompanied our lives for almost twenty-five years; they became the voice of the undespairing and insuppressible *narod* (people).

The Taganka actors learned how to work in a 'non-play'. Being co-authors with the director, they had a total grasp of the composition and put the whole of themselves into the stage time allocated to them within it. As a result, in the best of the Taganka's productions everything was as packed with meaning as a line of verse. There was not a second of empty 'realistic communication'. The dialogue was always individual and rich in nuances, but it was arranged poetically as part of the overall rhythmic movement of the play. During the performance, Lyubimov often stood in the dark auditorium and as it were conducted what was happening on-stage, using special torch signals.

Mayakovsky used to say that every poet has poems that are 'carriages' and one that is the 'engine' that pulls them all along. For the poetic Taganka of the 1960s the 'engine' was their show about Mayakovsky himself, *Listen!*, which opened in 1967. The set designed by Enar Stenberg consisted merely of large cubes with letters on them from which words could be constructed. This fragmentation of meaning was carried through the whole production and culminated in the brilliant idea of splitting the single poetic personality of Mayakovsky into several components: he was played by five actors on-stage at the same time. None of them looked like Mayakovsky; indeed the most lyrical Mayakovsky (Boris Khmelnitsky) had a beard and stammered. From these five conflicting forces arose an image of the poet of Revolution, the lyricist and fantasizer, utopian and satirist, who had 'stood on the throat of his own song', as he put it.

Mayakovsky had been shamelessly appropriated by the Stalinist system (after his suicide, the dictator had declared him 'the best and most talented poet of the Soviet epoch', thus killing him a second time by forcibly canonizing him). The Taganka was restoring to the poet's image the true depth of his tragedy. It was not fully recognized then that the Revolution was the source of his destruction. Lyubimov hardly touched on Mayakovsky's self-deception – on the fact that he carried his death within him. The Taganka endeavoured to understand what were the *external* forces that killed Mayakovsky. The actors very wittily created a series of quick scenes showing the poet's clashes with the main character in Russian history, the bureaucrat-cum-fool. Here Lyubimov was touching for the first time on the theme that would preoccupy him for the two decades leading up to his emigration: how is the artist/Master/performer to exist under an anti-human regime? Lyubimov declared his love for the impassioned Mayakovsky, who was for him then the symbol of genuine Revolution, just as the impassioned Fidel Castro in his field jacket was for him the symbol of the true revolutionary, compared with the beetle-browed party worker Leonid Brezhnev.

The high-mindedness of the 'True Revolution' that inspired those who created the trilogy at the Sovremennik, also inspired Lyubimov. Just as at the Sovremennik they revelled in singing the Internationale at the end of *The Bolsheviks*, so the trappings of revolution were glorified in Lyubimov's production, *Ten Days That Shook the World*. With what enthusiasm we handed our tickets at the door to actors dressed as Red Army soldiers, who impaled them on their bayonets; how raptly we listened to the outrageous revolutionary songs played in the foyer before the performance . . .

In *Listen!* it was not just the poet who was killed, it was the myth of the 'Great Revolution'. What we were shown was the slow, agonizing destruction of talent. The five Mayakovskys gradually left the stage one by one. Mayakovsky the lyrical poet left, unable to stand the mockery of the crowd; the satirical poet left; finally the tribune of the Revolution left, because he could no longer exist in a state full of functionaries rather than humans. The five Mayakovskys died and we were left with the lacerating lines from one of his notebooks:

> I want to be understood by my country,
> and if I'm not,
>> well so what:
> I'll pass over
>> my native country
> like slanting rain.

This was one of the most transparent, simple, and bitter of the Taganka's productions. The theatre's brief youth was over. A fresh breeze of sorts was blowing from Prague, and the concept of 'socialism with a human face' achieved some currency. In reply, the cursed volcano began to wake up again. The theatre and with it the whole country was on the threshold of major events. All of this lived in the play about Mayakovsky's destruction; in his own anxiety and foreboding.

A secret document has survived, compiled by the Moscow city bureaucrats who were supposed to decide the fate of this production. It is fairly typical of this sort of operation, so if I quote a few lines from it I shall not have to explain any further the nature of Soviet censorship and the principles behind it:

> The Taganka Theatre did everything to give the impression that the persecution of Mayakovsky was organized and directed . . . by representatives and institutions of Soviet power, officials of the State apparatus, and the Party press . . . The choice of extracts and quotations is extremely tendentious . . . A text of Lenin's is poked fun at by delivering it from a hatch with the letter M on as though it were a men's toilet. Mayakovsky is played by five actors simultaneously. However, this makes no difference: the poet comes across to the audience as an embittered and hunted gladiator. He is alone in Soviet society. He has no friends and no one to defend him. He has no way out. In the end, the only logical escape for him is suicide. Altogether, the production leaves a dismal and depressing impression. As you leave the auditorium, you think: 'What a wonderful man

they hunted to death!' Who did? The impression is created that
Mayakovsky's tragedy was the fault of Soviet power.[30]

Lyubimov made changes, toned things down, devised a more optimistic ending. He mutilated the production, doing to it what Yury Olesha
had once advocated at the First Writers' Congress. However, unlike
Olesha, Lyubimov did not poeticize his self-destruction. He tried to
retain his own voice at any cost. And for a while he succeeded.

Lyubimov devised a way of playing the game that demonstrated
no mean grasp of the inner workings of power in his country. Every
director played his own game and had his own mask. Yefremov was per-
ceived as 'socially recognizable' and therefore played at being 'socially
recognizable'. Efros set himself up as a 'pure artist', whose pranks were
dealt with the way a district party secretary would have had to handle
the eccentricities of Mozart. Tovstonogov pursued a long-range strategy of compromises that would enable him and his theatre to stay
afloat. Lyubimov, however, chose to play the part of an insolent artist,
almost a hooligan (in officialdom's eyes, of course), who dares do outrageous things because he has some aces up his sleeve. It was a dangerous
game, but no bluff: in a situation where all the sheep were obedient,
only a person with 'someone behind him' could behave provocatively.
And several times in Lyubimov's life the shadow of this 'someone' was
seen.

The first time it happened was in April 1968, as events were
moving to a head in Czechoslovakia and Moscow was caught up in a
new spiral of ideological terror. It was decided to remove Lyubimov from
his theatre. The campaign slid smoothly into operation: public meetings were held, there were attacks in the press, and finally the office of
the district party committee proposed to Lyubimov 'strengthening the
leadership of the theatre'. This formula generally meant a recalcitrant
director was to be sacked. But Lyubimov decided to go for bust: he wrote
a letter to Brezhnev and got one of his liberal patrons in the entourage
to deliver it. A saving telephone call followed from Brezhnev's office:
'Carry on working, Yury Petrovich old chap, don't have another worry.'
Even now it is not clear what happened. Possibly, in his desire to restore
Stalinism, Brezhnev was reviving the glorious Stalin tradition of life-
saving calls to writers who were out of favour.

Plate 4   Yury Lyubimov's production of *Alive*, by Boris Mozhayev, Taganka
Theatre, 1968–1989.

Alexander Solzhenitsyn would later call his spiritual and literary autobiography *The Calf Kept Butting the Oak*. This was a highly
accurate description of the game that artists played with the regime.
In time the 'oak', that is, the regime, learned not only to react calmly
to the pranks of the 'calf', but even to toss him a few overripe acorns
in the form of a medal on an anniversary, or permission to direct in the
'rotten West'. Lyubimov played this dangerous game for two decades
and nearly lost: the regime almost tamed him, almost turned him to the
greater glory of the reign. The idea in such cases was that they could
say: 'You see, we too have our "lefties" and anyone can stage what they
like here.' In 1983 the creator of the Taganka would leave all that
behind him; he would break his tether. But at the end of the sixties, his
tether was still strong and his aim was different. He had to preserve his
theatrical home and common cause at all costs, even if it meant making
a pact with the Devil.

Lyubimov embodied this ambiguous situation in his production
Alive, which he was rehearsing in the spring of 1968 in parallel, as it
were, with the 'Prague Spring' and against its background. This long
short story by Boris Mozhayev had recently been published in *Novy*

mir and met with howls of reactionary criticism. The image of Fyodor Kuzkin, a Russian peasant who wages a supremely cunning war with the collective farm system, probably moved Lyubimov because it appeared lyrically linked to his own experience of 'butting the oak'. Lyubimov and his actors (especially Valery Zolotukhin, who played Kuzkin) demonstrated with great clarity and simplicity the essence of what one might call 'how a talented person survives under a regime that strikes everything dead'. The fact that Kuzkin was a simple peasant, and not a director or a writer (the characters most favoured by Anatoly Efros in those years), was particularly significant. What was at stake was the gene pool of the nation – and here Kuzkin was an extremely important figure.

This was probably the first time that Lyubimov had put his peasant roots, his ancestral memory, into his art. It was a folklore production, full of bawdy songs and pointed travesties of Christian mythology. The director and his designer David Borovsky (who was working with Lyubimov for the first time) had rejected any rural naturalism of the Soviet 'power of darkness' type. A silver birch grove sprouted out of an empty stage. The thin, living trunks had little huts in their tops, rather like starling boxes. It was a simple, poignant metaphor for our lives: people without homes, without domesticity, without property, relieved of everything that keeps people's feet on the ground. An angel might descend from the flies in the form of a ragamuffin peasant in torn breeches, and sprinkle semolina from a jar on Kuzkin and his children ('manna from heaven'). But in defiance of all the laws of nature the Russian peasant Fyodor Kuzkin still existed, resisted, used all his wits to stay alive.

They tried to destroy *Alive*. At a special run-through with an empty auditorium, the Minister of Culture Yekaterina Furtseva clapped her bediamonded hands at the point where the poor angel was flying about, stopped the rehearsal, and bellowed: 'Does this theatre have a Party cell in it, or doesn't it?!' Answer came there none. She then tried to enter into a dialogue with the performers. 'Hey, actor, you there, actor!' she shouted to Ramzes Dzhabrailov, the peasant angel with his pot of manna. Lyubimov recalls that the tiny Ramzes, with his wisps of hair and torn tights, then stuck his frightened head round the wings. 'Aren't you ashamed to be taking part in this disgraceful exhibition?'

she asked him. But the frail little man ascended his Calvary: 'No, I'm not.' Thereupon the Minister bustled out of the theatre, dropping her astrakhan coat, which one of her retinue picked up.[31]

The show was doomed. Like its peasant hero, however, Lyubimov kept his head down and waited. Twenty-one years later it was revived when Lyubimov returned from emigration. It was a great theatrical occasion. The auditorium was full of prominent sixties survivors, there were tears, elation, amazement at the determination of the people who had saved Fyodor Kuzkin. There were the same classical silver birches with the starling box houses in their tops; the same Valery Zolotukhin was playing the lead; there were the same earthy songs, with some new, very daring ones in the spirit of *glasnost*. And yet, there was a feeling of tremendous sadness that the production had come too late, that it had withered, having been born in a different age and suffocated by silence.

The fact that *Alive* was banned did not break the Taganka. In fact their resistance became more conscious. A poetic theatre turned into a political one. In 1969 Lyubimov staged a production of Gorky's novel *The Mother*. August 1968 had happened, the tanks had settled in around Prague, and the soldiers in their barracks. A few brave dissidents had come out to demonstrate on a deserted Red Square, and promptly been thrown into camps. Lyubimov came out not on to the square, but on to the stage. The calf decided to butt the oak from a different, completely unexpected quarter. Gorky's novel had laid the foundations of socialist realism, but it enabled Lyubimov to mount a production of unprecedented social criticism. He packed everything into it: the impossibility of living with a noose round one's neck, the need to fight, and the fact that resistance was doomed.

At first David Borovsky wanted to cover the Taganka stage with a brightly coloured parquet floor, like one in the Winter Palace. Blood would have been split on this floor and soldiers would have come on and scraped it, washed it down, and polished it until it shone again. Then he thought of using the architecture of the stage itself and its technical accoutrements to suggest the Nizhny Novgorod factory where the play was set. The stage was stripped to a womb and the audience saw two staircases running up the side walls, along the top, and into the bare brick wall at the back. The space of the stage became a changing metaphor: when fly beams were lowered, for instance, and the actors 'worked' at them with files, you instantly thought of a factory. The back wall was made up to look like a series of bricked-up window frames with boarded-up doors below them. This alluded to a feature of the Russian mentality that the rest of the world has difficulty understanding. When a building is planned in Russia, it is always given a large number of doors; but once it is built they are all nailed up and only one narrow, awkward way in is left. Borovsky and Lyubimov succeeded in creating what one might call the affective-dimensional environment of the production. They also found a genuine steam train whistle from the turn of the century, with a frighteningly deep, uterine kind of sound which cut across the otherwise agitated soundtrack of the production.

The main idea of the director's, however, which transported this school set-text into the present, was to have a square of real live soldiers standing with fixed bayonets round the edge of the stage and for everything to go on inside this square. Lyubimov arranged with the local guards' commander to have several dozen young soldiers appear on stage. And insofar as there was a predominance of fellows from Central Asia in our security forces at that time, the selection of faces alone made a strong artistic impression. From time to time the soldiers would face the auditorium and with their somehow detached, narrow Asian eyes they would scour the Moscow audience, which cringed beneath their gaze. When a handful of people with a red flag came on stage to hold a May Day demonstration and found themselves inside the living square of soldiers, the setting was so familiar that one winced. It was a theatrical metaphor for the age-old Russian confrontation.

Lyubimov blurred the dating of Gorky's tale and brought in texts from other works by him – works replete with hatred for the slavishness of Russian life. He cast Zinaida Slavina, who was schooled in Brecht, as the heroine Nilovna. She used alienation effects to play her as a downtrodden old woman finding her way into the revolutionary movement. She acted not Nilovna's character and age, but her predicament. It was an imperceptibly mounting image of resistance, suppressed anger, and the hatred that was silently building up in the whole country. At the end, this theme emerged into a scene called 'Dubinushka', which was classical in its directorial composition and emotional impact.

In Russia everyone knows the song about the 'cudgel' (*dubinushka*), if only because of the superb rendition by Shalyapin. Nowhere will you find a better expression of the spirit of the workers' artel, of Russian oppression and Russian rebellion, than in this song of the people, which does not even possess a canonical text. The texts may differ, but the refrain is famous: '*Ey, dubinushka, ukhnem!*' In Lyubimov's production this song of the workers' artel grew into a musical image of an enslaved country threatening one day to straighten its back and lash out with this 'cudgel'. The dark expanse of the stage was filled with human faces slightly lit from below. The actors were standing on fly beams at different heights, so that not only the horizontal stage space, but the vertical space was filled. The effect was as if the air of the stage itself was thick with anger. And these faces, suspended in air, this Taganka artel, began to sing 'Dubinushka'. They began softly, not articulating the words, just intoning the stresses, winding the theatre up with sheer energy: 'I have heard many songs in my native land, folks sang 'em for joy and for sorrow . . .' Then, at the refrain, the faces swam through the air and this movement caught up the tune, intensified it a hundredfold. When the *forte* point came, the director lit the tableau more: all the actors had put the fly beams against their chests, swayed with them as though pulling barges, and moved towards the auditorium, drawn by a mighty burst of song: '*Ey, dubinushka, ukhnem*, heave and she'll go, hea-ve ho!' Suddenly Shalyapin's incomparable bass wove itself into the tumult of modern voices. It was as though the great Russian art of the past was experiencing with them what they were doing on the Taganka stage, echoing this movement, this heaving towards liberation. It is difficult to describe the impact it had on the audience. Probably it was one of the most sublime moments of sixties Soviet theatre.

Where we came from: Tovstonogov's diagnosis

Georgy Tovstonogov has already been introduced with his production of *The Idiot*. It is now time to say a bit more about him as a key figure in our post-Stalin theatre.

Tovstonogov wrote several books himself and even more have been written about him.[32] Nevertheless, he remains one of the most enigmatic figures on the Russian stage. He defies simple definitions. Of course, as has already been said, it was Tovstonogov's mission to bring together again the two halves of our culture that had been torn apart – the pre-war and the post-war. This is generally indisputable. He had

46

grown from a MKhAT root, but had learned the lessons of Meyer-hold and Tairov well. He understood early on what opportunities the Brechtian 'corrective' was opening up for the actor's art. He was one of the first of our directors allowed 'out', and he studied closely what was going on in European theatre. He acquired something more important from the West than his favourite tweed jackets. In the 1960s he began to experiment at grafting the poetics of the Theatre of the Absurd onto Gorky's plays. He took account in his art of the experience of Brook and Bergman, both of whom he knew well, and was one of the first to open up a theatrical window on Europe.

Tovstonogov is commonly thought of as a synthesist. However, mere synthesis does not produce great directors. There has to be some personal ferment that gives the synthesis its unrepeatable artistic individuality.

It is difficult to identify Tovstonogov's 'ferment'. He dissolved his own voice in his authors and actors. Sometimes he altered it beyond recognition, remaining true to himself only in one thing – his professionalism. He was a professional when he staged Dostoyevsky or Tolstoy, but he also remained a professional when he put on a play about Lenin or extolled collectivization in his version of Sholokhov's *Virgin Soil Upturned*, which had an extraordinary ensemble of actors. He was probably faithful to his craft even when (in the late forties) he put on Shalva Dadiani's monstrous play *From a Spark*, dedicated to Stalin.

It is said that words have a conscience. A true poet cannot wrench them as he wishes. When Mandelshtam attempted to force an ode to Stalin out of himself, he was destroying himself and began to go mad. How Tovstonogov brought himself to exercise his divine gift on *Virgin Soil Upturned* remains a mystery. Nor is it very clear what were the sources of his faith. He could not possibly have had any sincere affection for the regime. Its genocide had touched his family directly. Fear had implanted itself in him when he was a teenager. It was the force behind his life – but also behind many of his most moving theatrical creations, in which he was trying to get this fear out of his system (his production of Gogol's *Government Inspector* was about a country in which everything is driven by fear). He made professionalism his anchor and the symbol of his faith. It was his way of surviving and his response to the riddle of the Soviet sphinx.

He often said that he could not sit down and read a novel the way everyone else did. He reacted to every text as a director, attempting to identify what lay behind every conversation and what each person was really after. He translated everything into actions. He utterly subordinated his reading persona to his aims as a director. He revealed the whole of our life as an on-going play with certain *données*. He learned to read these *données* better than anyone else. He turned his own life into a play, attempting to anticipate and act out the role time had devised for him.

There were precedents for this way of life and for this attitude towards the profession. Again, Tovstonogov reminds one of Nemirovich-Danchenko. They both inclined towards epic theatre and could study a play and extract its hidden meaning with inexorable logic. They both collected talented actors and understood them from top to toe. Observing law and order was part of their code of social behaviour, as was the ability to enjoy life to a ripe old age. They steered their theatres' ships skilfully, aware of all that lurked in the Soviet sea. The co-founder of the Moscow Arts and friend of Chekhov ended up becoming the theatrical director-in-chief of the Stalin empire; which did not prevent him from remaining a first-class artist, who, at the age of eighty-three, created what may well have been the best production of *Three Sisters* in the Art Theatre's history. After Nemirovich-Danchenko, Tovstonogov was the only director who managed for three decades to head the Soviet theatrical Olympus and remain not only a professional of the highest calibre but a 'shaper of minds'. One can only imagine what this cost him.

Although he was flexible in his relations with the outside world, inside the theatre he was a dictator (like Nemirovich-Danchenko). He was feared and adored. He had been hardened under Stalin and he perpetuated the mentality of that era in his own theatre. He loved power and enjoyed the art of exercising it. His guttural voice, with its pleasant Georgian accent, the large ring he wore on his finger, his thick horn-rimmed glasses, his boldly sculpted face rather like a bird of prey, his deadly irony and his great diplomatic charm – all suggested he was one of the lords of life. This did not prevent him from being morbidly sensitive to what other people thought and said, and he tried very hard to manipulate the theatrical press. Behind his back, the whole theatrical world called him 'Goga', which made him more homely but also lent him a certain apocryphal stature. 'Goga' suggested a 'Godfather', that is, an unofficial authority in the theatrical world. And the official authorities in the theatre world had to reckon with this unofficial authority. More than once they tried to sink their fangs into it. For thirty years Georgy Tovstonogov ran an exemplary theatre in the cradle of the Revolution, Leningrad, which was the most unconducive city for art in the Soviet Union.

In terms of social memory, his productions were as accurate as a court record. Popular, even trite plays showed his analytical gifts to particular advantage. His fame began with Vsevolod Vishnevsky's *An Optimistic Tragedy*. Even by the standards of our literary herbarium, this author was a very poisonous specimen. He had been a machine-gunner and commissar during the Civil War, a Stalinist literary hit-man after that, and founded the Soviet genre of the 'optimistic tragedy', which was canonized in the early thirties with Tairov's celebrated production of the play.

Tovstonogov took this play and poured a different content into it. He changed its emphases, placing at its centre not the female commissar but the figure of Vozhak ('the leader'), in whom he expressed all his pent-up hatred of the regime. He rejected the exquisite geometry of Tairov's staging. Tairov had aestheticized and romanticized the Revolution, and to this Tovstonogov opposed the bloody reality of it, the indifference of heaven, and the vile machinations of people who were dragging the nation into a meat-mincer to satisfy their own lust for power.

Vozhak, the 'leader' of the anarchists, was played by Yury Tolubeyev. His gait was ambling, he spat out one-liners, his face was like stone, his brow low, and his eyes empty and unblinking. Konstantin Rudnitsky has written:

> This mass of flesh inside a sailor's striped vest exuded a terrifying absolute power that knew neither mercy nor compassion. Vozhak was the embodiment of unbridled violence and maniacal paranoia. When the revolve brought into view the fat hulk of this idol, reclining on a flowery carpet surrounded by obsequious henchmen ready to shoot anyone he told them to, the audience was overcome by an acute, if as yet powerless, hatred.[33]

49

The portrait does not mention who the prototype of Vozhak was; whose demise the audience was yearning for. There was no need to spell that out. It was December 1955. Stalin's body was still lying in the mausoleum and audiences understood the metaphor perfectly well. The criminal nature of the Stalinist state, dressed up in revolutionary slogans, had been presented by Tovstonogov for all to see. Vozhak died horribly slowly, and just before he went he summoned up all his energy to electrify the audience with the croaky words: 'Long live the Revolution!' By presenting this symbiosis of the criminal and the revolutionary, Tovstonogov had gone to the heart of one of the century's most subtle deceptions.

Shortly after *An Optimistic Tragedy* opened, Tovstonogov was appointed head of the Gorky Bolshoy Drama Theatre (BDT),[34] and began to reorganize it. He was fully aware of the problems. He did not hesitate to bring in new actors, but he was extremely cautious about introducing a new repertoire. French melodrama rubbed shoulders with unpretentious Soviet comedy, but both were staged with professional chic. It was only at the end of the second season that he launched *The Idiot* with Smoktunovsky. This was a breakthrough, an upheaval, a qualitative shift not only for theatre in Leningrad, but for the whole Russian stage.

After a production like this, the most difficult thing was to maintain the level. In the next theatrical season Tovstonogov rested with an Italian pot-boiler by Aldo Nicolaj called *Signior Mario Writes a Comedy*, and an equally mundane Soviet play by Ignaty Dvoretsky called *The Highway*. In 1959 he directed Aleksandr Volodin's *Five Evenings* and Gorky's *Barbarians*. Both productions unquestionably turned Tovstonogov and his actors into Russia's number one theatre company.

The action of *Five Evenings* was set in an ordinary Leningrad flat, where a certain Sasha Ilin had turned up after an absence of seventeen years in the Far North. He had decided to visit a girl called Tamara, whom he knew when he was a teenager and whom everyone in those far-off days called 'Star'. Who Ilin is, and why he spent so many years in the North, is left to the imagination. His 'Star' has certainly faded in the meantime: she has become a foreman at a factory, is childless, unmarried, submissively happy, and lavishes all her love on her nephew, whom she is trying to knock some sense into, where necessary with the help of Karl Marx. The faceless set was in keeping with the characters. It was a painfully familiar picture of semi-poverty: a table covered with a cheap oilcloth, a cupboard, a sofa with a dark blanket thrown over it, and the inevitable tin washtub hanging by the door. Tovstonogov did not even show a scrap of the city through the curtained-off windows, which might have relieved the sensation that everything going on was utterly trivial. An ordinary lorry driver from the North, with a pleasant, slightly over-assertive baritone and touches of the provincial Don Juan; and an ordinary woman who works in a factory, wears curlers and fills her voice with received optimism. Two cases of *Homo sovieticus* . . .

Love did not sweep these people off their feet. No, it flared up somewhere deep inside them, afraid to express itself openly. They just chattered, they said nothing important out loud, in case it scared their possible moment of happiness away. Volodin had written a tale about how feelings return to people who have been turned to stone. How the husk of a ready-made persona, complete with assimilated tones of voice and conventional social roles, gets peeled away. How a 'Soviet' person becomes simply a person; returns to being him/herself. This melody, as simple as the musical scale itself, was performed by Yefim Kopelyan and Zinaida Sharko. It was an achievement of a poetical order: through the magic of naive and almost meaningless words filtered the light of a time of great changes, when millions of Ilins were returning from camps and exile, meeting their near ones again, and thawing themselves out in faceless flats that were, however, home. The joy of normal words, of domestic humour, of unannihilated humanity, won the audience over. 'My dear sweet darling, take me with you' this woman sang to the guitar – and seemed to have become amazingly pretty. One was over-whelmed with love for the miracle of life that had come through.

Tovstonogov gave Volodin's tale the breath of history. Perhaps this was the strongest aspect of his directing generally. His talents were essentially epic. Not surprisingly, therefore, people called his productions stage novels. Behind any play he could see the chunk of life that had served as the source for it. The marks on the page then filled with astounding 'accidents' and discoveries, which seemed to have been brought forth from within the play itself, without doing any violence to its structure. Tovstonogov despised directing that was just a display of inventiveness. He did not like the noun 'concept', he preferred the verb 'unravel'.

Having unravelled Volodin, he gave a rereading of *Barbarians*. Gorky wrote it at the beginning of the century. It concerns two railway engineers, 'bearers of civilization', who arrive in a Russian provincial town that is a quagmire of 'barbarism'. As a result of their cultural activity, the dozy little corner is turned upside down and destroyed, and Nadezhda Monakhova, the excise officer's wife, kills herself after falling in love with one of the engineers. Obviously, the civilizers themselves were the barbarians.

Lev Tolstoy once waspishly called Gorky's plays 'ecumenical councils of know-alls'; and he was right. Every single one of Gorky's characters loves to talk in aphorisms and parables. They are clever with Gorky's cleverness, endowed with the crude sociology into which he had compressed his enormous experience of Russian life. His plays are as weak as his prose about Russian provincial life is strong. Gorky himself felt this, and disparaged his theatrical work. The success of two of his plays on the stage of the Moscow Arts was that of a slogan shouted at the right moment. Soon MKhT started turning his plays down. Apropos of *Summerfolk*, Nemirovich-Danchenko wrote him a stiff letter in which he identified Gorky's main sickness as a writer: he did not love any of his characters.[35] After that, the word 'Gorkiada' entered MKhT's vocabulary, to describe plays that were 'committed', tendentious and politically coloured; that is, everything that Chekhov's were not. After the Revolution, when Gorky was turned into a sacred cow, his plays were finally deactivated as works of art and used as object lessons in class hatred. No one sought in them any growing, living meaning addressed to new generations.

Tovstonogov used *Barbarians* to create a novel about Russian life. He took the play back, so to speak, to its origins. In the centre of his design he placed Nadezhda Monakhova, played by Tatyana Doronina. Gorky had written an anecdote in the Russian style about a very beautiful and very stupid provincial lady, almost an idiot, who had read too many novels and therefore saw the newly arrived engineer Cherkun as the man her soul had been longing for. Her suicide at the end of the play was pure parody: it was how Russian women of destiny were supposed to kill themselves in novels.

Tovstonogov turned all this round. He took seriously the beauty and the suicide of the excise officer's wife. Nadezhda was not just beautiful, she was *searingly* beautiful. However, it was not the sensuality of this that was played (sensuality did not mean much on the Soviet stage anyway); it was the Platonic aspect of a provincial lady who was dazzlingly beautiful. Triumphant, her head held at a proud angle, completely indifferent to the scrum on stage, she stood to one side of everyone else, fixing her bright blue eyes on Cherkun (played by Pavel Luspekayev). She spoke in a tense whisper, with the short, different length gasps that later became Doronina's trademark. At that time even these gasps were irresistible. They were the voice of the love for which she had been waiting. Nadezhda could babble what she liked, it changed nothing. Even arrant nonsense endeared her. Beauty need not worry about wit.

And she indeed had someone to fix her eyes on. With Luspekayev's arrival at the BDT, Tovstonogov acquired a performer of rare gifts and that reckless Russian energy which blazes brightly but not for long. He acted little, drank a great deal, got gangrene and had to have part of his leg amputated. He still tried to act in films, in parts where he could stay sitting down; and you could not take your eyes off him even in these 'sitting roles'. A passionate drama on an almost classical scale unfolded between Doronina's and Luspekayev's characters, one that baulked at nothing and nobody. The unfortunate excise officer Monakhov (Yevgeny Lebedev) played clarinet in the firemen's band and felt God had punished him by making him the owner of otherworldly beauty. At one moment, in a divine whisper, without raising her voice, Nadezhda said to him: 'Get away from me, corpse.' The production possessed every ingredient of the Russian nightmare: people shot each other, drank themselves stupid, made fools of each other, and tormented each other. In the end, you felt sorry for all of them, and Nadezhda Monakhova's death was devastating. 'You have killed a human being' Mavriky Monakhov said in the deathly silence. 'What have you done, what have you done?' he kept repeating stupidly, and his question was addressed not so much to the barbaric engineers as to the one responsible for ordering the world in this way. This sudden shift in meaning and emotion filled the play with precisely the compassion that the co-founder of MKhT had found lacking in Gorky's plays.

Two years later Tovstonogov gave a new reading of Griboyedov's *Woe from Wit*. As behoves a classic, the play was impenetrably encased in the acting tradition. Tovstonogov decided to sharpen the subject of the play immediately by hanging a placard above the proscenium with Pushkin's words: 'God help anyone born in Russia with wit and talent.' It caused a furore. The director let the epigraph be taken down, since every fibre of his production screamed the Pushkinian message anyway. The penetration of his reading was achieved by a simple yet irresistible ploy. Tovstonogov trusted Pushkin's criticism of Griboyedov's hero, namely that this hero, Chatsky, is not clever, because clever people do not cast pearls before swine, and submitted him to . . . the audience's judgement. It was a Brechtian alienation technique. These historical characters ceased communicating directly with one another. Chatsky and his opponents began to 'cast' all their passionate monologues before a modern audience. The characters communicated *via* the audience, which became both witness and judge of their irreconcilable conflict.

Phrases one had known since one's schooldays suddenly came alive with fresh meaning. Tovstonogov's own wit remained level-headed: he gave his Chatsky no chance of winning, but managed to glimpse the face of the new generation.

As with Smoktunovsky in the part of Myshkin, Tovstonogov found the ideal actor for the lead. Sergey Yursky was a complete unknown, but his star began to rise the day the production opened. He was a highly strung young man, not handsome, and even outwardly reminded one of Meyerhold. With his amazing feel for verse, his brilliant sense of irony, and eyes sparkling with intelligence, he became a lyrical focus of the sixties generation. He was one of those who had managed to inhale some of the air of freedom and he turned it into the theme of his art. His Chatsky loved, suffered, choked for air and writhed with pain. He could not get through to anyone, or make himself heard by anyone. He unburdened himself to the modern audience, who responded with a wave of bitter sympathy. In the scene at the ball, Tovstonogov surrounded his hero with a *danse macabre* of masks and pigs' snouts that undermined his sanity. Although not in Griboyedov's script, it was completely consistent with the truth of the production when Chatsky/Yursky fainted in the middle of this scene and the people in masks carried on whirling their endless waltz.

The director also completely reinterpreted Griboyedov's hero-ine. Tatyana Doronina's Sofya consciously preferred a fool to a clever man and took the snub-nosed lackey Molchalin for a hero. Boris Alpers, a critic of the Meyerhold generation, was disconcerted by such a distortion of the original, but left an accurate description of the key episode: 'Sofya/Doronina in a bright red velvet dress and with golden tresses tumbling down her back lies face down across the stairs, lit from every side by floodlights; Famusov and Chatsky deliver their monologues, and Sofya still lies there lit by the fierce floodlights.'[36]

This may have been one of Tovstonogov's bitterest intuitions. The sixties people conducted dessicating ideological battles with an impregnable centre of power, they cast pearls before swine, they butted the oak, and meanwhile the wonder of life itself was passing before their eyes. A few years later Vampilov's heroes would appear on our stages: as it were exhausted Chatskys who would dream of retiring at thirty and drowning their sorrows in a glass of cheap wine.

Tovstonogov's objectivity was of a particular type. He always started from the present, but managed to give it the pulse of history. In the classics he revealed where our contemporary problems had come from.

The end of the 1960s and of the Thaw was marked in Moscow by Lyubimov and Yefremov differently, and in Leningrad by Tovstonogov's production of *Three Sisters* and Gorky's *Philistines*. What interested Tovstonogov in Chekhov's play was the theme of collective murder. This was the unexpected phrase he used to refer to the fact that all the characters in *Three Sisters* know about the impending duel between Solyony and Tuzenbakh, but none of them lifts a finger to stop it. It was also no coincidence that Tuzenbakh was played by Sergey Yursky. This generation that had got freedom into its bloodstream was broken. The director was offering his own analysis of the situation and he focused first and foremost on the all-pervading paralysis of will. He was challenging the garrulous liberal intelligentsia who had voluntarily ceded their house to Natasha, the 'rough-coated animal' as her husband calls her. Very few, it has to be said, understood that Tovstonogov's analysis was coolly prescient. The coldness of his condemnation was interpreted as an excess of rationalism. People looked in vain in the production for a nerve, for passion and social protest (for which there was still a demand).

Three Sisters was staged in 1965 and in the following season Tovstonogov's production of *Philistines* opened. As we know, Chekhov did not like this play. He did not think that the disgusting old man at the centre of it could hold it together, because a petty domestic tyrant would not engage the audience's sympathy. Tovstonogov trusted Chekhov's judgement. He read his own historical experience into *Philistines* and realigned the conflicts in the play. Bessemenov became a tragicomic King Lear figure who, however, did not experiment with dividing up his property but did everything in his power to prevent his household from falling apart and his children from leaving.

The director found a magic crystal that transformed the domestic drama into a tragicomedy. People are trapped in a vicious circle of dead ideas and as one character puts it they keep 'acting out a scene from an endless comedy called *Neither This Way Nor That*'. The style that expressed this tug-of-war was borrowed from the theatre of the absurd. At the beginning and end of the production Tovstonogov presented Bessemenov's household as a kind of surrealist mural in the form of a family photograph. At the centre of the universe was Bessemenov, severe, grey-bearded, with all the appearance of a prosperous merchant who had led an upright life, scraped together his capital, and brought up his children. The latter were gathered round him: his own children Pyotr and Tatyana, and his adopted son Nil. But all this was against a studio backdrop with an erupting volcano on it, which they did not notice!

The play began with old Bessemenov, played by Yevgeny Lebedev, coming on to take his morning tea. The unoiled door produced a strange whine, suggesting some disorder, some secret ailment in the house (this whine would become a leitmotiv of the production, like the strangulated chimes of the enormous grandfather clock). The old man's movements were deliberate; he was clearly gnawed by thoughts, had not slept all night, and wanted to discuss with the members of his household something of great moment. He crossed himself – devoutly, deliberately and demonstratively, so that everyone could see he was suffering and asking the Lord for something important. His daughter Tatyana (Emma Popova) was standing behind him and also performed this ritual, but turning round he could see that she was crossing herself quite nonchalantly. Before they sat down round the family table, there was another rude departure from tradition: the daughter sat down on a chair before her father, he did not let this pass, waited until she stood up again, then sat down and began his morning 'sermon': 'Cube sugar is heavy and not sweet; therefore it is unprofitable.' He uttered this nonsense as though it had the most profound subtext – as though it were a revelation. So he continued throughout the play.

Bessemenov/Lear was trying to teach his household sense. But no one would listen to him except his frightened old wife, who timidly pushed a cheesecake in front of him in an attempt to shut him up and avoid a scene. In fact, though, the whole production consisted of erupting family scenes virtuosically presented in the style of absurdist theatre. The old man knew he was right. His concept of a household had stood the test of centuries and his animal instinct told him that something was up; that his children, to whom he had unfortunately given a university education, were on the wrong track. 'I can see he's going to be a shyster . . . an actor, or something like that', he said, raising his scrawny arm with clenched fist then bringing it down like a chopper. 'Maybe he'll even be a socialist . . . Well, serve him right!'

Tovstonogov demonstrated that this play, written at the turn of the century, was capable of a completely new interpretation. Nil, a factory hand in a Gorky shirt, was a marvellous fellow who had been fed and brought up in the Bessemenov household, but felt no gratitude to them whatsoever. He went around tossing off Gorky slogans, which in the Soviet period became clichés, such as 'He who works is boss!' In Gorky's conception, Nil represented the future. From the vantage of that future, Tovstonogov decided to take a closer look at this workman. It was all done in a style of utter objectivity – one in which Tovstonogov had no equals. Kirill Lavrov played Nil as a good chap, one of those termed in the Stalinist period 'socially recognizable'. Frank, content with everything, foreign to all introspection, in love with Polina, whom he had brought into the house without consulting his father, Nil was striding confidently into the future. He had only one failing: he was a bit thick-skinned. He was not in the habit of noticing other people's lives. He did not notice the drama of the old man, and he did not notice Tatyana gazing at him with lovestruck eyes. When she came across him kissing Polya in the dark, he raised a lit match to the face of his grief-stricken adopted sister and this realistically motivated gesture sent a shiver down your spine: it evoked associations of an interrogator dazzling his victim with a lamp.

Tatyana tried to poison herself; everything was collapsing around their ears; the old man kept making Herculean efforts to save the House. Every new scene was accompanied by the ghastly twanging of a balalaika, a sound that gave the action a touch of the Devil. The children were leaving. However, they did not leave in a human fashion, they did it churlishly. 'I *knew* he would leave,' the petty bourgeois Lear said with hopeless lucidity, 'but not like this!'

What was collapsing was not a household, but the nucleus of how Russia had lived. It was accepted to despise this 'nucleus'. To some extent this was the fault of Russia's 'ideological' literature, since it had made the very concept of the middle class contemptible. Tovstonogov did not justify the petty bourgeois Bessemenov, he merely rehabilitated the life of an entire section of society. Through Gorky's play written sixty years before, Tovstonogov touched the very heart of Russian life that would be destroyed by the Revolution.

At the end of the play, Bessemenov was suprisingly calm and finicky. He took the flowers off the windowsill one by one, very slowly, as if it was a ritual. Before standing on the *chaise-longue*, he carefully wiped his feet. The mesmerized house was watching Vasily Bessemenov go mad. Finally, he opened a window, shouted to the police, and only then did the final grand 'scene' begin. The house was empty, the old man alone, and he fought to get his breath back. Then, leaning on his chair, he slowly got up and went off to his room. In the deathly silence the door whined yet again and we heard the diabolical balalaika in the distance. A drop curtain came down and on it again was the respectable family portrait: the father with his spade beard, the mother and the children. And behind them was the smoking Vesuvius with a few palms, so incongruous in the Russian climate.

Within the bounds of tenderness (Efros in the sixties)
Anatoly Efros was born in Kharkov in 1925, studied at GITIS in Moscow under Aleksey Popov, and began his career as a director in the provinces at Ryazan. In the early fifties he was invited to work at the Central Children's Theatre (Moscow), which was then run by Mariya Knebel, a pupil of Stanislavsky and Michael Chekhov. Efros did not create a

theatrical 'church' of his own, as he was not allowed to. However, this did not prevent him from becoming one of the greatest directors of the post-Stalin period.

In his book *A Love of Rehearsals*, Efros attempts to explain the essence of how he works with actors. He speaks of the 'zigzag filament' of the human soul, its contradictions, which have to be uncovered and expressed on the stage. He compares it with a cardiogram, in which the jagged peaks convey the workings of the pulsating heart, and only a straight line signifies death.[37]

For a quarter of a century, the art of Efros himself was a kind of stage cardiogram. The jagged peaks and troughs of his productions showed us the rhythm of our own heart. His lyrical talent naturally predisposed him to this role, although he started out next to Oleg Yefremov and continued together with Yury Lyubimov and Georgy Tovstonogov, who were his friends and artistic rivals. Unlike them, he did not have his own theatrical home. Fortunately, his management of the Leninsky Komsomol Theatre swiftly ended in dismissal. I say 'fortunately', because it spared him from the kind of responsibilities towards the regime that went with any official position. He did not have to play the part of 'first Soviet theatre director' and sign open letters against Solzhenitsyn, as did Tovstonogov. He did not have to conform to the image of officially endorsed dissident that was foisted on Lyubimov. He did not have to put on productions for revolutionary and Party jubilees, as Yefremov did. Basically, Efros was ignored and left with only one thing to get on with – his art. He was fortunate indeed!

He believed that great performers had a low pain threshold, as it were lacked skin, and this was true of himself. His response to a theatrical moment was so strong that he might burst into tears or faint. Even when he laughed, a dark anxiety flickered in his oriental eyes. Moreover he was alien, if not hostile, to 'social gestures' or 'commitment', as it was then called, and was not a hard drinker – something virtually unheard-of in our theatre. His favourite modern dramatist was the boneless, lyrical Aleksey Arbuzov, who was both theatrical and humanly universal.[38] This 'lack of principles' irritated and shocked people, but for him it was a means of escape and self-preservation.

Absorbed in the problems of art, Efros did not accept, and then more and more despised, the modern world around him. He seemed to unlearn how to stage modern plays, even Arbuzov. His 'struggles', as Pasternak would have said, were largely 'with himself'. Amidst the general collapse, he attempted to find an ecological niche in the classics. It was the metaphysical problems that he relished in them. He confronted the spiritual experience captured by Chekhov, Shakespeare, Dostoyevsky or Molière with the experience of Soviet life – his personal experience. From this confrontation he produced impressions that meant something to everybody.

He created his actors, who then became mysteriously joined to him. Outside his vision they simply ceased to exist. In the end this led to a terrible breakdown in their relations, a war in which there were no victors. He taught his actors to move strangely, as though weaving a spell. His staging did not seem fixed, it was more like Brownian movement, and had an hypnotic effect. Efros's best productions are as difficult to describe as good jazz (which he adored). What won you over was the improvisatory lightness within the clearly marked boundaries of the plot. He taught his actors how to create a tough emotional geometry. He taught them to improvise within the established rectangle, the 'bounds of tenderness' as he sometimes called it at rehearsals. He had no special theory; to a large extent he relied on intuition and was simply expressing what engaged his soul at a given moment.

He started with the plays of Viktor Rozov, which won us over in those days with their truthfulness to life. Like Yefremov (who acted in these plays), Efros was discovering for himself the live Stanislavsky. The creator of MKhAT was out of fashion, 'rehabilitation' was coming in, and people were beginning to whisper the names of Meyerhold and Tairov. Versions of entries from Vakhtangov's diary were circulating, and just before his death Vakhtangov had rebelled against the Teacher. But Efros and Yefremov were faithful young Turks ready to hurl themselves at anyone attempting to disparage the author of *An Actor Prepares*. In the mid-fifties Efros even wrote an article entitled 'Poor Stanislavsky!', in which he attacked Okhlopkov and Ravenskikh for false theatricality and a tendency to 'presentation', which had been a term of the strongest abuse in Russia ever since Stanislavsky.[39]

The kind of acting that Efros and Yefremov then cultivated was above all natural. They survived on this naturalness for several years. Then Yefremov left the Central Children's Theatre and started the

Sovremennik. He pursued what Stanislavsky called the 'sociopolitical line' of his own art, whereas Efros, who was stuck at the Central Children's Theatre for ten years, began to develop the 'line of intuition and feeling'. One of the most important productions in which Efros became aware of his new opportunities was *My Friend Kolka!* by Aleksandr Khmelik, which opened in December 1959.

In a theatre intended for children, Efros began to destroy the aesthetics of the Soviet stage. The play is set in the back playground of a school. Initially, the designer Boris Knoblok presented it in great detail with a realistic wall, broken desks piled up against it, and so on. The director and the designer fumbled with this design, then hit on something different: they decided to deconstruct the box-set, strip the stage space, put a kind of yellow carpet in the middle, and on it install PE apparatus, including the unforgettable 'horse' of our schooldays. Around the edge of the stage there was a vertical strip of white canvas with washed-out drawings by children on it – outlines of houses, cranes, trees and above them a flock of birds soaring into the sky. Efros never went back after this to the enclosed, prison-like space of the box-set.

The play was performed by the theatre's drama students, who were only a few years older than the characters they were playing. For Efros it was important that the characters should be as recognizable as possible. These student actors changed sets in a trice, mimed scenes from school life, and so on. You felt you were watching a new kind of psychological art that had rediscovered its theatrical roots. The psychology ceased to be boring; indeed it was sharp, mischievous and exciting. With the box-set walls gone, the actors seemed to have come out into the fresh air. A new sense of stage space had come about, and a new relationship of the actor to this space. It was precisely in this production that Efros's young pupils began to practise the 'Brownian movement' that would become his trademark for decades.

My Friend Kolka! began with a vignette, a kind of epigraph. The schoolchildren were frozen in various attitudes, as if on a still from a film: one had a ball in his hands, another a skipping-rope, a third was just about to leap on to the horse. All movement had stopped and there was not a sound. And suddenly someone shouted joyfully, disrupting the dead stasis: 'Breaktime!' Whereupon everything came to life, tumbled and turned; the ball reached its destination, the children somersaulted all over the PE apparatus, in a word, life returned.

The school 'breaktime' coincided with an historical one. The apprentice became a master. He learned to shape space on the stage as a sculptor shapes clay. The air of the stage became as obedient to him as colour to a painter. Furthermore, he discovered his hero/protagonist in the boy Kolka Snegiryov. Unsociable, a bit rough, painfully shy and absolutely honest, this lad could not stand the phoniness of the Pioneers (Lenin Scouts/Guides), which were a microcosm of the hell that we all lived in. Efros had captured the atmosphere of this hell, its laws and *mores*. All of the bigotry of our society seemed to be concentrated in the pretty little, fairylike Pioneer leader, who was acted by Antonina Dmitriyeva as a Russian version of the Nazi Ilse Koch. They began to bully the boy, to corner him. Finally, they put him up against a wall and stripped him of his Pioneer's red neckerchief. In Soviet school terms this was tantamount to a 'civil execution'. All one heard in the silence was the bony drumming of the Pioneer leader's fingers on a desk-top. Then it was answered by a drum roll that grew and grew. This sent shivers down your spine. It appealed to our emotional memory; it opened the floodgates in our minds, lifting this tale about school on to a different emotional plane. It was the reaction of a country that had survived fascism but simply could not free itself from fascism's drumbeat.

In 1964, just before the end of the Khrushchev decade, the regime made two mistakes: it opened the doors of the Taganka to Yury Lyubimov and it allowed Anatoly Efros to head the Leninsky Komsomol Theatre (Lenkom). The three years Efros spent there became a watershed in his life and in that of the modern Russian stage.

Topical issues and misgiving about the future now acquired more and more resonance in his life. He shifted his focus away from society itself to the position of the artist within this society. Whether he was directing Chekhov's *The Seagull*, Bulgakov's *Molière*, or Edvard Radzinsky's *Shooting a Film*, he was talking about himself.

Shortly before, Federico Fellini had been awarded first prize at the first Moscow Film Festival (1961) for *$8\frac{1}{2}$*. Muscovites were taken aback by this lyrical confession, but it was the confession of a Western artist and Western artists, of course, were allowed to do such things. In

Efros's case it was the confession of a Soviet theatre director who had long lived encased in the uniform of a 'state employee in the arts'. What he created were delirious, searing confessions into which a modern man had poured his soul. The fact that the artist was presenting himself in the name of everyone, that his state of mind had ceased to be his personal business and suddenly become of general significance, gave the whole art of the theatre a new tone. Efros turned the Lenkom into a new theatrical church and Moscow immediately began to beat a path to it.

In Efros's hands the theme of the artist acquired crucifixional overtones. Instead of the enchanted lake, his 1966 production of *The Seagull* focused on the extremely discordant image of the theatre as a scaffold on which the artist is executed. The stage was strewn with new timber from which the unpainted platform had been erected, and there was also a high, louring fence across the 'real' stage. Treplev rushed about this scaffold like a man condemned, frantically tried to balance across a plank that had not yet been fixed, fell on his back, and shouted that 'new forms' were needed and 'if they don't exist, it's better to have nothing'. The production was staged for Treplev and about Treplev. Every other character was defined by his relation to the boy rebel (who, as played by Valentin Smirnitsky, was blatantly younger than Chekhov had written him).

Efros was looking for new approaches to the classics. He seemed to have the knack of extracting red-hot meaning from any tired phrase in world literature. *The Seagull* opens with the teacher Medvedenko asking Masha: 'Why do you always wear black?' 'Because I am in mourning for my life', she replies. This means that one can fall into the tired old way of doing Chekhov from the first line, from the very first intonation. But Efros exercised his imagination: no, this dialogue is not whingeing, it is an immediate outburst of passion, almost a yell. It is the *teacher* asking, the teacher who is paid twenty-three roubles a month, is humiliated, has no prospects; so he is saying: 'Look, I'm a teacher, worse than that you cannot get, but I'm not whingeing, so why are YOU wearing black?!' And everything was turned round and came alive. Human pain flooded into the play – the electric current of life that was the real object of Efros's art.

In his *Seagull*, with one blow Efros overturned all the clichés of how Chekhov was played on the Russian stage: the lumbering pace, the way characters communicated 'at room temperature', the famous pauses, the 'mood' and the poetic haze that had seemed an intrinsic feature of Chekhov's plays ever since early MKhT. He revved up the pace as far as it would go, he made the characters communicate directly and brusquely, but this did not lead to them understanding each other; on the contrary, it completely isolated them from one another. Continuous active communication combined with complete misunderstanding became the style of the whole production.

From every corner of the stage one heard howling, shouting, groaning and hysterical sobbing. It was as though the young Chekhov had lived in one of our *kommunalka's*, with a kitchen and one lavatory between twenty people. The actors were no longer embarrassed by their modern manners; they had boldly appropriated Chekhov to their own experience and level.

It was also Chekhov interpreted through Rozov and Radzinsky, two authors to whom Efros was then very close. The theme of uncompromising youth cutting into the adult world, in this case the world of official art represented by the ageing prima donna Arkadina and the pining Trigorin, came from Rozov. The biting, ironical tone, which Efros had completely mastered in his productions *104 Pages about Love* and *Shooting a Film* (both before *The Seagull*), originated in Radzinsky. In *Shooting a Film*, which was about the split soul of a modern film director, Efros had lifted a corner of the curtain on the hell in which every artist in Russia found himself who had talent and tried to fulfil himself. He showed the ghastly compromises, the habit of self-abasement, the pangs of conscience and the self-betrayal followed by more agonies of conscience, and soaring above it all at the end was the beautiful sound of a magical trumpet – the sound of pure art, the unattainable and spat upon ideal. The trumpet, of course, was also a grateful quotation from Fellini's $8\frac{1}{2}$ mentioned earlier. Fellini taught Russian directors of the 1960s freedom of expression, and in *The Seagull* this freedom was shouted from the rooftops.

Everyone betrayed Treplev, but Efros took a particularly close look at how Nina did it. She was played by Olga Yakovleva, whom Efros encountered on the stage of the Lenkom and subsequently rediscovered for Moscow in the plays of Radzinsky and Arbuzov. He brought out her incomparable voice, her fragile tenderness and alluring frankness, the passion and incisiveness of her reactions. From one part to the next he moulded her appearance and image into the lyrical centre of all his major theatrical compositions. Olga Yakovleva opened up to his art the previously unknown world of desires, suffering, vice and love. He broached the 'fateful passions' which from then on began to nourish his most important productions.

In Nina Zarechnaya the director discovered an insatiable appetite for fame and for furthering her own career, which turned her into Treplev's chief betrayer. At the beginning of the play she was a delicately chiselled figure in black on the boards of Treplyov's theatre. To be on the safe side, she distanced herself slightly from the text of the 'decadent play', as she declaimed her monologue kneeling at the edge of the platform. Young, captivating, she flirted with the text in order to impress the celebrities from the city, rather than the excitable author of the play. She was in a conspiracy with them. When Treplev ran off, humiliated by the lack of understanding shown him, Nina came and joined 'the audience': the boy genius with all his complexes no longer interested her. She was interested in Trigorin (Aleksandr Shirvindt). The long scene with the writer she conducted with great feminine charm. She did not understand, did not even listen to his outpourings. She was conducting her own intrigue, her own game, which had one aim. She was seducing a writer. At the end of the scene Efros gave the actress a remarkable, wordless piece of performance: Nina seized the thin, whippy fishing-rod and began slicing the air with it – ferociously, and with a glee that promised extraordinary carnal delights. A stunned Trigorin, and with him a stunned Moscow audience, saw a predatory animal awakening in this provincial doll, against whom Arkadina would not have a chance.

Efros's *Seagull* was met with indignation. People leapt to Chekhov's defence and said all the kinds of things that are said on such occasions. Efros did not protest. After a while, he even published an article in which he criticized his work with Chekhov more fiercely than any of his critics. He wrote that in his production the play had lost its poetic 'bloom', that Chekhov is not Chekhov without this 'bloom', and that it was difficult for today's actors to play *The Seagull* because their inner experience was horrendously narrow – hence the *kommunalka* intonations of their voices, their shouting and ranting, which they ought to get rid of, but how could they escape from their own selves? He also wrote that one must not 'frighten' the performer by handing him a classical part and telling him it was a crystal bowl and if he broke it no one would ever forgive him. He defended his right to free artistic utterance, the right to be himself, although he was under no illusion about what that freedom might throw up.[40] Several years later he was to say that his actors' overwrought nerves in his first Chekhov production were caused by the fact that an impoverished spirit is hyper-receptive. This was probably one of the most devastating verdicts not only on his Chekhov production but on his whole theatrical generation.

He kept looking for new sound boards for his own pain. Having 'Efrosized' Chekhov, he turned to Bulgakov's *Molière*, which was, of course, a much more appropriate vehicle for the feelings that gripped him. The play had not been performed since 1936, when it had been banned at MKhAT.[41] The prohibition of *Tartuffe*, Molière's relations with Louis XIV, the theme of Molière's theatre, and, actually, his confused personal life – all of these became for Efros emblematic of the life of the artist generally.

In his dealings with absolute power, Bulgakov's Molière chose what may well be the most difficult path. To save his play, the artist was prepared to become a helot, to lick his boss's boots and behave like a worm. Stanislavsky disliked this aspect of the play intensely. He wanted a Molière who would be a genius doing battle with the king. This attitude was very much of its time. The Soviet regime, which itself made artists crawl like worms, would only allow on stage the image of the 'fighting' artist. It was a special form of social sadism and Stanislavsky was prone to it too.

Efros went even further than Bulgakov in his unwillingness to present Molière as a hero. In his very first stage direction, describing Molière's dressing-room, Bulgakov has a large crucifix with the words 'LES COMEDIENS DE MONSIEUR' underneath it. To this Efros added his own detail: the crucified figure was also wearing a theatrical mask, and on either side of Him, instead of the thieves, hung 'crucified' theatrical costumes. This threw a double light on the theme of the play: not only did Christ become an actor, the actor became a Christ. 'Crucified' costumes hung all over the stage, as though echoing the main theme. The designers Viktor Durgin and Alla Chernova had decorated the proscenium arch with monkeys scrambling up it, which accentuated the tragicomic perspective.

Molière, indeed, not only did not fight, he did not want to fight. He was incapable of fighting. In a deathly silence, he came backstage, where the terrified actors were waiting for him. The *comédiens de Monsieur* were shaking, because Monsieur was sitting in the royal box. They reminded one reviewer of a group of refugees huddled together at some tiny railway station. Molière came off-stage clutching at his heart and asked tersely and matter-of-factly for water. 'He was revived like a boxer between rounds', Aleksandr Asarkan remarked in his brilliant portrait of the production published a quarter of a century later. This Molière was not attractive; he was irritable, hysterical and a cuckold. He was so unheroic he even put you off, rather as Andrey Sakharov sometimes did when giving a speech – swallowing his rs, speaking with difficulty and breathing asthmatically.

The truth rarely speaks with a golden tongue; it prefers to wear rags and stumble with its words. Compared with Molière, the indolent, majestic and witty Louis (played by Aleksandr Shirvindt) was irresist-ibly sun-like. In the scene at supper, the king commanded that Molière be given a chair, but no one actually did, so the actor pretended they had and ate his ritual chicken leg squatting as though on a chair.

Another personal question of the director's could be heard in *Molière*, and heard very clearly. It was: is *Tartuffe*, or any art, worth the kind of humiliation that the author of this banned play decided to put himself through? If you abase yourself and tell so many lies, can you achieve what you set out to? 'What else do I have to do to prove I am a worm?!', the prostrated Molière shouted into the emptiness, addressing the invisible golden idol. 'But Your Majesty, I am a writer: I think, I protest.' Asarkan's comment on this key point in the production was: 'But you can see that he is *not* a writer any more, that he does *not* think; he rants, yes, but does *not* protest.'[42]

Molière was dying on the stage, the candles were being put out, the actors gathering up their costumes, taking their crucified counter-parts off the wall and putting them into chests. They had to leave the king's theatre and go somewhere else. The ending of *Molière* anticip-ated the biggest upheaval in Efros's own life. Soon after the opening night of *Molière*, he was sacked from the Lenkom. External forces got their evil way, but they had been abetted by forces inside the theatre. Efros was, of course, a hopeless manager. Some actors he indulged, others he hardly ever used. The Moirrons in the Lenkom wrote their denunciations of him, in which they said he had no right to be running it. In a sense this was true: the art of Anatoly Efros had nothing to do with either Lenin or the Komsomol. Yury Zavadsky, Oleg Yefremov and Yury Lyubimov went to see various people and put their case, and Lyubimov even threatened to hand in his Party card (which would have been like a jester threatening to tear off his cap and bells!). Nothing made any difference. Efros's theatre was wiped out. All he was allowed to do was 'take some costumes with him': ten of his actors transferred with him to the theatre on Malaya Bronnaya.

It was 1967. The writers Sinyavsky and Daniel had been sent to labour camps in Mordovia; Solzhenitsyn had decided to go over to open warfare with the 'oak'; the magazine *Novy mir* was on its last legs. At the Taganka five separate Mayakovskys were dying and at the Sovremennik the subject of 'Red terror' was being debated. Efros was an artist and only an artist. He therefore responded to the challenge of the times as befits an artist. Exiled to the Malaya Bronnaya, he immediately started rehearsing *Three Sisters*.

Everyone for whom the theatre means something probably has one production which for them sums up the very sensation of theatre. For me, and I daresay my generation, that production was *Three Sisters* at the Malaya Bronnaya. I remember the bare stage, the back-cloth with black trees drawn on it containing empty birds' nests, the strange mythological tree-cum-clothes-stand centre stage with metallic golden leaves, the huge ottoman, the gramophone with its trumpet, the grand piano, and the clock with no hands that had been positioned next to the proscenium. I remember the green colour scheme of the whole stage, which was as it were clad in tsarist military uniform. You could contemplate all this calmly enough until the action started, but then it was like a plane hitting turbulence. The performance was heart-stopping. In it raw pain was coupled with a vision of things past and future suddenly revealed through Chekhov, and the acting had an absolute penetrative power like X-rays. It may have been the first time I understood what happens when people on a stage exchange their theatrical blood for human blood.

Efros said later that the image of the production came to him in desolate, wintry Yalta, where he experienced what Chekhov had probably experienced in his 'warm Siberia'. It was an image of exile, of being cut off from life, of the impossibility of reaching Moscow. The railway motif (Mandelshtam once joked: 'Buy the three sisters tickets to Moscow and let them go there') was transmuted into a metaphysical problem: the production was about a lost spiritual homeland.

However, Efros certainly did not begin *Three Sisters* with the theme of exile, longing or hopelessness. Life in the Prozorovs' house began with joy, a nameday party and a marvellous waltz that Tuzenbakh called on everyone to join. *Invitation to a Waltz* was how Vadim Gayevsky entitled his excellent portrait of the production.[43] The waltz gave the first act a strong, impetuous pace that was very unusual for Chekhov. The director had found this waltz in the Czech film *The Shop on the Square* and simply used it as the soundtrack for a classic. The fact that Chekhov's people were dancing to a sixties hit immediately dissolved the historical distance between them and the audience and established a friendly trust in what was going on.

As in the old days, the play was performed with three intervals. However, I think this was the only concession to tradition. Everything else was provocatively unexpected. Viktor Durgin had designed the production in the style of the Russian *moderne*. There were the modest, elegant lines of Shekhtel's MKhT interior, but also the garish colours of the merchant *moderne* suggestive of the usurping Natasha. The famous tree with the golden leaves was particularly prominent in this regard, and had a depressing effect. There was no house, or garden, or avenue of birches as in the 1940 MKhAT production. You could say the action was unfolding in a theatre and the demise of this house was also the demise of a true Theatre, above all the Art Theatre (the Shekhtel quotes were no coincidence).

The designer gave the sisters amazing dresses whose colour changed in the course of the play from green to ash-grey, and then to funereal black stripes, mirroring the movement to despair. Apart from anything else, it was a virtuoso portrait of a group. The actresses' movements somehow suggested a flock of birds, perhaps of the cranes mentioned in the play. They sometimes looked as though they had broken wings. Their performance was about some wonderful women who were not destined to take off; not destined to love and be loved. The men in the production, from Andrey (whom Natasha literally tumbled on to the ottoman) to Vershinin with his mad wife and two little daughters, were capable only of moaning, talking incessantly, and philosophizing about what life would be like in 200 years' time.

Efros gave a completely new intonation to every part. His interpretation of Baron Tuzenbakh (played by Lev Krugly) was a particularly violent break with tradition. Krugly not so much acted his role as danced it. It was a form of intellectual clowning, in which even the most serious things were presented ironically. The audience got its first shock during the famous monologue in Act 1 about work, which begins: 'The longing to work, goodness how I understand it! I've never worked in my life.' Krugly fell into a state of mock exaltation, turned words inside out, and clowned about as he approached his punch line. 'The time has come,' the text continues, 'an avalanche is moving towards us, a mighty, healthy storm is brewing, it is on the move, nearly here, and will soon blast from our society all its laziness, indifference, prejudice against work, and rotten boredom.' The contrast between Chekhov's prognosis and what actually happened in Russia was devastating, but no one acting Tuzenbakh before had ever made anything out of it. Efros's 'heresy', which subsequently provoked an ideological inquisition, merely consisted of causing a short circuit by bringing the two centuries into direct proximity with each other. And at this point, when the auditorium was bursting to know what would come next, Tuzenbakh pronounced deliberately and with deadly sarcasm the crowning words: 'I – shall – work, and in another twenty-five to thirty years time every – person – will – work. Every one of 'em!'

I do not remember actually doing the sum in my head and seeing in my mind's eye the Stalin camps that were being put up everywhere in exactly 'twenty-five to thirty years time'. One's response was not arithmetical but deeply emotional. Purely theatrically, by means of the air brought into the words, the tragic clowning of the Russified little officer, the hysterical laughter of the Prozorov household, the agonizing waltz and goodness knows what else, the director did what real theatre must: he threw open Chekhov's text to the twentieth century.

The irony restored what the bombastic Soviet approach to Chekhov had destroyed. When the baron exchanged his officer's uniform for a black suit and bowler hat in order at last to 'get down to work', he was also removing his buffoon's mask. His slightly Chaplinesque gait and his slightly upturned eyebrows retained something clown-like, but now the clownery was tragic. We were looking at someone extremely vulnerable, to whom death was beckoning. Solyony was carrying out someone's predetermined plan and in this production he was full of philosophical significance. And he did not like waffle – the 'cluck-cluck-cluck' of the chickens. Tuzenbakh's dispiriting farewell smile before the duel, his half-skipping departure upstage, and then his return, were acted with all the power of modern tragic ballet. 'Say something to me' – and he moved towards us, towards the auditorium, with Irina (Olga Yakovleva) standing on the forestage. His voice seemed to be conquering the no-man's land, the endless dead plain, that already separated them. The commonplace words were filled with blood, despair, an impossible thirst for love. And back came Irina's brusque, hopeless echo: 'What? Say what? What? What? What?' This intensification, these glacial hysterics, triple italics, told us one thing: there was no love between them and there never could be. Even the premonition of death did not alter this simple, irreparable fact.

Each of Chekhov's heroes was given such moments. I shall never forget Irina's desperate cry in Act 3: 'Throw me out, throw me out, I can't take any more!' Masha (Anna Antonenko) literally had to be torn away from Vershinin (Nikolay Volkov) in their farewell scene, which, as one critic finely remarked, she played not as a general's daughter but as a female soldier herself, not afraid of letting all her emotions hang out. However, the inner theme of the production was heard at its most penetrating in Chebutykin's monologue in Act 3. Chebutykin was played by Lev Durov as another tragic clown and this monologue was undoubtedly the emotional and semantic climax of the production.

First we heard his drunken, sobbing laughter off-stage. Vadim Gayevsky has likened it to the way in ancient tragedy the actor's groaning preceded his entry. Then the short, dishevelled doctor shot on to the stage. He was propelled by an inarticulate grief, a nervous spasm, which had somehow to break out, to be resolved. Then his eyes alighted on the gramophone in a corner of the stage. He rushed over to it, wound it up, and started a wild dance to its strange, parp-parping sounds. He jerked about in time to the music, writhed, leapt on to the ottoman, fell to his knees, and carried on dancing on his knees. A stump of a man was shouting that his life was finished, that a woman patient of his had died through his fault, that he was tired of putting on a show and pretending that he understood anything. 'I know ab-so-lute-ly nothing', he intoned to the jazz quartet on the record. He jerked about like a marionette, kept feeling his arms, legs and head to convince himself that he was human, again despaired, and howled that it would be better if he did not exist. After this heart-rending crescendo, the music suddenly broke off and for a few seconds Chebutykin blacked out – hung there limply, as though something inside him had broken. Then he wound up the gramophone again and started to flail and shake to the broken beat as though being electrocuted.

Of course, it was a scandal, an affront to the 'nice', academic Chekhov. Every single person sitting in the auditorium could have put his own experience and memory into that dance of despair. The whole meat mincer of the twentieth century, all its nightmares and lies, were placed on general display. The drunk doctor was confessing what the audience carried in its own soul. It was a monologue from the under-ground. And it was also the end of the ideology of optimism that had dogged Chekhov on the Soviet stage. There was no dream of a better life in this production. It was replete with the terror of what people had lived through and their fears for the future.

They flocked to the theatre and some even fainted during per-formances. In order to strangle such a production, the name of the Moscow Arts had to be invoked. Angelina Stepanova, who had played Irina in Nemirovich-Danchenko's legendary 1940 *Three Sisters*, was approached. She signed the appropriate article in *Pravda*, and in the spring of 1968 the production was rubbed out; almost at the same time as *Alive* at the Taganka. One era was ending, and another beginning. A decade and a half later, Stepanova, who had been a pupil of Vakhtangov and was the widow of Aleksandr Fadeyev, General Secretary of the Union of Soviet Writers under Stalin, had a small part in Efros's pro-duction of *Tartuffe*, which she performed brilliantly. I was at the rehearsals and neither of them breathed a word about the past. Efros showed a wise understanding of the inveterate weakness of actors, entirely *à la* Chekhov or Bulgakov. Both then and later he knew only one cure, only one salvation: work. Almost like Tuzenbakh.

The Thaw (1953–1968)

In the Russian theatre, the sixties ended with a series of massacres spread over a year from summer 1967 to summer 1968. This was a run-up to the domestic version of the Prague invasion. As well as *Alive* and *Three Sisters*, they banned Ostrovsky's *A Profitable Position* directed by Mark Zakharov, and Pyotr Fomenko's staging of Sukhovo-Kobylin's *Tarelkin's Death*. To this list I would add Aleksey Tolstoy's *Death of Ivan the Terrible* at the Theatre of the Soviet Army, directed by Leonid Kheyfets. It was not actually banned, but it was used as a pretext for settling scores with the director, who was ejected from this theatre and immured in Moscow's Maly Theatre where the breath of life could not reach him. By a quirk of fate, Boris Lvov-Anokhin was also exiled there for many years. He was a very promising director, but was later used to produce a stage version of Brezhnev's memoirs! This kind of sea change became the order of the day.

I shall return to the directorial 'undergrowth' that the regime did not manage to chop down at the end of the sixties, in the final chapter of the book. Let us now continue the stories of the figures we already know. The heroes of the Thaw – Oleg Yefremov, Yury Lyubimov, Anatoly Efros and Georgy Tovstonogov – will now appear within a setting that is known in Russia as 'the stagnation' (although at the time it was described as 'advanced socialism'). Continuing the meteorological analogy, we shall call the second chapter 'The Frosts'.

2 The Frosts (1968–1985)

Immediately after Prague, people's faces in Russia became mute again. A cold wind blew through every cranny, the ideological inquisition started up again, and all the methods and trappings of life under Stalin began to be restored. Public opinion, which had only just begun to stir, remembered in its bones the crack of the policeman's whip and cringed as it awaited its punishment.

The punishment was not slow in coming, but the 'collective leadership' was no longer capable of plunging the country into a blood-bath. It therefore devised a policy of creeping, low-key repression that would penetrate everywhere. It began to bring to heel anyone who could think and had made a name for themselves in the previous period. If it did not succeed in taming them, they were sorted into two categories: those for the camps and those to be expelled to the West. The regime was pumping the country's intellectual potential out of it. Sometimes it exchanged political dissidents for spies or Western communists and exported/deported artists for pin-money, the way it did Russia's mineral resources. Those who were left had again and again to swear allegiance to the regime. All open forms of resistance were cut short, driven inwards or pushed underground.

However, this hiatus in the history of the country was not a hiatus in the history of its theatre. Paradoxical though it may sound, the Brezhnev era was one of the most important periods in Russian theatre. Art learned to survive on the edge of disaster and even to keep a shorthand record of this extremely complex act. The art of the stage made the life of those whose faces had become mute into its principal theme and subtext.

Plate 5   Oleg Yefremov receiving the Order of the Red Banner of Labour from
Leonid Brezhnev, 1977.

Oleg Yefremov resuscitates the Art Theatre

We left Oleg Yefremov at the point where he had moved from the
Sovremennik to the top theatre in the country, MKhAT SSSR imeni
Gorkogo (The Gorky Moscow Artistic Academic Theatre of the USSR).

When he was a teenager, Yefremov had been medically exam-
ined with others to see if he would be suitable for a career in sport. He
was the only one the doctors predicted could run a marathon, because
he had the right heart. The marathon that he set off on at the Moscow
Arts in the autumn of 1970 cannot be compared with any other, unless
perhaps the one that the country itself has come through.

Yefremov arrived at MKhAT with the outlook of the man who
had created the Sovremennik. He had no other ideas than those he
practised at the Sovremennik, and still has not. If you like, this is the
'matrix' of his theatrical consciousness. He 'prints' from this matrix as
unselfconsciously as we bring children into the world who resemble
ourselves. We might like it to be otherwise, but it cannot be. It is in
his theatrical genes to work with people who are close to him in spirit

and have something to them. Theatre for him is above all duty, and only after that a celebration or joy. If it were acceptable these days, he would always write 'theatre' with a capital T. Miraculously, his mind has remained impervious to cynicism about the theatre. At rehearsals, he follows what is happening on-stage and mouths each word with the performer, as though casting a spell on him. Sitting next to him in the stalls, I often see him tense up his whole body and lean forward if something talented is coming about on stage. Yefremov has a super-sensitive nose for genuine acting – acting that catches life unawares.

Born under an authoritarian regime, Yefremov is (like Tovstonogov) cut from its cloth; but the cloth has been enriched with talent. A wall can only be brought down by a battering-ram. He has developed 'battering-ram' qualities in himself, after dedicating his life to bringing the 'wall' down. This made him the leader of the Russian theatre, but also in some sense stunted his psychology. He trained himself to see in life and art only that which is connected with the 'wall'; which means that he cut himself off from many other, very important aspects. The regime tried to domesticate him, it gave him medals and patted him on the head, but he kept breaking free – his legendary drinking bouts were, amongst other things, a form of inner protest against the unbearable grotesqueness of his official life.

In the autumn of 1970 Yefremov began to reform the Art Theatre. Like the country generally, it was suffering from creeping degradation. By the time Yefremov arrived, the company contained 150 actors, many of whom had not been on stage for years, and it was exhausted by infighting.

First, Yefremov revived some of the traditions of Stanislavsky's time. He set up a 'council of elders' and attempted to divide the personnel of the theatre into a main force and an auxiliary force. He interviewed everyone personally to find out what made them tick. These interviews nearly drove him mad: it transpired that it was not a home, a family, but a Petri dish of people all thinking the same, and this Petri dish had grown used to being the showcase of the regime. The way of life of the Art Theatre, its customs and its high opinion of itself, were dictated by the 'USSR' bit in its name. When it arrived on some special state mission in a Soviet republic, the actors were always met by the First Secretary of the Central Committee there and accommodated in special government residences guarded by KGB troops. I remember that Yekaterina Vasilyeva, one of the excellent actresses who had been brought in by Yefremov and was not used to MKhAT's ways, found herself staying in one such 'reserve' in Kirghizia and shouted to some-one down the phone: 'Get me out of this gilded cage!'

After two years of changes, Yefremov found that the company had increased to 180 actors. Having failed utterly to reform MKhAT from within, he set about entrenching himself. Inside the Art Theatre he gradually began to create another company, selecting for it some actors from the old MKhAT and some who took after himself – above all, of course, actors from the Sovremennik. 'With the old-timers it was easier', he said years later. 'Yes they were corrupted by the official pampering, many of them had lost their courage, they had lived through terrible years, breathed stale air all that time and been poisoned by it. But it was easier with them because as soon as you got on to artistic issues some-thing in them woke up. Say what you like, they were great performers; and they proved it one last time in *Solo for a Chiming Clock.*'[1]

This was a play by the Slovak dramatist Osvald Zahradník and it acquired super-theatrical significance. Acting in it were Mikhail Yanshin, Olga Androvskaya, Pavel Massalsky, Aleksey Gribov and Viktor Stanitsyn – leading lights of the so-called 'second generation' of the Art Theatre.[2] They were very old actors with an illustrious past, who lent a rather weak play flashes of brilliance from their own legendary lives. It was the story of their youth, loves and nostalgia. The public understood that the 'solo' would not last long. It came to the produc-tion to say farewell to its favourite actors. Soon, one after another, the MKhAT veterans really did begin to take their leave. The 'council of elders' ceased to meet because there were none left.

Yefremov was left alone with his 'corrupted' company, the so-called middle generation educated during the worst years in the country's history. He started the resuscitation of MKhAT by staging *Dulcinea del Toboso*, a play by his favourite dramatist Aleksandr Volodin. Yefremov himself played the Knight of the Sad Countenance, opposite Tatyana Doronina, who had left Tovstonogov's company by then and set out on her wanderings through the theatres of Moscow. He then directed Mikhail Roshchin's *Valentin and Valentina* and *Old New Year*. As at the Sovremennik, the new artistic director of MKhAT felt it was important to bring back to the theatre 'living life' and natural voices. He was attempting to reintroduce to this stage people for whom entry had been barred for decades.

The quality of a play often did not matter as much as the desire to say something about a burning social issue. This was the case with Bokarev's *Steel Founders*, and many others. The flagship for this trend was Gorky's *The Last Ones* (1973). Its main characters define its genre as 'tragic *balagan*' (fairground theatre), and this proved highly appropriate for the beginning of the seventies, when the Brezhnev regime was stabilizing itself. Yefremov attempted to expose the nature of the ranting blather that kept police officer Ivan Kolomiytsev's house going. In reality this house was falling apart. Children were being raped, perverted and morally crippled. Any manifestation of independent thought was immediately gagged. It was a witches' sabbath of terror, torture and corruption, and through it all those in charge kept talking, talking, talking. The worse things were, the more they bandied about high-flown words and exhorted people to lead 'moral' lives.

Yefremov revealed the effrontery of a regime that believed it was here for ever. He cast off the cosy psychological togetherness so beloved of MKhAT's actors, made the characters relate to each other aggressively, and introduced parodic elements in the most rhetorical scenes. He reoriented the text of the play so as to expose the pain at the centre of it. For instance, he moved to the very beginning of the play the dialogue between the police chief's children – the 'last ones' – about how the blood spilt by their fathers would be upon them. In another place, the drunken bosses sang 'The Wreck of the *Varyaga*', with its priceless line: 'And the comrades are all above, in place for the last parade.' This scene was virtually the first theatrical expression of what might be called the 'post-Prague syndrome': a victor's feast that lasted nearly twenty years.

In the mid-seventies Yefremov discovered for himself a new author, Aleksandr Gelman, whose name would be closely associated with MKhAT and the history of the Soviet theatre for the next ten years. Gelman's credentials were impressive. He had been a builder, a Party worker, a soldier and a journalist. In short, he was a man of the world, one of the kind that Yefremov was always attracted to. Gelman was born in Romania before the war and as a teenager lived in a ghetto, where almost all his relatives were murdered before his eyes. He survived and came out of it not only with an abhorrence of fascism in all its forms but also with a certain wisdom about life. In the mid-seventies he wrote his first sociological tale about Soviet life, called *The Bonus*. It started life as a film, then he adapted it for the stage as *A Meeting of the Party Committee*.

Gelman presented a social paradox that anticipated the main slogans of *perestroika*. The building foreman Potapov, and with him the rest of the workforce, had turned down a bonus (unheard of!) because they regarded it as a disguised form of exploitation and humiliation. Notebook in hand, Potapov tried to explain all this to the Party Committee of the building project. This country, which had extolled labour as dignified, honourable and heroic, had in fact degraded the working man more than any other system on earth. Gelman was investigating the irreversible changes that occur in a person once he is deprived of property and drawn into a system of depersonalized, all-levelling labour without incentives. He touched on the consequences of a totally unnatural socioeconomic order that crippled people. Moreover, he did it in the only possible form acceptable to the system. At first it looked as though he wanted to improve this system. The film was seen by government ministers. I do not know what their reasoning was, but they passed it, and then the play. A few years later Lech Walesa said that foreman Potapov was one of those who inspired him in his struggle.

Like a man thirsty for the truth, Yefremov drank in the paradoxes of his new author, which were presented in a vivid, flexible theatrical form. He did not have to look far for confirmation of what Gelman was saying: his experience of the Art Theatre, which was intractable to improvement, fed his directorial and actorial imagination. The problems of MKhAT's rebuilding mirrored those of the building site in *A Meeting of the Party Committee*.

All the time Potapov/Yefremov came on with his notebook and demonstrated that lies were uneconomic, he was left in peace. At the 25th Party Congress, Brezhnev even said something about the whole country having gone through this meeting of the Party Committee. The country had, but it had learnt nothing from it, of course. Two years later, in *Feedback* on the new MKhAT stage (the old one was being modernized), the Czech designer Josef Svoboda helped create a powerful image of a grey bureaucratic state in which people were literally turning into extensions of their desks. These highly polished desks stretched for as far as the eye could see, one bank piled above another to dizzy heights. Behind each desk was a secretary, phones were ringing all the time, and everyone was rushing about getting things signed. At the base of the gigantic pyramid was a building site, a town, a municipal committee. At the top was the regional committee. At the end of the play the First Secretary of the regional committee descended like a *deus ex machina*.

It was an image of a state in which there is no 'feedback' in the true sense: all channels of information are distorted, all production relations are deformed, lies are fed upwards and disastrous decisions sent downwards. It was a Soviet looking-glass world in which the ubiquitous lying thwarted the very basis of human personality. Here too Yefremov did not have to look far for material: the Art Theatre, with its drones who did no work but drew the same pay as everyone else, was a microcosm of the situation in the country as a whole.

A Meeting of the Party Committee met with state approval, but *Feedback* provoked irritation: it rocked the boat. The third play, *We the Undersigned*, encountered open hostility. Director and playwright radically altered the focus and offered to the public a confession by Lyonya Shindin, a 'cog' in the system and one of those fixers whom it could not survive without. This cog was suddenly declaring his right to human dignity, which was being trampled upon daily. He was no longer defending his job – in this case the unfinished bread factory that was supposed to be ready for a particular revolutionary date – he was defending a person, who could be destroyed if the commission did not pass the botched piece of construction. He was defending a person against the system. At the end of the play Yefremov swung the front of the electric locomotive in which this part of the action was set round to face the auditorium. The monster, which had been constructed virtually life-size by designer Valery Levental, turned its headlamps on the audience and dazzled them. One got the feeling that the hero was about to throw himself under the train. Critics immediately remarked on the ironic parallel with MKhAT's vintage production of *Anna Karenina*.

'Production drama', as it was called then, was a unique offspring of the period of stagnation and died with the period that begat it.

Gelman's fourth play, which he offered to the theatre at the beginning of 1981, suggested that the regime was in its death throes. It was
entitled *Alone with Everyone*. For the first time, the dramatist dispensed
with the Aesopic language that had enabled his dangerous tales to get
past the censor. He demonstrated black on white where the madness
of the system was going to end. The head of a large construction project, Golubev, was part of the system of universal lying and maimed his
own son. The son's hands, torn off in an industrial accident, became a
metaphor for the impending disaster. The theatre was performing what
happened five years later at Chernobyl.

The play was banned. The 'battering-ram' attacked the 'wall'. As
usual, Yefremov took everything upon himself. Despite the ban, he not
only rehearsed the play, he acted the main part. The fate of the production was to be decided by the Minister of Culture of the USSR, Pyotr
Demichev. In an empty auditorium, basically for the benefit of one
bureaucrat, Oleg Yefremov and Tatyana Lavrova began the performance.
Never had he put so much of himself into his acting. He poured the whole
of his enormous experience as a theatre leader – not only at MKhAT but
at the Sovremennik – and the experience of his own evolution between
1956 and 1970, his compromises, his drinking sprees, the accursed
medals and the Kirghizian 'gilded cages', into his hero. The latter was a
major figure endowed with diabolical astuteness, nauseating sincerity,
a complete understanding of the situation, and an utter inability to resist
it. 'It's people like me who move everything along!', Golubev shouted
at his wife, who he thought could not possibly understand all the wise
reasons of state for his actions. 'But where to?' she replied. Suddenly he
was deflated. He snapped back: 'Wherever they say.'

The woman's simple question hung in the air of MKhAT's auditorium. It was a question about changing the purpose and meaning of
life, and evidently it penetrated even a government minister's soul. The
quiet, grey-haired former chemist decided not to ban the production.
Both those on stage who were bashing their heads against the 'wall' and
the one in the auditorium who represented the 'wall', understood in
the empty silence that the system would not come crashing down just
because of this production. Soviet 'production drama' ended, then, on
a note of hopeless longing. This longing would be resolved not in the
theatre but by *perestroika*, which began in April 1985. For Gelman,

however, *perestroika* brought crisis: in ten years of freedom he did not write a single play.[3] He entered politics, became a deputy in the last Soviet parliament, was given his own column in the newspaper *Moskovskiye novosti*, but wrote no more plays. Play-writing as a statement of political interests that cannot express themselves in the natural way, blows itself out.

In 1976 Yefremov directed Chekhov's *Ivanov*. It suited the period of stagnation well. Social apathy, cynicism, lack of belief, stricken conscience – all of these long-standing problems of the Russian intelligentsia were floating to the top again. Yefremov put into his production all the horror of a situation where people have no beliefs or ideals left; a sickness of the soul that Chekhov described as 'worse than syphilis or sexual impotence'.[4]

MKhAT's production came straight after one by Mark Zakharov not far away at the Lenkom. At the latter, Ivanov was played by Yevgeny Leonov; at MKhAT, by Innokenty Smoktunovsky. Leonov and Smoktunovsky were totally different types of actors, exemplifying their directors' different views of the play. Leonov was one of the country's most popular comic actors and played not Ivanov the 'Russian Hamlet' but an ordinary intellectual, Ivanov Number One Million and One, as a contemporary of Chekhov's called him. What was important for Leonov was to be so recognizable that every member of the audience could identify with him.

Smoktunovsky played an out-of-the-ordinary person, someone genuinely big, who had been struck down by the sickness of the age. David Borovsky gave the director and actors a space that was unusual for Chekhov: an empty stage with the front of a landowner's house around its edges, complete with colonnade. The branches of a leafless autumnal garden were superimposed on the walls of this house as dark shadows. Interior and exterior became weirdly mixed. Ivanov existed in a deserted, as it were plundered space, in which he languished, unable to find a niche for himself. To begin with Smoktunovsky would not accept this set at all because he was afraid that it would leave him too exposed in what was a realistic play. Yefremov insisted, and in the end it was precisely the spatial design that conveyed Chekhov's sensibility best, for Chekhov had once written that in Europe people commit suicide because there is not enough space, but in Russia because there is too much.

In Mark Zakharov's production the hero's place was taken by a woman. The consumptive Sarra, played by Inna Churikova, still saw in Ivanov the hero of her youth who was capable of out-of-the-ordinary actions (marrying a Jewess in Russia was always an unusual action). Even at his worst, when Ivanov shouted at her 'You are going to die' and 'Shut up, you Jewish bitch!', she could find an excuse for him. Her face suddenly lit up with an extraordinary smile. All in white, she went up to him, embraced him in a solemn, liturgical fashion, and as it were blessed him. It was an act of compassion towards a fallen man; a smile of farewell and forgiveness.

Yefremov's anthropology is purely masculine. Woman does not determine anything in Ivanov's fate: only he can solve his problems, inside himself. The director took note of Chekhov's remark that 'the women should not be allowed to obscure the play's centre of gravity, which actually lies outside them'. The 'centre of gravity' of Yefremov's production consisted in the fact that a man had fallen into a deep depression which happened to coincide with the depression of the times. Having 'flipped' like this, there was nothing Ivanov could do with himself; moreover, he was intelligent enough, as Chekhov put it, 'not to hide his illness from himself, not to lie to himself, and not to cover his emptiness with other people's rags, e.g. the ideas of the 1860s'.[5]

The predicament of Chekhov's hero, like that of the main character in *Alone with Everyone*, Yefremov had filtered through himself. He performed an artistic experiment on himself. It was the same at the end of the seventies, when he directed Aleksandr Vampilov's *Duck-Hunting* on the stage of the Art Theatre. This too was a kind of public confession, in which Yefremov's personal themes proved unusually close to what Vampilov had written back in the sixties (*Duck-Hunting* had been banned for ten years).

Vampilov's play was the first in a totally different dramaturgy that stood in opposition to Soviet official drama, its heroes and anti-heroes, its plots, its language, and its conception of human beings. The hero of *Duck-Hunting*, Zilov, was a person formed by the system. All its consequences were focused and imprinted in him. He was an engineer in some research institute and despised his job. Unlike Gelman's Golubev, he was not 'moving' anything anywhere. It was our life that was moving him; crippling him, not giving this clearly gifted man the chance to develop.

Zilov's life consisted of compulsive lying, exhausting idleness, heavy drinking, and a string of infidelities and betrayals. All these had become second nature to him. The play began with him waking up with a hangover and discovering a wreath that had been delivered to his flat by a funeral parlour (a prank played on him by his friends); it ended with him 'forgetting' to go to his own father's funeral. Duck-shooting had become the ideal of this anti-life and the waiter Dima had become its hero – a crack shot and a fascist who is painted by Vampilov in colours usually reserved for the most positive characters in Soviet drama. Against this background, the figure of Zilov evoked the deepest sympathy. Vampilov had learned the lessons of Chekhov and world drama well. A man was measured not only by his outward actions. Zilov was endowed with spiritual torment – a sure sign that he was talented and had ideals that were being stamped on.

Yefremov assumed that Vampilov's play had been written about his generation and himself. He played it accordingly, forgetting that in the course of its ten-year ban the play had aged and he himself was no longer a 30-year-old Zilov for whom there was still some light at the end of the tunnel. He brought to his hero something that the latter did not possess by nature: the tragedy of a big man who had known different times when life had had meaning. Yefremov did not emerge the victor from this tussle with the play. He had not felt the language of the new drama – its subtleties. These demanded a different kind of directing and an acting technique that was not accessible to the MKhAT ensemble.

Duck-Hunting was staged at the end of 1978. A year later the war in Afghanistan started. The sixties ended with tanks in Prague, the seventies with tanks in Kabul. The end of the Brezhnev regime's stability can be very precisely dated to its Afghan gamble. The oil dollars that had made the USSR look quite respectable in the world economy became a thing of the past. So did the cosy 'stagnation', with its medals for performers and memoirs of the General Secretary acted by the stars of the Maly Theatre. The regime went into terminal decline. It was consuming itself. In July 1980 the Taganka actor Vladimir Vysotsky died at the age of forty. His obsequies were held in a half-empty Moscow that had been sterilized for the Olympics. Every conceivable military precaution was taken in case of demonstrations. Taganka Square was cordoned off and people tossed flowers on to it; apparently this was the only form of protest that we were capable of. There was a complete lack of public reaction to the outbreak of the Afghan War, as there was to the exile of Andrey Sakharov. The Art Theatre kept silent, like the rest of the country. The martial music struck up, a Party Congress was called to rubber-stamp what had been done, and every theatre was obliged to bring a 'present'. Yefremov observed this ritual, but tried to do it his way. For the 26th Party Congress he decided to put on a new production about Lenin.

I must explain what this all meant. Soviet artists responded to the issues of their day through Lenin; by filling his image with topical content. Thus, in the Soviet art of the late thirties Lenin was a vindication of terror. In the mid-1950s he was a vindication of the anti-Stalin policy. In the early 1980s he was an attempt to discuss the death throes of the Soviet regime, which saw itself as directly descended from him.

This plan of Yefremov's, in which the present author was directly involved, was flawed from the outset. The true sources of the tragedy of the revolution were not discussed, and Lenin's ideas were not subjected to any doubt. On the contrary, Lenin was called as a witness against the present regime. In restrospect, it was a dangerous, pointless game which we were wasting our lives playing.

Mikhail Shatrov, who as always was working with a group of well-informed liberal historians, offered a rather novel twist. It was known that on 18 October 1923 Lenin, who was convalescing outside Moscow after a severe stroke, demanded to be taken to the Kremlin. By then he had lost the use of speech and his right arm was paralyzed. He spent only a few minutes in his office, completely alone, stayed overnight in his Kremlin apartment, and returned next day to the sanitorium. He had three months left to live.

The idea of the play was to show Lenin in these few minutes, to flash back in time and forward, and pose questions to Lenin as it were from our own day. The socioeconomic dead-end that the country had reached, the problems of democracy and dictatorship, the debate about trade unions (we had Solidarność in mind), and policies towards other nationalities and their culture, were all 'read into' the play, which was written in collaboration with the theatre. We argued for days, until we were hoarse, and it kept looking as though relations between the director and the playwright were about to break down. Of course, we were arguing not about Lenin, but about the world we lived in, about what sore points we could touch upon and how we could steer through all these reefs while remaining honest.

Yefremov invited Aleksandr Kalyagin to play Lenin. Kalyagin was a splendid comic actor not obviously suited to such roles. At first he declined, because he knew what had happened to many Soviet actors who had played Lenin before. Some had gone mad for fear of assassination. Others had joined the *nomenklatura* (Party oligarchy) and been forbidden to play funny or 'negative' parts. Yefremov needed precisely Kalyagin because of his normal human reactions and, in fact, his attitude towards Lenin as the source of the ongoing disaster. Yefremov was right. An unprecedented Lenin came into being on MKhAT's stage: cut off from people, hemmed in, understanding much of what the country was heading for. Kalyagin found very subtle ways of heightening the meaning in places, which redirected Lenin's utterances to the present day, juxtaposed them with that reality, and struck the spark of political theatre from them. The audience picked up every allusion. They burst into applause when this Lenin called for the recognition of private property in order to feed the country, and froze when, cut off from the world, virtually a prisoner, he dictated his political testament.

The production went into rehearsal without the play having been cleared by the censor. We had decided to push through a finished production because we thought 'they' would not dare to ban a production about Lenin at MKhAT and cause a scandal just before the Party Congress. But they did dare. No one came to 'accept' the finished work from us, which used the entire gigantic company of the Art Theatre.[6] The production was banned at the highest government level and remained so for almost a year.

It was a year of deceptive calm. The theatre did not rehearse anything new. It was preoccupied with cutting and pasting the play in the hope of offering it 'upwards' again. We had to provoke the top leadership into a decision. The period of 'stagnation' should not be imagined as monotonous. Life in this swamp was highly active, as is any form of decomposition. 'Up there' were various people, including liberals, who wanted to help the theatre (some of them would subsequently gather around Gorbachev's standard). On the advice of one of them, we decided to write to Konstantin Chernenko, Brezhnev's second-in-command.

The style of this letter may be of interest to future historians of etiquette. We had to get through to someone who was a bit thick; to find a ploy that could not fail. The Art Theatre therefore requested him to allow it to 'improve its production about Lenin'. They could not refuse us permission to 'improve' such a production, and we did: we switched scenes round, added bits here and there, took bits off, and generally made the kind of daft changes that would appeal to people who read a play without understanding what a production is. They then permitted us to give them this 'present'. The first performance was before Moscow Party activists and their leader, Viktor Grishin. They were invited without their wives, and 1,200 deerskin hats appeared in MKhAT's cloakrooms (it was December). The Moscow Party boss sat in a special box and his 'flock' looked not so much at the stage as at the box, in an attempt to guess his 'mood'. The production was not only passed, it was decided to treat it as a paean to Leninism. The Art Theatre was in raptures. It very soon became apparent, however, that our victory was a hollow one.

In March 1982 Brezhnev came to a performance, surrounded by his comrades-in-arms. It was the swan song of Soviet political theatre and the end of the myth about 'refurbishing the revolution'. Brezhnev never went to the theatre (except for a ritual *Swan Lake*): he preferred ice hockey. He had only a few months to live, had difficulty understanding anything, could hardly stand on his feet, was almost entirely deaf, and was looked after by his batman Chernenko. We were destined to discover all this in the course of the performance. Brezhnev was supported like a dummy and shown to the world when it was necessary. He was literally carried into the box two metres from the stage. Being a man of ritual, he bowed to the audience. He received a ripple of applause in reply, and the historic performance began.

He evidently did understand that he had been brought to a play about Lenin. When Kalyagin appeared in a spotlight in Lenin's Kremlin study, Brezhnev began to fidget – to get worked up, in fact. He could not decide how he should respond. In our ritual theatre the form was to clap when Lenin came on. There was no applause on this occasion, because Yefremov had rigged the staging in order to break the tradition. Lenin had come on in the blackout to disturbing strains of Wagner.[7] The audience was silent. Then, so loudly that the whole auditorium could hear, the inimitable, half-paralyzed voice known to all the world asked Chernenko: 'Is that Lenin? Should we greet him?' Without turning his head, Chernenko said curtly: 'No!' The audience went cold. We realized we were assisting at an exceptional event. It was impossible to laugh: a hundred agents seated in square clusters were scrutinizing the audience. All one could do was watch the box, where another show was going on that was no less interesting than the one on stage. Brezhnev gave a running commentary at full volume and tried to communicate with those around him. 'Can *you* hear anything?' he asked Andrey Gromyko, and without waiting for a reply complained: 'I can't hear a thing!' They were the reactions of a sick old man fallen into second childishness. 'She's pretty', he suddenly murmured, staring at Lenin's secretary. The aged entourage preserved its stony silence. In the second row of the box, in shadow, sat Yury Andropov. In a box opposite Brezhnev's, which was reserved for the Politburo, sat our friend Demichev, the Minister of Culture, hunched up and wearing dusky-lensed glasses that presumably concealed horror. The KGB men kept looking all round the auditorium, and the actors strained every muscle to shout loud enough for the chief spectator to hear them.

In the middle of the second act Brezhnev suddenly left his box. A rustle went through the audience. What was happening? Twenty minutes later he was brought back. In the meantime, on stage Lenin had had a chat with Armand Hammer. When Brezhnev sat down, one of those next to him informed him very loudly, straight into his ear: 'They've just had Hammer on.' 'Hammer in person?' the old man asked, and this time the audience could not restrain itself. A peal of laughter rolled across MKhAT's auditorium, followed by wave upon wave. The *narod* were laughing out loud and only those in the square clusters were impervious to it.

This period in our country's history was ending in a shameful farce and the Art Theatre was inevitably playing a part in it. After Brezhnev's visit it was impossible to deceive ourselves any longer with the flattering notion that we were 'fighting' or 'confronting the "wall"'. We had to get on with our lives and somehow do our duty. One after another the old men went to their graves. Along the way they managed to shove Lyubimov into emigration. Yefremov found himself in a vacuum and gritted his teeth. They decided to sack him too, but certain famous actors leapt to his defence, went to see the Minister, the Central Committee even, and saved him. The regime was humouring them.

In spring 1985 MKhAT visited Poland. Kalyagin was in his dressing-room being made up as Lenin and asked me about the circumstances surrounding the recent murder of the Catholic priest Popiełuszko. As I recounted them, his eyes widened in horror, yet all the time the features of the leader of the revolution were emerging on his face. It was pure Brecht! Then, in a half-empty Warsaw auditorium, in a country under martial law, Kalyagin/Lenin tried to address the Poles through the words of his stage character: 'No one in the world can compromise communists, unless communists compromise themselves.' I can vouch as an eye-witness that Kalyagin gave a brilliant performance. The Polish audience understood what he was saying.

We returned to Moscow in April. In February, Yefremov had opened his production of *Uncle Vanya*. Five years before that he had staged *The Seagull*. The deepest note sounded in both of these productions was one of reconciliation and forgiveness.

In *The Seagull*, Yefremov and his designer Levental brought to the fore the gazebo-cum-theatre, which became another character in the play. The cries of seagulls were often heard above the garden. The production was a symphony of light, a ballet of gauzes. Chekhov's heroes became part of nature. They dissolved and died in the beauty of the world. At the end of the sixties Yefremov had turned *The Seagull* into a pamphlet. Now he wanted to listen carefully to each character – and he succeeded. They were garrulous, these strange Chekhovian people, they were so garrulous that they did not even notice when a man like Sorin was dying. But the theme of faith in the midst of collapse prevailed over all the disillusion. At the end of the play Treplev's theatre stood there in ruins, the wind whistled through its timbers, and the torn curtains flapped. Nina Zarechnaya, played by Anastasiya Vertinskaya, appeared and recited her monologue again, but this time it did not sound like a parody. Treplev's death brought out the true sense of his abstract words about the World Soul, people, lions, eagles and partridges. Moreover, these words were now being uttered not by a provincial teenager but by an actress who had trodden her path of suffering and penetrated to the source of his symbolist visions. The idea of the fusion of spirit and matter, of life's eternal cycle, was given real human content.

'I must do it, if I am honest.' This is where the Sovremennik began. Thirty years later, in Yefremov's *Uncle Vanya*, the theme of creative patience re-emerged. Yefremov did not give Vanya's 'I've wasted my life' an heroic dimension. It had *not* been wasted, because his life is what life itself is by definition, in essence, in purpose. Far away, at the back of the stage, Levental had painted a house into an autumnal Levitan landscape. As darkness descended front of stage, through the mist that rose from the cooling earth we suddenly saw a small light in the window of this house. The light shone in the darkness not very brightly, but it shone, it beckoned, it pointed the way. This was how the production ended, early in 1985 on the eve of unpredictable changes.[8]

Mikhail Gorbachev came to see *Uncle Vanya* on 30 April. The next morning, of course, he was due to be standing on Lenin's tomb for the May Day parade. Never before had a General Secretary taken the liberty of devoting the evening before the proletarian holiday to Chekhov. A week later, he rang Yefremov and gave him his impressions of the production. He said that he had liked Astrov (played by Oleg Borisov), but Vanya (Andrey Myagkov) was simply heart-rending. He then said that he had a lot to do, that they ought to meet and talk about what concerned the theatre, and that altogether he had to 'get our fly-wheel moving again'. Did he have any idea at that moment where this 'flywheel' would spin off to?

Yefremov and I were alone in his study. Yefremov appeared to be talking normally, not playing up at all to the person he was speaking to. But when he had put the receiver down he suddenly mopped his brow. He noticed my surprise and explained with a sheepish grin, quoting Chekhov: 'You know, squeezing the slave out of oneself is not easy.'

Yury Lyubimov's 'black cross'

By the beginning of the 1970s Lyubimov's *Sturm und Drang* period was over and the Taganka's style had settled down. It was a style saturated with metaphor. The actors and the director had learned to express themselves by creating a series of flashes of insight. Their metaphor factory used Eisenstein's 'montage of attractions' method, which was mastered to perfection.[9] Actors and audiences alike got used to parallel montages, counterpoint, deconstruction and contrast. The light curtain acted as scissors for cutting up the montages. Director and designer continued the search for expressive techniques latent in the stage box itself. They spiritualized it. Instead of the borders, you had a theatrical heaven consisting of battens and fly bars which performed new roles in every production. The stage surface was the theatre's 'earth', and what was below the 'earth' was capable of a multitude of unpredictable meanings, from grave and dungeon to swamp or Hell. The Taganka's natural 'backcloth', that is, its diagonal off-white back wall, was equally suggestive, because it could adopt any light or colour as though it were a clean canvas. This saturated space transfigured everything that came within the production's force field: objects accreted layers of meaning.

For many years, the freedom of Lyubimov's theatrical language enabled him to do without a Soviet play. His poetic theatre moved smoothly into a 'theatre of prose'. Side by side with a production about Pushkin, he would put on stage adaptations of Dostoyevsky and Bulgakov, Fyodor Abramov and Yury Trifonov, who were the best contemporary prose writers. At the very start of the seventies he turned to Shakespeare, who became the ideal sound board for his theatrical ideas.

The tragedy of the Danish prince was prepared and anticipated by a production called *The Dawns are Quiet Here*. Those who took part in it recall that it came together very quickly and easily, almost by accident. Boris Vasilyev's story about five women anti-aircraft gunners killed in the war lasted two hours without a break and really was played in a single breath. The breath was imparted by a confident style that was extremely successful with this rather simple Soviet prose, but would not have been equal to the responsibilities of doing Shakespeare.

The stage was covered in greenish, blotchy tarpaulin. Across the centre was the chassis of a one and a half ton truck, with the girls in the back. They were singing and laughing and had no forebodings. The game of hide-and-seek played by life and death began with the wooden slats and planks that lined the back of the truck. The planks became the barn in which the women were billeted, then the fence on which they hung their underwear to dry, to the consternation of Fedot Vaskov, who was put in charge of them. Then the planks were used to enclose the *banya* (steam bath) and an extraordinary scene followed, in which the contrast between the warm, living human body and impending death was almost unbearable. The back of the truck

Plate 6   Vitaly Shapovalov as Fedot Vaskov in Yury Lyubimov's production of
The Dawns are Quiet Here, by Boris Vasilyev, Taganka Theatre, 1970.

was dismantled again and the slats used by the women as poles to probe their way through a swamp. Then, attached to fly lines, the poles removed themselves from the humans and began to dance to Matvey Blanter's sad waltz 'Soundlessly, weightlessly, the yellow leaf drifts from the birches'. The least change of angle or lighting was enough to spawn more and more meanings. In the end, each girl met her death against a wall of planks.

It was a virtuoso score of light, music and voices, which revealed the very deepest sources of the people's war with fascism. Lyubimov laid bare the main paradox of a war which for many had been their 'moment of stardom'. For those who had survived the pre-war terror and the ordeal of silence, the war was a return to clarity in life, to a definite purpose. The war was like being freed from ideology, like getting one's country back. All of this lived in Lyubimov's production, in its subject matter, its cultural semiotics and its musical organization. Although the play began with brash Stalinist marches of the 1930s, it gravitated more and more towards the people's own songs and funeral laments. The death of each woman was preceded by a vision and a song, which actually lifted the military subject matter on to a universal national plane. Here too Lyubimov very cleverly 'blurred' the production's 'targets'. Fascism in this production was not merely a German product, it was a sullen force diffused throughout the world; it even existed in those fighting it.

The war brought light into the brain of the girls' commander Fedot Vaskov (played by Vitaly Shapovalov). He was a peasant bloke from a God-forsaken corner of Russia, who had known no poetry in his life, only military discipline. He was humanized by witnessing death. Charged with guarding part of the Stalin Canal, and having laid down the lives of five future mothers for this canal, for the first time the sergeant-major discovered in his heart feelings not governed by military regulations. When he had buried the last of the girls in the swamp, he collapsed in tears. But this is saying little. In this most symbolic of plays, this moment was the least artificial, a devastating human outburst and a breakthrough to the true self. It was also the high point of the style Lyubimov had been evolving. All of the theatre's potential, all its metaphors and 'attractions' had been necessary merely so that these few seconds of absolute actorial, human freedom could happen.

Plate 7   Vladimir Vysotsky as Hamlet in Yury Lyubimov's production, Taganka Theatre, 1971.

Lyubimov was making new theatre, but the theatre was also making a new Lyubimov. As I have said, his peasant mind possessed enormous magpie abilities. He was always absorbing and storing things in it, in order to bring them out at the right moment. Shakespeare's play was such a moment. The production of *The Mother* gave him a feel for a pulsating space. The living ring of soldiers that expanded and contracted was the prototype of the living curtain devised by David Borovsky for *Hamlet*. Some critics suggested that this curtain should be named in the cast list before all the other characters. It could move up, down and across the stage, at any angle, replete with the energy that came from moving in an enclosed space. The metaphorical meanings of this curtain have been described in dozens of articles. The curtain was the earth, the state, a 'wall', a murderer, and decay – it evolved endless images, some of which its creators had not foreseen.

It was knitted out of dark wool. This was an indirect allusion to the leather that the main characters wore in Peter Brook's *King Lear*, which had been seen in Moscow in the early sixties. In Russia, leather was associated with Bolshevik commissars. Borovsky countered it with a coarsely knitted wool, that is, a material that like leather, iron or wood retains something timeless in it, or rather something that links all times. It was these elements that became the basis of the Taganka production. All of the main characters were dressed in dark brown jumpers, except for Hamlet, who wore a black one. On the forestage, immediately in front of the audience, was a grave filled with real earth, from which Yorick's skull would be produced. In an upper window stage-left a live cockerel appeared at the beginning of the performance and crowed to announce the dawn. Down right was a coffin, on which the grave-diggers shelled their hard-boiled eggs and Hamlet tortured his soul with the question of death. Poetic naturalism penetrated every pore of the show. The unrealistic curtain and the real cockerel were the extreme poles of Lyubimov's directing, and represented a freedom of style that was to echo the free spirit of the great play.

There were no genuflections to the latter. From the very first seconds *Hamlet* was an utterly modern spectacle. The actors relieved the play of the rituals of theatrical medievalism. There was no 'royal entry', 'court', operatic splendour, or business with Fortinbras's soldiers carrying off the corpse. Only the earth and the grave, life and death, which lorded it in this space like the awesome curtain itself.

Vladimir Vysotsky began the performance by singing Zhivago's poem *Hamlet* to the sound of his guitar. This, of course, was a calculated polemical act; a response to the audience's expectation and a challenge to the gossip that 'they've got Vysotsky playing Hamlet!' They had, and with his guitar even. 'The buzz subsides. I come out on the boards.' Through Pasternak and his guitar, Vysotsky set the tone for the whole production: 'The order of the acts has been thought through, / The end is inescapable.' It was not about a man who discovers that Denmark is a prison, but one who knows everything in advance. Lyubimov needed the 'Mousetrap' scene not for Hamlet to get confirmation, but entirely for the purposes of theatrical parody. His Hamlet had received confirmation long ago and now had somehow to take action before our eyes in these few hours. To exact revenge or not; to spill blood or not.

Vysotsky's jumper was a sign of the generation of the sixties. The sixties men regarded jumpers not only as a democratic uniform suitable for real men, but as a signal for distinguishing 'one of us' from 'one of them'. However, it was not just his jumper that marked Vysotsky out from other Hamlets of the post-Stalin stage. He put into his Hamlet his poetic soul and his legend as imprinted on millions of cassettes. Remember that by the beginning of the seventies Vysotsky's songs were being secretly listened to by the whole country.

The order of the acts had been thought through to the end: Hamlet chose struggle, and consequently death. This Hamlet could not live stained with blood. There was no Fortinbras at the end, just the curtain moving slowly across the whole stage. Previously it had swept aside people and fought with them. Now it was moving in an empty space. There was no one to sweep aside. The curtain's farewell solo became an image for what happens after death. People die, but the clock carries on, the Earth continues to revolve. Maybe it was an image of continuing time, or of the eternity in which there is no death.

At first Lyubimov wanted to finish his *Hamlet* with a conversation between the grave-diggers. They had led the action throughout and the idea was for them to spend five minutes at the end retelling the plot of Shakespeare's play as though it were a rumour that was going the rounds. 'This Hamlet drank like a fish, wanted to grab the crown', and so on. A text was suggested from Stoppard's *Rosencrantz and Guildenstern are dead*, in a translation by Joseph Brodsky. This bathos would have been entirely in the spirit of Lyubimov's theatre and, even better, would have brilliantly combined Hamlet's posthumous biography with the legend that had sprung up around Vysotsky, actor and poet, in his own lifetime. Unfortunately, the bureaucrats objected that Stoppard's play had not been passed by the censor. Lyubimov would not risk playing this text as an improvization, without permission, as Hamlet proposed to the players with 'The Mousetrap'. Nothing at the Taganka, however, was ever forgotten. Ten years later Yury Lyubimov would create a mystery play about the dead Vysotsky and recall the grave-diggers' conversation on Hamlet's grave. The short life of the Taganka's Hamlet did end in gossip. Things came full circle.

After *Alive*, Lyubimov began to take a very close look at contemporary Russian fiction, which in the 1970s consisted of two opposing camps. The first was associated with village life (so-called 'village prose') and the second with urban problems. Lyubimov's soul had its roots in both the town and the country, and this enabled him to rise above the literary barricades. In Fyodor Abramov's *Wooden Horses* (staged in

1974 for the Taganka's tenth anniversary), and in *The Exchange* (1976) and *The House on the Embankment* (1980) adapted from Yury Trifonov, the director presented his own image of rural and urban Russia. The 'village writers' looked back in time and were inspired by a patriarchal Utopia. The 'town writers' looked forwards, but their diagnosis of the world they lived in was astonishingly similar. Both were talking about the degeneration of the nation as a result of the crushing blow dealt it by the system.

For a long time, no serious theatre would look at 'village prose'. The Soviet stage confections of rural life had put serious directors off. Apparently the conventions of the stage were incompatible with the naturalism of village life. The attempts of urban actors to imitate rural speech were faintly embarrassing.

Lyubimov took all of this into account in his *Wooden Horses*.[10] The idea that Russia's two worlds – city and village – were alienated from each other, was introduced right at the start. We entered the auditorium not by the usual doors but across the stage, which was already set for the performance. You could touch objects whose names, I suspect, I was not alone in being unsure about: this, apparently, was a harrow with its teeth digging into the Taganka's floor, and this (someone volunteered) was an old flail, polished by time. You could touch the faded calico curtains and shudder at the pitiful choice of goods in the village shop (townspeople were better off in those days). The audience felt they were in a museum; and the director and designer had deliberately provoked this response, in order to plunge us a few minutes later into a fierce world where people were fighting for their very survival.

It transpired that poetic theatre was uniquely suited to recreating the rural way of life. Without going into the naturalistic details, but by stripping the stage bare and seating all the actors round its perimeter like a Greek chorus, Lyubimov enacted these three stories by Abramov as though they were a peasant saga. It told the story of the destruction of the village by showing how the essential peasant type was replaced and died out. This 'type' was represented by different women, who by their nature were destined to defend and preserve the very foundations of the home, family and life.

The old woman Vasilisa Melentyevna was played by Alla Demidova. A Moscow intellectual, a superb Gertrude in *Hamlet* and a no less beautiful Ranevskaya in *The Cherry Orchard*, she brought poetry to Abramov's old woman from the village of Pizhma by conveying the music of a soul that had survived. She was a dispossessed kulak, had dragged a home and children onto their feet, had starved and suffered everything, yet retained the light in her soul. The light shone through her face as on an icon, through her peasant hands that never knew rest, and through her speech which was full of dignity. The actress did not imitate the northern Russian accent, she seemed to let it into her own city speech and to demonstrate the beauty of an organic intonation. It was a miracle, indeed the cream of our national spirit; a spirit that had been wrenched out of shape but not finally broken.

Melentyevna was a type on the way out. In her place came Pelageya (Zinaida Slavina), who represented a different village and different times. She burst on to the stage being bawled at by her daughter, who accused her of spending all her life hoarding 'rags'. There was screaming, hollering, wailing, the irrepressible energy of acquisition. Incapable of telling right from wrong, incapable of tears ('They boiled away by the stove ages ago'), Pelageya ran, crept and crawled to scrape together what she thought were the most important things in life: a little gold watch for her daughter Alka, a job for her at the bakery, or a mock-velvet jacket (a great status symbol in the villages then). Basically, this animal that had been thrust into a situation of natural selection was the product of our common hell. Her aims were paltry and she paid a terrible price for everything: her body, her soul, and in the end Alka, who was propelled from the village into a restaurant in town and set for a 'life of fun'.

Wooden Horses showed the degeneration and extinction of the peasant type – what might be called the gene bank of the nation. In Trifonov's *The Exchange*, produced two years later, Lyubimov broached this theme from a different angle. Engineer Viktor Dmitriyev's confession was the confession of the middle stratum that formed the bulk of any Russian town. Theirs too was a world that had become fixed and compacted by the whole course of post-revolutionary history.

It was an 'exchange' in at least two senses. There was the exchange of an apartment and the exchange of a soul. The first sense needs explaining. During the Soviet period accommodation was practically the pivotal problem in people's lives. After the Revolution, the spacious apartments of the upper classes were 'settled more densely' and as a result so-called 'communal flats' sprang up everywhere, that is to say flats with far more families living in them than the 'facilities' were ever designed for. For decades it was impossible to buy or sell a flat, all one could do was exchange it. This was a way of life in which whole generations grew up and were schooled. And Soviet literature – at various levels – described this extraordinary human termitary, where people lived without a shred of privacy. Trifonov was one of the most perceptive chroniclers of the seventies. In *The Exchange*, Viktor Dmitriyev and his wife lived in a single room in a communal flat, whilst his mother, an Old Bolshevik, had a flat of her own. His mother had cancer and they had to move into her flat as soon as possible in order not to lose the living space. It was a typical Soviet affair, known to millions every day. The only complication was that by suggesting to his mother that they move in, he would be telling her that she was soon going to die, and it is not done in Russia to disclose to people that they have cancer. This was the narrow threshold that Dmitriyev had to cross, and with him the Taganka audience, who were transfixed by a horror all too familiar to them.

Lyubimov and Borovsky piled up old furniture front of stage, as though it were about to be removed. It was in various styles and of various ages, from which one could tell what kind of life had been lived here. All over the furniture and props, in the most unexpected places, little handwritten adverts were fixed, offering exchanges of accommodation. In the middle of the cluttered stage was a bare space that acted as the theatrical equivalent of a television screen: here parodies of figure skaters whirled before Dmitriyev (Aleksandr Vilkin) as he struggled to resolve his 'to be or not to be'.

Lyubimov selected the most characteristic visual features of the era of 'decomposition'. Strange though it may sound, the television equivalent of the era was figure skating. Prime viewing time was devoted to fancy dancing on ice. 'Stagnation' proceeded to the merry tones of 'Kalinka'. On-stage, Lyubimov opened up a gap in domestic time, through which poured all kinds of people more suited to a novel. Viktor's relations and forebears appeared as figure skaters: revolutionaries, fanatics, executioners and their victims. The engineer's short step to self-betrayal took on a spiritual dimension. In order to accentuate this, Lyubimov invented a kind of Soviet middleman/devil in black (played by Semyon Farada), who was a genius at property exchange, forged invisible chains of people, decreed who moved where, how many square metres they got, and what could be exchanged for what.

The main character of the play was selling his soul. At the end, he came to his mother and, writhing with self-disgust, suggested that she leave. At this moment, the shadow of a washing-line hanging from one wing to another fell across Dmitriyev's face and seemed to strike it out. He went back to his communal flat and without taking off his mac sat down in front of the 'screen'. 'Kalinka' struck up again and the figure skaters danced. It grew dark. A huge, transparent polythene cover came down over the stage, like a shroud. It began to rain: streams of water beat down on the cover, coursing above the furniture, the adverts, the figure skaters, Moscow, and the whole of this country in which people who were basically guilty of nothing were being tormented to death.

The rot was at work everywhere. Soon it would even penetrate the Taganka; and from a most unexpected quarter.

In 1977, immediately after *The Exchange*, Lyubimov staged Bulgakov's novel *The Master and Margarita*. In the ten years since its publication, this book had become for Russian readers something akin to the Bible, which itself had not been published since the Revolution. The adventures of the Devil in Red Moscow, the comparison of the Stalin period with life in ancient Judaea, and of the prophet from Nazareth with a modern writer incarcerated in a lunatic asylum – this whole extraordinary *Satyricon* of Soviet life was made for Lyubimov's theatre. He was about to be sixty, as was our Revolution. He decided to celebrate both anniversaries with a Bulgakov production that to some extent would be a summing-up.

The set contained elements of all Lyubimov's and Borovsky's previous designs. There was the pendulum from *Rush-Hour* (Margarita swung to and fro on it as though flying above Moscow), the curtain from *Hamlet*, the truck from *The Dawns are Quiet Here*. The handling of the theme of the artist (the Master) grappling with a moribund state also had the air of a summing-up. Lyubimov and Boris Dyachin very skilfully brought together the main themes of the novel. They had an inspired scene on the subject of 'manuscripts do not burn', they included the black magic show at the Variety Theatre in which Woland put Muscovites to the test, and a superbly conceived Satan's Ball, in which a naked Margarita received the world's wrong-doers as they emerged from a grave as through the gates of eternity. The stage was thickly populated by Pharisees/writers, informers, and a crowd of Judaean/Soviet types. The production culminated in a display of portraits of Bulgakov, from the Kiev schoolboy to the writer of the 'sunset novel' wearing dark glasses and already marked by death. Before each of them a candle was lit.

The Master had been passed by the authorities. This triggered important changes which were not at first appreciated. The showy and not very profound production initiated the Taganka's own 'exchange'. Gradually, the audience that had been born with this theatre and educated by it accordingly, was replaced by another. What caused this, whether it was Bulgakov's legendary book or the rumour that they were 'offering' a nude actress at the Taganka, I do not know, but starting with *The Master and Margarita*, the Taganka's auditorium began to be filled with Moscow's élite, including the Party élite. The Taganka was 'recognized'; it became chic to go there. The regime felt itself sufficiently secure to allow itself to be criticized. It even espied a certain advantage in this. From *The Master* onwards, until the war in Afghanistan, the Taganka's productions 'got through' relatively easily. Nikolay Potapov could print an article in *Pravda* entitled 'Black Magic at the Taganka' and lecture Lyubimov ideologically, but its general tone was indescribably deferential: he called Lyubimov 'the Master', equating him with Bulgakov's hero.[11] There was no higher praise in the Soviet critical vocabulary!

An ambiguous situation had arisen. The establishment had recognized the Taganka and begun to show it marks of favour. These marks were extremely dangerous for a theatrical 'priest's' reputation. To be a tame dissident was intolerable and even shameful. Lyubimov did not solve this problem until the autumn of 1983, when he abruptly changed the rules of the game and burned his boats. However, there were some fallow years until then, in which the creator of the Taganka had to do battle on two fronts: with the outside world and with the bureaucrats who had 'taken a shine' to the Taganka and were creating a reputation for it as an officially authorized 'political theatre'.

In the last few years before he emigrated, Lyubimov tried to expose his theatre to a new range of artistic challenges. Gogol, Dostoyevsky,

Chekhov, and finally Pushkin were all signposts on an important, if interrupted, path that was to lead the theatre out of its ambivalence.

In 1978 the production *Revizskaya skazka* (which means both *An Inspector's Census* and *A Fairytale about Inspection*) attempted in the Meyerhold tradition to recreate the 'whole of Gogol'.[12] It was a significant experiment in grasping the mystical reality discovered by the author of *Dead Souls*. The director created a mishmash of Gogolian texts, in which he sought his own cherished themes. With his designer Eduard Kochergin, he fashioned a theatrical underworld bristling with evil growths that shot up through the stage to become three-metre-high monsters. Gogol's apocalyptic vision of 'the earth on fire, the heavens being rolled up, corpses rising from their graves and terrible monsters growing from the seeds of our sins' was transferred literally to the stage. Gogol's landowners sprouted up like ghastly mirages before the stocky Chichikov (played by Feliks Antipov), who alone had both feet on the ground.

One of the main themes, naturally, was that of the artist and power. But this time it was radically different. Lyubimov had turned to Gogol's story *The Portrait*, which shifts the subject of the artist on to a quite different plane. It deals with the relationship between the artist and reality – any reality, not necessarily Russian reality. The Tagankans had acquired a taste for metaphysics. 'Reality' was choking the artist-hero of *The Portrait*, as he stood alone on an empty stage covered with the cloth that military greatcoats are made of. For, as was often the case at the Taganka, the air was stuffed full with human faces. They all wanted their 'portrait' painting. They demanded to be made flesh. They begged, besought and tempted the creator. Amidst this universal madness, the artist had to define himself and choose his path.

Through the literary chaos of a hastily assembled script, you suddenly heard the authentic note of Gogol's own fate, paired with that of the modern artist. '*Rus*, what do you want from me? . . . And why has everything in you turned on me eyes full of expectation?'[13] No other Lyubimov production had focused so much on the theme of the deadly stasis of Russian life, its habit of spiralling back on the same old problems throughout its history. The production began with some mischievous business involving the pre-revolutionary monument to Gogol and the Soviet one, but ended in a quite different mood. The theatrical

Plate 8   Yury Lyubimov at a rehearsal of *Revizskaya skazka* (1978). Foreground:
Yury Lyubimov. Immediately behind Lyubimov: the composer Alfred Shnitke.
Right of Shnitke: the designers Eduard Kochergin and David Borovsky.

underworld created at the Taganka resounded with Gogol's *cri de cœur*,
which was uniquely despairing even for the Russian classics:

> And the earth burns with incomprehensible ennui; life becomes
> like hard, stale bread; everything grows pettier and more trivial;
> and before us all there arises the gigantic image of tedium,
> growing vaster and more immeasurable every day. All is hollow
> and desolate, the grave is everywhere. God, how empty and
> terrifying it becomes in Thy world![14]

The 'gigantic image of tedium' became a metaphor for the stagnant
quagmire of Soviet life at that moment.

Revizskaya skazka demanded of the Taganka's actors a completely different level of artistic response and even a different ethical
talent. Lyubimov overcame the inertia of his well-tried methods for
'butting the oak', but discovered in his Gogol production that he and
his theatre were ill-equipped for achieving a complex artistic task of
this kind. Gogol had little to contribute to the call to fight the regime.
The Taganka's usual method of communicating with its audience by

a wink and a nudge, and its heightening of Gogol's texts, were totally at variance with the nature of his art. The fear of death, the awesomeness of retribution, the thirst for redemption, the dream of universal repentance and above all the examination of one's own vices, that is, everything that formed the basis of Gogol's spiritual drama, was reinterpreted in terms of Soviet psychological experience. The three-hour show had its moments of sublimity, but there were wearisome stretches in which it was just stuck in one place.

Similar problems afflicted *Crime and Punishment* (1979). Lyubimov narrowed the meaning of the great novel right down to the present. He was not inspired by the spiritual drama of a man who had transgressed. He was not interested in the Christian themes that were so important to the book. He discovered in Dostoyevsky the theme of the 'intellectual with an axe', and this coloured the whole production.

Lyubimov began by experimenting on the audience, who were channelled into the auditorium through one door. As you entered, you received a jolt: front of stage, where you could not possibly ignore them, lay the corpses of two women. One was spread-eagled on the floor, the other seemed to have slithered down the wall. Their faces were covered with blood-stained towels. All 'literary' notions were swept aside. It was as though no novel existed and the theatre was starting from scratch to tell the story of how two innocent women were murdered.

Lyubimov's production was based not so much on Dostoyevsky as on Karyakin, the author of the adaptation and of the book *Raskolnikov's Self-Deception*.[15] Readers feel compassion for Raskolnikov because he killed something in himself, as well as two women; but the theatre presented him as an ideological maniac in the revolutionary mould. From the very first seconds when he played a spotlight over the audience and dazzled us, and his enormous, baleful shadow fell across the screen of the Taganka's back wall, he started shouting to us about Napoleon, the termitary, lice, and the rest of his 'philosophy'. Dostoyevsky's famous technique of manifesting the inner workings of a character in outward action (which has given rise to the legend that his prose is incredibly adaptable to the stage), here led to an unexpected result. Lyubimov translated into outward action all of Raskolnikov's latent potential and thereby deprived him of any inner drama. The early Russian Nietzschean was brought down from the high horse of philosophy and reduced to an axe. Dostoyevsky wrote a novel about 'Thou shalt not kill'; Lyubimov staged a production about 'Killing people is wrong.'

At the Taganka the spiritual make-up of Dostoyevsky's hero was replaced by that of someone formed by the Russian Revolution. The idea of violence for the sake of good, of a new 'arithmetic' according to which it was all right to cut short a million human lives if they did not fit a theory – this was the thrust of the Taganka's production and the source of its ecstatic style.

However, in this production, as in *Revizskaya skazka*, the political intention did not succeed in drowning the polyphonic prose entirely. Something remained and this artistic 'residue' was apparently the most important thing. The 'residue' here was Svidrigaylov, played by Vysotsky. He gradually pushed Raskolnikov out to the periphery and took over the space of the production. Compared with Raskolnikov, who seemed rather one-dimensional with his 'self-deception' (although Aleksandr Trofimov played him with the kind of nervous energy that few actors dare to expend on the modern stage), Svidrigaylov was complex and unpredictable. Vysotsky played him as a Russian Mephistopheles, but always kept him recognizably human. Svidrigaylov's nihilistic irony, his self-pity, his protest about the immortality of the soul, his denial of eternity, which he reduced to the image of a peasant bath-house with spiders, and finally his mysterious suicide – all of this was acted with tremendous force.

It was in fact Vysotsky's last part. He handled Dostoyevsky's text as a musician and poet, feeling every nuance. Svidrigaylov's soliloquies sounded like rhythmical prose, taking on the beauty and finality of poetic utterance. 'So eavesdropping on people is / wrong / but bumping off old women with / whatever comes to hand / is / right?' he asked. For the first time in the performance the audience laughed, and the psychotic tension was suddenly relieved by irony. A most unlikely tenderness and longing began to be heard in Vysotsky/Svidrigaylov's voice, which had previously sounded like sandpaper. It was as though the stuff of life itself were breathing hoarsely in this tormented man.

The death of Vysotsky in July 1980 was a turning point for the Taganka theatre. The soul left it. Gogol's image of an empty and terrifying world, the image of colossal boredom, became absolute fact. Clearly, something also went out of Lyubimov's soul. For January 1981,

Vysotsky's birthday, he mounted a production about the poet who had been 'hunted like a wolf'. Vysotsky's song about this 'hunt' was the emotional climax of the show. There were several rows of old theatre stalls on the stage, as it were continuing the Taganka's auditorium, and these were wound with a strip of white cloth. Through the cloth could be seen bars, lit from below with a blood-red light. Stage and auditorium were united by the agony of a hunted, unique living person. It was a production about a deceased poet and a theatre that was exercising its right to remember him.

Done in the style of the 'old' Taganka, it threw fresh light on the history of this theatre. The fates of Pushkin, Mayakovsky, Yesenin and all the 'fallen and the living' accompanied the fate of the Taganka actor. The very aesthetics of the theatre were here no longer a means to but an object of portrayal. The marketplace frankness and audacity of their style, the montage of attractions, the light curtain, the planting of leitmotivs and the factory of theatrical metaphors – all this was presented as a kind of digest of the Taganka in tribute to its top performer. Through Vysotsky, the Taganka had enacted the mystery play of our life. Its stage had been filled with the characters of his songs: winos, heroes, *zeks* (convicts), KGB men, circus performers and actors. They all yelled and joked and struggled to become free. His songs touched on eternal Russian themes: prison and poverty, the camps, war, 'Abroad', and over them all the eternal question of 'to be or not to be'. A cor anglais marked off each episode in the Taganka's hagiography. Vysotsky's raucous voice was projected from behind us and on-stage, the performers entered into a dialogue with it, as though he were still alive; they joined in his songs, questioned him and argued with him. In another second, it seemed, he himself would come onstage in his jumper carrying his guitar.

However, 'they' did not let the theatre exercise its right to remember. Lyubimov therefore turned to the powers of darkness for help. The chief of the KGB, Andropov, deigned to let him perform it once. For this performance the theatre was cordoned off with military precision. Inside, it was full to bursting. All Moscow was there.

Lyubimov was burning his boats. In his next production, of Trifonov's *The House on the Embankment*, he did something unprecedented even for the Taganka. The main character was a Soviet intellectual who had toed the line and at one point a gobbet of spit flew from backstage towards the audience, only incidentally aimed at the conformist's face. Then, in *Three Sisters*, Lyubimov placed the Prozorovs' house in the context of an army barracks (the idea was simple: if the officers visit the house so often, they cannot live far away, so the barracks are close by). In fact it was less of a barracks than an army latrine. The stage was surrounded by suspiciously filthy walls with yellow water stains on them. In the middle of the stage a kind of platform was erected, on which Lyubimov made his Chekhovian officers watch *Three Sisters*. At one point, he opened the outside wall of the theatre (the performance was in the new building, where this special effect was possible) and we saw a fragment of old Moscow: a church, cars and passers-by, who did not know that they had become part of a performance of Chekhov.

Our life was interpolated into Chekhov's world rudely and provocatively. However, as with the spitting in *The House on the Embankment*, people tried to ignore the challenge. As soon as the Grundies exclaimed 'But it's not Chekhov!', a well-meaning chorus of liberals drowned them out. As usual, the 'progressive' critics deactivated the production's message.

Meanwhile, following its historical nose, the Taganka began rehearsals of Pushkin's play *Boris Godunov*. The part of Boris was offered to Nikolay Gubenko, who had started at the Taganka in the mid-sixties and then gone into films. A few years later Gubenko would become the last Minister of Culture of the USSR and play a part in the division and demise of the Taganka. In 1981 this was still quite unimaginable. This remarkable actor's ambitions were then restricted to Pushkin's tragedy, which was chosen in anticipation of a 'change of guard'.

The dress rehearsals of *Boris Godunov* coincided with Brezhnev's funeral. He was succeeded by the patron of the arts from the Lubyanka, Andropov. This completely demoralized the arts bureaucrats. They began to suspect subversion everywhere. Lyubimov's production terrified them with its allusions. The False Dmitry wore a sailor's vest, so they interpreted this as a reference to Andropov's past (in his youth he had been in the navy). The prologue itself was seen as an insult to the regime, because it involved all the characters joining hands, singing, groaning

Plate 9   Nikolay Gubenko (centre) as Boris Godunov and Valery Zolotukhin
(right) as the Pretender in Yury Lyubimov's banned production of *Boris Godunov*
at the Taganka Theatre, 1982.

and bellowing, and this was immediately identified as the Russian
people. The production was banned. This meant an end to Lyubimov's
most important piece of work for the theatre; one that far transcended
political allusions.

In December 1982, when the fate of the production was still
unclear, the Taganka invited friends of the theatre to take part in
a recorded discussion of *Boris Godunov*, which would be a kind of
defence of it. I was not able to be there, so I sent Lyubimov a letter,
which I should like to quote from now as a testimony to the times.
It is important to understand how the production was received in
December 1982, rather than seven years later when Lyubimov returned
from emigration, recreated *Boris Godunov*, and basically could find
no place for it in the new era.

I wrote that Lyubimov had brought *Boris Godunov* alive for the
first time on the Russian stage. It had been a great museum piece originally intended for a theatrical revolution that never happened, and
Lyubimov had elicited from it for the first time a living, incisive historical meaning that was truly theatrical.

With the ease of a Master, you have achieved what Meyerhold was girding his loins for at the end of his life. The experience of a people's theatre in the true sense of the word, the experience of the early Taganka's *Pugachov* period, the experience of your best work in recent years, in which you attempted to acquire new values – all of this has gone into making *Boris*. The play has turned out to be an ideal sound board: it answers all the questions [that we are agonizing over now] and echoes a hundredfold one's intellectual hesitations or mental anguish.

Pushkin dreamt of a theatre writer who would combine the ability to think historically with a vivid imagination. No prejudices or hobby-horses, and so on. Lyubimov, however, had never fitted into this ideal. On the contrary:

> There are hobby-horses in all your productions; you often fight to the finish with an author's own intentions or prejudices, thus disappointing people who above all look for *literature* in the theatre. But in *Boris* you are not even 'fighting the material' in the usual sense. The nature of the political tragedy, the nature of Pushkin's reflections about Russia and our people on the eve of the great silence with which it met the Decembrists' 'ghastly riot crushed by three whiffs of grapeshot', and the 'boundless power of the government rooted in the *force des choses*' – all of these famous themes, which made Pushkin shudder, nourish *Boris Godunov*. On this occasion your hobby-horses happen to be Pushkin's, and just like him you have not strictly observed the tragic *hauteur*: here and there your 'ears stick out'![16]

The Pretender was convincingly revealed in this production as a prophetic figure and at the end Boris moved towards self-knowledge and religious composure.[17] In fact the whole production moved from the problems of social evil in their baldest form to those of a much more important and profound 'metaphysical' evil. I wrote to Lyubimov:

> You have created an historical production in the original sense of the word: in it the whole of our history has been thrown wide open. Sometimes, through stylistic inertia, you attempt to interpret what is obvious, to give the audience little props and

pointers, such as the light that comes on in the auditorium when particularly relevant lines are spoken. I think this is all superfluous. The inner movement of the production is quite clear enough. Its free spirit and untamed down-to-earth frankness echo the play so closely that no prodding is needed. The production contains no hidden meaning or secret hints: it is straightforward, honest and open, like Pushkin's text itself.

I was not the only person to write such letters at that time. Many Soviet critics, theatre historians and scholars came to the Taganka's defence. As always, Lyubimov changed one or two things, removed the so-called 'Andropov vest' from the False Dmitry (played by Valery Zolotukhin), tinkered with Godunov/Gubenko. None of it was to any avail. The production was killed off.

In the summer of 1983 Lyubimov left for England to stage *Crime and Punishment*. Whilst there he gave an interview to *The Times* headed 'The crosses Yuri Lyubimov bears'. This caused panic in Moscow. Never since Michael Chekhov had a Russian theatre director conducted a dialogue like this with the Russian authorities, let alone from abroad. The stand-off lasted several months. Probably Lyubimov was counting on Andropov. He did not know that the latter was already hopelessly shackled to his kidney machine.[18] Theatrical Moscow awaited the worst. Everyone understood that Lyubimov had staked not just his Taganka home but the fate of our theatre generally.

Lyubimov was waiting for Andropov, but Andropov's men were waiting for his death. It came, and within a few weeks a decree was issued relieving Lyubimov of his post as artistic director – 'for neglecting his duties without good reason'. There was nothing mysterious about this ludicrous formula, nor about the fact that in his absence Lyubimov was expelled from the Party. It was totally routine. The mystery lay elsewhere. The head of Moscow's Cultural Administration, Shadrin (the 'Man with a Gun', as Lyubimov called him, after the soldier Shadrin in Pogodin's play of that name about Lenin), suddenly turned up with a new artistic director to replace him: Anatoly Efros.

In Bulgakov's *Molière*, La Grange used to put a black cross in the company's book as a sign of mourning. Such a cross should probably have been put in the Russian stage's book on 20 March 1984.

The Frosts (1968–1985)

The man from outside (Efros in the seventies and eighties)

Anatoly Efros arrived at the Taganka theatre escorted by the 'Man with a Gun'. The changeover from one artistic director to another was widely seen as a human and theatrical disaster. One of the major directors in post-war Russia, Efros had dared to enter someone else's theatrical home without asking its master, his friend, for permission, and actually against his will. One has to know what the Taganka meant to the Moscow public in order to appreciate the situation. At the Taganka, as at the Sovremennik or Tovstonogov's BDT, everything was held together by shared memory. It would have been very difficult here for any newcomer, but the situation was aggravated by the fact that it was not the home that had changed its master, it was the detested state ('man with a gun') that had foisted a new owner on it with his own rules. The word *betrayal* was on everyone's lips.

Lyubimov called down curses on Efros's head from abroad, whilst the latter made no comment. He was met in the theatre with stony silence and promised the orphaned company only one thing: 'We shall work very hard.' He was assuming that he would put on a few productions and not only the Taganka rabble but the whole world would understand that he had come not to destroy someone else's home but to save it. He understood perfectly, as did we all, that Lyubimov would never return to Russia. No one had ever yet come back alive from the place that the creator of the Taganka had disappeared to. Efros was not a politician, he was an artist, and he believed that art would be able to overcome 'public opinion'.

One of the main reasons Efros went to the Taganka was that by the beginning of the eighties his own theatrical 'family', which he had spent fifteen years building up at the Malaya Bronnaya, was falling apart. His move to the Taganka was therefore prompted by a crisis in the very idea of the theatre-home and theatre-family. In Soviet conditions, this vital Russian idea had turned into a situation where the performers were feudally owned not only by the state, but by their own theatrical 'family'. No one had any freedom, that is to say the natural right to leave – to be 'divorced'. In such conditions the threat of losing one's theatre was for both actor and director tantamount to a death threat. The melancholy fate of so-called 'free' directors and actors (of whom there were only a handful in the whole country!) was plain to everyone.

The phenomenon of Anatoly Efros and the collapse of his theatrical family in the early 1980s therefore acquires a wider interest.

As the reader will recall, Efros started to create his own home under someone else's roof, having been expelled from the Lenkom in 1967. The banning of *Three Sisters*, his first production at the Malaya Bronnaya, did not break his will, it only fractured it. From then on his art hardly ever tackled modern reality directly. Sometimes he would put on Aleksey Arbuzov, and do it extremely well; but what interested him in Arbuzov's fairytales were the same eternal themes that excited him in Shakespeare or Dostoyevsky. If he touched anything 'Soviet' at all, it became strange, unexpected, as though pierced by another light. This is how he staged Korneychuk's *Platon Krechet* (1968) and *The Man from Outside* by Ignaty Dvoretsky (1971).

The latter instance is particularly interesting, because with it Efros sparked a whole trend in the Soviet theatre – that of the 'production drama' already referred to. It was about a man who has to deal with an idiotically topsy-turvy situation in a foundry. For Efros, however, the fact that it was set in a foundry and the hero, Cheshkov, was an engineer, was irrelevant. It could have happened in a theatre or a hospital, and the hero could have been a theatre director or a doctor. It was only the situation that mattered: the 'man from outside', that is, a normal human being, up against a well-orchestrated campaign by men who had their mythology and their methods for destroying anyone who was not in their pack.

Efros had studied the mechanics of this sort of thing not in Dvoretsky, but in Shakespeare. In *Romeo and Juliet* (1970) he endeavoured to conduct an audience through all the circles of an inveterate hatred between two clans. In *Othello* (1976) he made a meticulous study of the intrigue woven by Iago (Lev Durov). He attempted to understand the common roots of human hatred. He looked for the simple causes that set in motion awe-inspiring events. Iago, this balding little man filled with a malevolent energy, was not just getting his own back on Othello, he was putting to rights a world in which the Almighty had allowed an injustice. Efros was discovering hatred's depressingly simple formula. Someone had not been given the job they were counting on and this was enough for them to destroy the best people. Efros was interested in the mechanism by which harmony is destroyed.

The Frosts (1968–1985)

Desdemona was played by Olga Yakovleva, as was to be expected. However, Efros offered the part of Othello to Nikolay Volkov, who was probably less suited to it than any other actor in Moscow. Philosophic, slow in his reactions, with a deeply hidden emotional life, which occasionally broke the surface but even then only modestly, a very Russian actor in all his ways, Volkov portrayed not so much the Moor's soul as that of his director. For many years he was Efros's *alter ego*, just as Olga Yakovleva was Efros's female *alter ego*. Volkov was not a soldier but an intellectual. He shocked the audience by putting on a pair of delicate, silver-rimmed glasses and burying himself in a book. He reminded you of a Chekhov character, of the Vershinin whom he had played in *Three Sisters*. To destroy such a 'man from outside' was easy, and Iago spun his intrigue brilliantly.

The first ten years that Efros spent at the Malaya Bronnaya were happy ones. The plays he put on were gory, but there was a sense of complete artistic achievement to them. They were full of the joy of creative self-fulfilment, a joy which is so rare in Russia. The small team of actors that he had nurtured understood him instinctively. They turned the failings of the feudal theatrical system into virtues. They were in exile, but they put down roots and seemed not to notice their surroundings. The official senior director of the Malaya Bronnaya, Aleksandr Dunayev, treated Efros totally loyally and did not interfere with Efros's theatre within a theatre. For many years Moscow regarded Efros's productions as the creations of a particular theatre with its own artistic logic which was present in everything it offered to the public.

The classics became this theatre's ecological niche. They gave Efros the opportunity to touch on the eternal themes that had been eliminated from the Soviet repertoire. He brought back to our stage the human being striving to understand what belief, lack of belief, truth, death and retribution are. These themes made totally new demands on the actor's art, on the psychological realism that Russia had been so proud of ever since Stanislavsky, but which actors had forgotten how to apply because they were starved of material. Efros began to rediscover the complexity and unpredictability of the human being. He revelled in stage dialectics and taught his actors to express themselves complexly, to seize both of life's poles – its exterior and what lives deep down but sometimes breaks everything up and makes the actor speak not with the text of a part, but with his/her blood-soaked soul.

Stanislavsky was once watching a capable young actress at work and remarked with bitterness that the disadvantage of his method was that it led to actors being afraid of genuine stage truth: they would only go as far as its boundary. In order to experience this boundary you have to cross it, that is, move into the sphere of 'un-truth', then step freely back and forth. This in fact is the actor's supreme art.

Efros 'made' his performers as Professor Higgins 'made' Eliza. They learned to roam along the boundary of truth with unusual daring. A prime example was *Brother Alyosha*, Viktor Rozov's adaptation of *The Karamazov Brothers*, in which Olga Yakovleva played Liza Khokhlakova. This spoilt, invalid little girl in a wheelchair weaved mad patterns with it on the stage, and her soul was equally tangled. Yakovleva achieved the most complex things Dostoyevsky could offer: fits of goodness coupled with a deep, often unmotivated wickedness; a capacity for self-sacrifice and sadism; a child's ignorance of sin and yet a secret, morbid desire to be depraved, to experience everything to the last drop. This was not 'psychological realism' but 'fantastical realism', to use Dostoyevsky's own term for it.

Inevitably, when he turned to the classics, Efros found himself hemmed in by other people's interpretations and the obligatory clichés that often kill a modern creator's imagination. He himself had to learn to roam truth's 'boundary'. In his debate with a particular canon – whether Chekhovian or Shakespearian – he made mistakes, but this was part of the vital process of finding himself within the flow of history. He attempted to discover in a classic the site of the pain in which all the centuries met.

In Molière's *Dom Juan* (1973) the director swept aside the idea of a lady-killer. He sensed in Dom Juan an inner emptiness and a morbid desire if not for faith then for some stability in a world without God. Efros's Dom Juan (played, of course, by Nikolay Volkov) resembled a seductive lover even less than the Chekhovian intellectual resembled Othello. He was more like a peripatetic scientist conducting a ghoulish experiment on himself. If heaven is empty, is everything permitted? The Muscovite Dom Juan was preoccupied with this Dostoyevskian question of old. It was a parable about a man who was not only experiencing

Plate 10   Anatoly Efros (left) and Lev Durov (Sganarelle) after a performance of Efros's production of *Dom Juan*, Malaya Bronnaya Theatre, 1973.

moral disintegration but measuring it as he went. Even as he was dying he kept feeling his own pulse to make sure that retribution existed.

David Borovsky, who worked both with Lyubimov and Efros in the seventies, gave him the space of a parable: a kind of coach house made of old timber, with one window high up in the form of a cartwheel containing some bits of stained glass. Further down stage there was something like a gravestone, with a worn inscription. Above sat some doves ruffling their feathers, and there were theatre lamps on stands dressed in skirts and caps: the only reference to the outward plot of Molière's play.

In the echoing coach house of the world, Dom Juan and Sganarelle (Lev Durov) began to sort out their complicated relationship. The stage was too cluttered for them to continue circling each other endlessly. Sometimes one of them went into the auditorium and the other, attempting to find yet another convincing argument, looked for his opponent in the darkness among the audience, thus drawing the Moscow public into a philosophical discussion. There was nothing boring about this

Plate 11   Nikolay Volkov (left) as Dom Juan and Lev Durov as Sganarelle in
Anatoly Efros's 1973 production of *Dom Juan*, Malaya Bronnaya Theatre, 1973.

discussion. It was a passionate debate about final things, conducted not
so much by two people as by the two halves of one split consciousness.
Durov bound his Sganarelle to his master with very tough cords. He tried
to use popular, peasant methods to save the atheist's soul. The atheist
mocked his servant but could not live without him. He needed him as a
constant opponent. For this Dom Juan yearned to be proven wrong.

Sganarelle represented the interests of heaven. Breathlessly, with enormous gusto, he demonstrated to his master how well God's world and the human body had been conceived. He called the sky and a tree as his witnesses, he shoved his hand under the atheist's nose and showed off his veins, his blood vessels and his ribs, which were all so cleverly joined together. As a final argument, he tore off his shirt, literally flew up on to the vertical wall of the barn, and . . . dropped lifeless from the top. Some touching chords were heard, which were joined by a choir of angelic children's voices lamenting our faith and loss of faith.

Sganarelle believed in emetics and rhubarb. Dom Juan believed only in 2 + 2 = 4. The women along his path were merely another line of argument. He did not seduce them. He was experimenting with heaven's patience. Each time it was as though he were saying to the Almighty: 'If you exist, show yourself, punish me after this deception I've perpetrated!' But heaven was silent and its defender in the form of a benighted peasant could not, of course, win the debate.

This unselfish villain Dom Juan was, like Chekhov's Ivanov and Vampilov's Zilov, looking for faith and not finding it. His despair fed more on the atmosphere in Moscow than on Molière's text. His punishment was more like an execution. The Commander, in the shape of an unprepossessing little man, simply came on, went over to the 'scientist', and touched him – not with a vicelike grip, but with the palm of his hand. (A surgeon had once told Efros that he had patients who were so sure they were going to die from their operation that it was enough just to touch their bodies with the marker.)

Dom Juan lay dead on the forestage and those he had abused and deceived sat around him like mourning relatives. Sganarelle rushed about grief-stricken, kept poking the corpse, and wailed about his lost wages. 'Lost wages' had a special emphasis put on it. Efros was a past master at loading the most trivial phrase with new meaning. It was not his wages Sganarelle had lost, but a part of his soul. Now he had no one to argue with and prove the meaningfulness of the world to. There was no one to try the patience of heaven any more. The world had grown empty without this sinner – such was the paradoxical ending to this parable acted in 1973 on the stage of the former Jewish theatre.

Efros had been raised in a caste system which he 'made strange' with the help of the classics. He learned to understand human beings and feel compassion for them. He once called this 'overcoatizing', after Gogol's story. To 'overcoatize' meant to humanize, to find a method that would unlock the human meaning of a masterpiece (it is a sad fact that elevating a thing to 'masterpiece' almost automatically kills its living meaning).

In 1975 he turned to *The Marriage*, Gogol's early farce which, despite its reputation as a masterpiece, had never had any serious success on the Russian stage. It seemed to be a mere anecdote about a bored bachelor whom people attempt to marry off, but who just before the ceremony jumps out of a window. As such, it did not comply with the image of the 'great Gogol' who laughed through tears. The laughter seemed primitive and no one sensed any tears.

Efros did. He read the play lyrically, discovering to his amazement moments when he identified not only with the fugitive Podkolyosin but with the very least of the weird suitors. It was a lesson in theatrical insight into the author's vision. This vision was revealed by the simple but extremely effective device of realizing on the stage what was desired, imagined or existed only in the consciousness or subconsciousness of the characters. Thus Podkolyosin (Volkov) and Agafya (Yakovleva) began by stepping forward as though just married, to the swelling voices of a church choir and surrounded by well-wishers; then suddenly this all disappeared like a mirage, dark shutters flipped down all round the edge of the stage, and each showed the strange figure of a man running. Left alone with himself, the hero uttered the first line of the play: 'Yes, I suppose I really should get married.'

The audience burst into applause. The masterpiece was coming back to life. The director was removing the upper layer of the characters' consciousness and probing deep into their souls. Podkolyosin was playing a mixed-up game with himself. He was obsessed with what people said or thought about him, but he also lived tightly surrounded by his dreams, which were richer than the real world. These dreams surrounded Agafya with a clutch of beautifully dressed children and wove themselves into an image of future domestic bliss. Gogol's thinly populated play turned out to be densely populated.

Ivan Kuzmich Podkolyosin immediately appeared amongst the suitors in Agafya's imagination, then became her *idée fixe*. The designer, Valery Levental, had separated them spatially: 'She' was in a chintzy little theatre of her own, 'He' in his cosy bachelor space from which attempts were made to drag him by force. As Dostoyevsky would have said, the heroes' fantasies leapt over time and space, over the laws of existence and reason, lingering only in the places their hearts had dreamt up.

Agafya went up to the suitors and stared right into their faces, in an attempt to identify 'Him', the Only One. She was deciding her fate, and she was so frightened it gave her a headache. So she drank a powder, tore the paper in which it had been into several pieces, wrote the favoured names on them, and put them in her reticule. Fate could decide. But this was no use: all the pieces came out together. There was no 'He'. 'He' was an impossibility: the absurd plot suddenly revealed its inner tragedy.

These characters lived in the quotidian dimension of *The Marriage*. Opposite them stood Kochkaryov, who was from the fantastical dimension. He was played by Mikhail Kozakov as a friend-cum-tempter, who put a veritably demoniacal energy into seeing his friend married. In the original, Gogol does not make it clear what motivates Kochkaryov. Efros solved this mystery by endowing the character with a maniacal idea. Kochkaryov was himself a mass of complexes, and wanted to bring happiness to mankind. He thought he knew the secret of how to do this. He invaded another person's world, shattered it, and demanded that the person get married immediately. But Podkolyosin could not understand what the hurry was. For him marriage was a quandary and a mystery, and the idea of getting married in half an hour was vulgar and insulting. This tussle between them, in which the strange, whimsical nature of man was uncovered, ran through the whole play.

Finally Podkolyosin stood on the threshold of his happiness, pronounced the words expected of him as a fiancé, and realized that he 'could not escape'. But even at this moment some insidious voice, wholly in the spirit of Dostoyevsky's 'Man from the Underground', whispered to him that he could. And the more his reason told him he must go ahead with it, the more his 'voice from underground' whispered the opposite. 'What about the window?' – 'No, I can't.' – 'But why not?' – 'How can I without a hat?' – 'But what if you tried, eh?'

Quintessential man! He will jump out of a paradise that has been forced upon him, and run away, simply so as to live according to his own, maybe stupid, maybe ridiculous, free will.

Plate 12   From left to right: Viktor Shternberg as Gayev, Alla Demidova as Ranevskaya, Gotlib Roninson as Firs and Vladimir Vysotsky as Lopakhin in Anatoly Efros's production of *The Cherry Orchard* at the Taganka Theatre, 1975.

The Marriage was the high point of Efros's art – of his 'esoteric' theatre in which audience and stage were united in their being unfree and 'in the know'. Efros cultivated vagueness, Lyubimov clarity. Efros got his actors to enact the 'zigzag filament', that is, the living contradictions of the human soul, as their supreme achievement. If Lyubimov discovered such contradictions, he immediately tried to iron them out. Lyubimov would turn even philosophical tragedy into topical journalism. Efros made even topical journalism sound like philosophical tragedy. The two theatres argued, but audiences went to see their theatrical metaphors as though going to political rallies.

These two opposites met only once, and then they nearly blew each other away. Soon after *The Marriage* opened, Lyubimov invited his friend/adversary to put on *The Cherry Orchard* at the Taganka. It was a kind of joust. Finding himself on enemy territory, Efros decided to use the weapons for which the Taganka was famous. He interpreted Chekhov in Lyubimov's style, that is, openly, aggressively and very audibly. Whereas Efros had 'complicated' *The Marriage*, he tried to simplify *The Cherry Orchard*, to clarify it and liberate it from all its symbolic meaningfulness. They bundled Chekhov along, the actors played with their usual chutzpah, very bluntly conveying the theme of the production: that these people, who are deaf to fate's footsteps and do not want to face reality, are doomed.

Efros invited Levental from the Bolshoi Theatre to design the production. In order to survive on the Taganka's territory and to remain himself, he needed a strong ally. In defiance of Lyubimov's and Borovsky's style of 'anti-decor', the Taganka's stage became temporarily 'like the Bolshoi'. It was draped in white, the characters wore white, white curtains fluttered in the wind, and in the middle of the stage was a grave covered in white flowers, on to which was piled everything left of the house at the end of the play. The furniture was toy furniture and the characters' psychology childish. The image of children walking through a minefield unaware of their imminent destruction permeated the whole production.

Not having Lyubimov's frank temperament or the experience of communicating with the audience that the Taganka actors had, Efros was on a losing wicket. His 'zigzag filament' became ominously straight. The transparency of the overall metaphor looked more like poverty of invention. The production was heading for disaster. It was saved only by Alla Demidova as Ranevskaya and Vysotsky as Lopakhin.

Ranevskaya had an amazing smile that humanized the whole production. Even when she asked at the climax of the play in Act 3, 'Who bought it?', she smiled as though asking about something trivial. But it was the calm before death of people who have suffered long. Her sheepish smile before being slaughtered was, probably, the most moving 'Efrosian' moment in the play. After that it was pure Taganka again: hysterics, screaming and shouting, all of it outside the classical framework of the play.

Lopakhin/Vysotsky was driven by a secret love for Ranevskaya, which the latter seemed not to notice and which was full of a rare masculine nobility. It was the first time that their relationship had been portrayed with such complexity on the Russian stage. Up to the third act, Lopakhin behaved like a doctor trying to tell his unreasonable patients that there was a plague outside and they had to get a grip on themselves and take action. It was as though they had gone deaf. Ranevskaya had laid on a Feast in Time of Plague, the Jewish band were playing, and to crown it all Lopakhin turned up. In a wild outpouring of grief at his successful purchase, Lopakhin performed his *pièce de résistance*, the 'dance of the new master'. 'We missed the train and had to wait till half past nine', he said, and tapped the side of his neck with the back of his hand to indicate how much they had knocked back in the meantime. This plebeian Soviet gesture was the signal that freed the actor from all his previous constraints. Lopakhin now freaked out and a bacchanalia of loutish freedom ensued – a metaphor for Russia's future. The theme of the destruction of the 'cherry orchard' was resolved *à la* Taganka.

Lyubimov did not accept Efros's Chekhov. Whether he saw the production as a parody of his own style, or was simply jealous of an outsider working with his actors, I do not know.[19] What nobody could have forseen in their wildest dreams was that Efros himself would one day play Lopakhin *vis-à-vis* the Taganka.

The air of those times was infected with putrefaction and everyone breathed it in. You could not hide from it in aesthetics as Efros fancied, or in the somewhat journalistic theatre that Lyubimov was creating. After *The Marriage* and *The Cherry Orchard*, the theme of the excruciating discrepancy between beauty and reality entered Efros's productions. In *A Month in the Country* (1977) he created an apology for Turgenev's heroine and Turgenevan culture generally. He began to wallow in the 'epic tranquillity of the landowning life', as Stanislavsky called it, to the point of losing his sense of humour and historical perspective. His artistry, which until recently had been brilliant and provocative, became somehow limp. He started to be careless in his work with actors. Even in *The Cherry Orchard* he had left many characters alone with themselves. In his own theatre he stopped noticing what was happening to his performers, who were not living in stately houses. His theatrical home began to crumble. His productions started to resemble violin concertos, in which he ceased to bother about the orchestra. All that interested him was the 'violin' – Olga Yakovleva.

He equated Turgenev's heroine's secret with the secret of life. 'You're all so dreadfully perceptive', Natalya Petrovna/Olga Yakovleva drawled in an inimitably tender and yet penetrating voice to those who were trying to 'solve' the secret of her *ennui*. There was no solution; only the whirling of the heart as life went through its endless cycle from flowering to withering. 'The avant-garde can very easily become the rearguard. It only takes a change of marching order.' This saying of Dr Shpigelsky's was offered by Efros as a revelation.

He staged Turgenev's play as a study in dying love, in the passing of youth, in how we yearn for what is leaving us, what has not been lived or felt to the full. He did not succeed in keeping himself out of the picture. At the end of *A Month in the Country* he added a coda that revealed his own predicament and sensibility with devastating directness. Natalya Petrovna was left alone on stage holding the kite that the young student/tutor had made for her son. Instead of the usual elegiac Turgenevan calm, the emphasis was placed on the heroine's utter despair. Something ugly was invading her life, something unsettling, terrifying. Before our eyes the stage hands began to take down the set and with much clattering and clanging they dismantled the elaborate wrought-iron arbour. Then they took the kite away from Natalya Petrovna as though it were a prop she no longer needed. She flattened herself against the proscenium. The magic circle of the estate was broken; the hammers dismantling the arbour sounded like the axes being laid into the cherry orchard. The demise of this cosy world was expressed by destroying the theatrical illusion. With one fell blow the director was returned to the reality he loathed so much.

An age was coming to an end whose cardiogram had been recorded by Efros's art. The peaks and troughs were settling into a deadly straight line. Suddenly one became aware of a shortage of oxygen in Efros's productions. In Lyubimov's wake, and polemicizing with him, Efros staged a production called *The Road*, in which he endeavoured to present 'the whole of Gogol'. He, too, attempted to penetrate to the source of Gogol's inspiration, in order to understand how anyone could create in this country at all. He wanted to produce a highly complex symphony, but it was divided into small pieces that did not cohere. The image of a great Road, experienced by Gogol mystically, could not be reconciled with our real, extraordinarily tacky Russian soil. Like a wheel on Chichikov's carriage, the production spun round on one spot. The actors' Brownian movement became a mess and the attempt at 'overcoatizing' failed. The author of *Dead Souls* was brought into the production, unmasked his characters, and despised them: there was none of the love here that had filled *The Marriage* to overflowing; the love that a creator has for the very least of his creatures. The production ended with the Author being absolutely cut off from his characters, from the life he had wanted to make flesh. Chichikov was left in one corner planning a new scam, and the Author, curled up in solitary despair, on the brink of madness, kept praying to heaven and repeating the word *work* as the only way out of life's chaos.

The Road bore the marks of some very negative experience of life that Efros had been through. The failure of the Author in this production turned out to be bigger than that of any single role. It suggested a general malaise; that the artist was not spiritually at peace with himself. After *The Road*, the ground began to slip from under Efros's feet.

The production opened as the war was beginning in Afghanistan. This, of course, was pure coincidence, but the sense of collapse was not. It was no longer possible to serve beauty and ignore what was going on around you. It was impossible to remain a 'man from outside'. A classic theme now entered Efros's life, one known as 'the tragedy of Art for Art's sake'. Given the nature of the director's profession, he could not experience the crisis alone. His crazy team started a rebellion that he could not contain with his previous methods, that is, another successful production. By their very nature actors do not forgive failure. In these circumstances they should have disbanded immediately and left each other free. This did not happen. The serf-owning theatrical system, which for many years had enabled Efros and his team to stay together, now showed its deadly power. The 'home' turned into a communal flat from which there was no escape. The director began to rush hither and thither. He staged two productions at MKhAT – Molière's *Tartuffe* and Tolstoy's *Living Corpse* – which for a while brought him the joy of working with new actors. He was allowed to see the world, he put on Chekhov and Bulgakov in Japan and America, and he returned to Russia enigmatic, tired, but happy. His actors, sitting in Moscow like animals in a cage, took an even dimmer view of his success abroad. He then tried to beat life at its own game by recapturing the past. In 1982 he restaged *Three Sisters* at the Malaya Bronnaya and met with an indifference that he was not used to.

Shortly after the production opened, I bumped into him on the street by the theatre. He was taking a stroll before the interval. We talked about Chekhov and lady experts on Chekhov. He lost his cool:

'I don't believe *any* theatre people any longer, the circle has fallen apart, they all lie through their teeth.' He kept saying that we should put our faith only in fresh young audiences. We turned to walk to the theatre, arriving just in time for the interval. The fresh young audience was leaving his *Three Sisters* in droves.

On 20 March 1984 Efros arrived, or was brought, to the Taganka. Lyubimov's company, among whom were some of Efros's favourite actors, said nothing. He had convinced himself that he had come to carry on Lyubimov's work. Deprived of his own family, he had come to save someone else's. The job was booby-trapped and he blew himself up. We still do not know who devised this fiendish plot, but the purpose was to destroy two of Russia's major artists in one go.

Efros began to work like mad, harder than he had for years. He opened one new production after another.[20] Each of them was immediately supported by the official press, which made the situation look even more dubious. The productions varied, but none of them had the joy, the light of art, that had won over Moscow for two decades. Efros was working in a dead space, in a situation of social ostracism. He thought he was saving the Taganka, but it was himself he should have been saving. Some of the Taganka's actors, plus Borovsky the designer, left. Others stayed and were waiting for Lyubimov. A third group worked with Efros very well. In spring 1985, when Gorbachev came to power, the concepts of 'never' and 'forever' took a knock. The mystical curve of Russian history was going off in an unforeseen direction. The Taganka company began to stir. Efros gritted his teeth and kept on working. His latest production was a highly autobiographical one of Molière's *Misanthrope*, which opened in the autumn of 1986.

So as to leave no doubt about the nature of the production, Efros positioned a large mirror upstage in which the hydra-headed Taganka audience was reflected. Stage left there were costumes (an echo of his production of *Molière*) and on the bare boards old-fashioned stall seats alternated with modern chairs of the kind used in rehearsals. Once again, the action was set in the theatre. We heard piano music, then a mournful saxophone weaving in and out of it. Alceste, played by Zolotukhin, was trying to live without faff: he was trying to reduce the necessary delay between desire and act. He was upsetting the balance on which civilization depends. Alceste's complex conveyed Efros's complex. It was obvious that he was fed up to the back teeth with everything. The line 'We don't have critics, just assassins' came across particularly clearly. If only one could live without these conventions, without all these people round one, without this hydra-headed Moscow public reflected in the mirror. Alceste put a noose round his neck and tried it for size. The world was as threadbare as people's lies. What he had felt for Célimène/Olga Yakovleva (the only actress who had followed Efros to the Taganka) was exhausted; as wrinkled as an old apple.

Gorbachev came to one of the opening performances and stayed behind to talk to Efros. The new GenSec said a few flattering things about the former Taganka. Something miraculous was happening . . . Lyubimov could come back! The 'man from outside' had to leave. But he had nowhere to go. I saw a copy of the letter that all the Taganka actors signed, as well as Efros. He wrote something like: 'I support Lyubimov's return to the theatre if that is what Yury Petrovich himself wants.'

Less than six months later, in January 1987, Efros died. He therefore did not live to see the creator of the Taganka return to Moscow and begin his 'life after life'. He did not witness the final theatrical scandal of the empire and the break-up of the Taganka. The noise of the actors' squabbling was swallowed up in that of the country collapsing around them. Anatoly Vasilyevich Efros took no part in any of this. The secret of theatre directing lies in relating one thing to another. He possessed this secret. This is probably why great directors not only come along at the right time, they leave at the right time, too.

Georgy Tovstonogov: encapsulating 'stagnation'

In May 1987, following a long drawn-out row inside MKhAT, the Government officially divided that theatre in two. A few years later internal politics also destroyed the Taganka. It is pointless to look for scapegoats for these events. The break-up of the Soviet theatrical 'churches' was a portent of the great collapse itself. As is often the case, the theatrical brawling was merely symptomatic of a wider crisis.

Tovstonogov's stamina, therefore, is all the more amazing. Only he persevered, only his home survived. He not only stood his ground, he succeeded in expressing the final phase of 'stagnation' in sharp-edged theatrical forms.

The Frosts (1968–1985)

To those who did not live in this 'stagnation', it may look as though society simply stood still for almost two decades; as though it did nothing and expected nothing and a thick layer of duckweed covered the bog. As a character in one of Yevgeny Shvarts's fairytales puts it, that is true but incorrect. The bog only looks motionless. As I have said before, decomposition is one of the most active biological processes. Beneath the duckweed an extremely rich anti-life goes on.

In the most respectable of Soviet theatres, Tovstonogov attempted to capture the nature of this 'anti-life'. He endeavoured to understand and express the process by which a person adapts to social decay and yet resists it. He did not have to look far for examples. The process of survival, that is, adaptation and resistance, was implicit in Tovstonogov's own theatre. He was conducting an experiment on himself.

The last two decades of Tovstonogov's art clearly show how he managed to survive. He employed a strategy of 'fire-and-recoil'. Every serious 'shot' at the system was accompanied by a 'recoil' designed to offset the impression. After *The Government Inspector* (1972) he put on *Khanuma*, a charming Georgian vaudeville which it is impossible to imagine Lyubimov or Efros directing. After Tolstoy's *Story of a Horse* (1975), which was regarded with extreme suspicion by officialdom, he directed an adaptation of Sholokhov's *Quietly Flows the Don* for the sixtieth anniversary of the Revolution. Tovstonogov did not let a single major revolutionary date go unmarked, now concocting a montage of scenes about Lenin (1980), now offering a 'new reading' of *An Optimistic Tragedy* (1981). It was a very deliberate, very difficult balancing act which not only enabled him to survive but, paradoxically enough, to sustain a reputation as a pure artist. A conformist himself, he staged at the Sovremennik a production based on Saltykov–Shchedrin entitled *Balalaykin and Co.*, which was possibly the strongest attack on intellectual cowardice in Soviet theatrical history. And although utterly moulded by fear himself, he managed to stage Gogol's *Government Inspector* as a mystery play about fear deforming people's minds. Tovstonogov's famous 'objectivity' was partly directed at himself.

There were three productions that most completely expressed Tovstonogov's art and the social situation in the empire as it headed for collapse: *The Government Inspector, Balayakin and Co.,* and *The Story of a Horse.* Let us look at them in some detail.

The Government Inspector opened at the BDT in Leningrad in the spring of 1972, at the same time as Valentin Pluchek's production at the Satire Theatre in Moscow. The fact that classical plays were often put on simultaneously by different directors bemused many critics. In practice, it was yet another way of describing reality. By touching base with the classics, theatres were offering not so much different versions of the past as of the present. So it was with *The Government Inspector*.

In articles that they wrote for the opening of the productions,[21] Pluchek declared that he was staging not just the play but 'the whole author', whilst Tovstonogov spoke of the method of 'fantastical realism' which would finally unlock Gogol's mysterious satire. In Pluchek's case, things went no further than declaration: in spite of a brilliant Khlestakov (Andrey Mironov), his production was a copybook 'comedy of situations and fairground of comic types'.[22] Tovstonogov, however, produced something breathtakingly new. 'We must forget that we are acting a comedy', he wrote, 'and that it must be funny: we must declare war on the vaudeville.'[23] He was as good as his word: he tore off the layers of accreted cliché and presented the play as Gogol's mystical insight into Russia's future. The fundamental idea was that *fear* was the motive force behind this great national play.

The setting was archetypally provincial. An enormous puddle was projected onto the curtain, in which was reflected a painfully familiar Russian townscape (Tovstonogov himself was the designer, or rather architect, of the space, and the costumes were produced from Dobuzhinsky's original sketches). The world reflected upside-down in water is one of Gogol's favourite images. Suddenly, into this puddle dropped a pebble: the picture wrinkled, was distorted, and the action began. Behind the curtain puddle a fantastical space was revealed, which went down in one place and rose vertically in another. These different areas provided an underworld into which Osip and Khlestakov descended at the end, and a parodic purgatory in which the Mayor's unhinged reason was confronted by the new Inspector wearing a black Inverness and dark glasses.

Tovstonogov had obviously been reading Merezhkovsky's *Gogol and the Devil*.[24] This was the source of the surreal dimension and the idea of Khlestakov returning at the end as the new Inspector.

Tovstonogov himself was not inclined to mysticism, so he interpreted these themes rationally. He made it clear all the time that the black droshky hovering below the flies with the dummy inspector in, the replacement of Khlestakov by a dummy, and Khlestakov's final return, were all figments of a sick imagination warped by the universal fear.

To regard fear as the all-pervading note of *The Government Inspector* was not new. The author himself had pointed to it as the mainspring of the plot. But in Tovstonogov's case the theme filled the whole play. Fear became a metaphor and a synonym for life. And the Soviet authorities' reaction was swift. Yury Zubkov inquired on the pages of *Pravda* why a gendarme not in Gogol's text had been brought into the play, and why a 'mysterious man in a black cape and dark glasses' was always on stage and 'at the end whispers to the gendarme what to say'. In classic *Pravda* style, as though defending Gogol against mindless modern interpretations, the critic asked a string of rhetorical questions that made him sound like an interrogator: Why are the masters of the town obsessed by fear? Why was a complete non-entity like Khlestakov almost free of it? Why was Osip, Khlestakov's servant, not afraid and got more and more bumptious as the play progressed? 'After all, in Gogol's comedy Osip is a representative of the least privileged class in Russia . . .'[25] When *Pravda* used three dots like this it was pronouncing sentence.

Everyone in *The Government Inspector* was terrified, but in different ways. What made the Mayor (played by Kirill Lavrov) break out in a cold sweat was no phantom but the thought of the very real misdoings of his past (Tovstonogov turned the fact that Lavrov specialized in playing Soviet leaders to splendid effect). The postmaster, the judge, the merchants and the policemen were all afraid, but Luka Lukich Khlopov, the inspector of schools, was more terrified than all of them. After all, his speciality, science and culture, was a dangerous one: 'God help anyone working in education! You're afraid of everything – everyone pokes his nose in, everyone wants to show he's as clever as the rest.' In the opening scene, Khlopov (Nikolay Trofimov) fainted and this happened many times afterwards. The others were used to it, and someone was always standing behind Khlopov to catch him. In the dumb-show at the end of the play, to all appearances Khlopov simply gave up the ghost.

What happened when Khlestakov was shown Zemlyanika's hospital, where the patients 'recover like flies', we do not know. What happened on the way from the hospital to the Mayor's house also remains 'off camera' in Gogol's text. But Tovstonogov decided to fill this gap in. Far downstage, a carriage appeared. In it, the well wined and dined Khlestakov reclined in the arms of the town's officials, asleep. They were holding his body like a precious vessel. The schools' inspector pressed Khlestakov's foot to his chest and the higher ranks were supporting more important limbs. Sometimes the carriage passed members of the town's population who, seeing their bosses face to face, removed their hats. For their part, the bosses stiffened and very gingerly, condescendingly, waved. To complicate the mood even more, Tovstonogov accompanied this jaunt with a piece of highly lyrical Russian music.

The director was not interested in satire. He had taken to heart Gogol's advice that in *The Government Inspector* 'the human note is audible throughout'. Consequently, immediately after the 'government carriage' had disappeared one of the twin landowners, Bobchinsky, appeared in the middle of the dark empty stage in a spotlight, running along trying to catch up the carriage. Those in the carriage called to him: 'There's no room for you, Pyotr Ivanovich, no room!' Goodness, what a loss of face this was, what a slight, not to have taken him with them; and now the fat little man was having to patter along after the bosses, dripping sweat, out of breath, and heart-broken at the injustice of life. There was more of the real Gogol in this metaphor for human vanity and conceit than in all the production's dummy inspectors and strobes put together. Here Tovstonogov's imagination was not only socially true, it conveyed the complexity of the author's tone. The portrayal of human *poshlost* (vulgarity) broke off on a note of intense, searching bitterness.

It turned out to be extremely difficult to restore to *The Government Inspector* the sense of a 'collective town', to reinterpret its artistic space, to bury the clichés of its acting tradition and return the comedy to the fold of fantastical realism. The fantastical became over-illustrated and the quotidian dimension was destroyed by the incongruity between the rules that Lavrov acted by as the Mayor and the theatrical game that Khlestakov (Oleg Basilashvili) and his servant Osip (Sergey Yursky) played. Their ebullient duet was dominated by Osip, who had his master under his thumb. In fact Osip was the 'devil' of the whole piece: not by chance, the pair of them entered from under the stage at the beginning and went back down into this theatrical hell at the end.

Basilashvili lost weight specially for the part of Khlestakov and he brought to the fore the hilarious childishness of Gogol's fibber. He was staying on the first floor of the hotel and therefore engaged in the favourite sport of all young louts: spitting down on passers-by. He derived a genuine pleasure from this. Actually, it was a quote from Michael Chekhov's interpretation of the part,[26] and there were other moments that owed Michael Chekhov a lot, especially in the compulsive lying scene (Act 3 Scene 6) that is the climax of the role. Altogether, Khlestakov was not in control of his actions; he had delegated his life to a flunkey.

Sergey Yursky played Osip to one side of the rest of the production and against the stage tradition of the part. In his own explanation of the characters, Gogol had even felt it was not necessary to expatiate on Osip: 'The Russian servant of advancing years is . . . familiar to everyone. So the part has always been played well.' And now it was precisely the bumptious, lazy and always hungry flunkey who had elicited a tirade from a central Party organ determined to stand up for the only representative of the toiling masses in the play!

Yursky and Tovstonogov demonstrated a new way of reading a classic. Gogol's Osip wore a cracked, gold-framed pince-nez and white gloves. He immediately reminded you strongly of Korovyov, a demonic figure in Bulgakov's *The Master and Margarita* who accompanies the Devil on his visit to Soviet Moscow. Grafting Bulgakov's novel, which was genetically extremely close to Gogol, on to the play was unexpected and singularly productive. It made the text of the old comedy sparkle with new life.

Tovstonogov adored giving his productions epigraphs. On this occasion there was one in the original. The voice of Innokenty Smoktunovsky began each performance by saying: 'There's no point in blaming the mirror if it's your own phizog that's crooked.' Then the voice of Smoktunovsky/Myshkin ended the performance with the same words, only this time there was not a trace of slyness in them. His laughter broke off in sobbing that was almost convulsive.

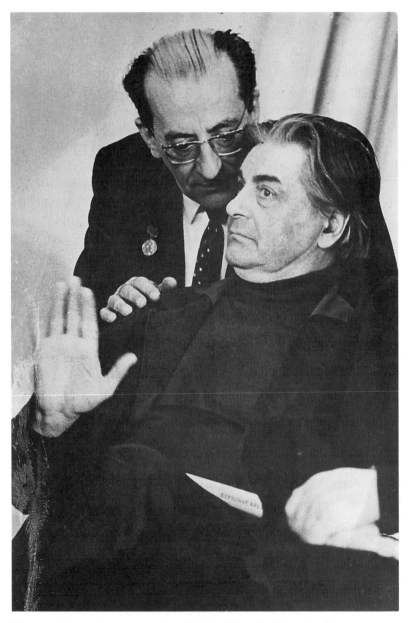

Plate 13　Georgy Tovstonogov (standing) and Yury Lyubimov in the 1970s.

The director continued his theatrical study of fear as the motive force of Soviet life by following *The Government Inspector* with an adaptation of Saltykov–Shchedrin's novel *A Modern Idyll*. This time Tovstonogov had found the ideal instrument. The tendentiousness of Shchedrin's satire, which was directed at the Russian liberals of the 1870s, matched the tendentiousness of the director's task. Post-reform Tsarist Russia and post-Thaw Soviet Russia overlapped. In both cases you were dealing with the average Russian liberal intellectual trapped in another of history's doldrums and having to 'wait'.

The play called *Balalaykin and Co.* was compiled with the help of Sergey Mikhalkov, the famous children's writer, author of the Soviet national anthem, and favourite of Stalin's. He could well have been a character in the play. Among his many talents was that of cynicism on a virtuoso scale. This is probably another reason why he agreed to 'shield' Tovstonogov's daring experiment. He was a classic writer of Soviet fables and therefore knew exactly how to prepare the official reaction to the production. In an interview with *Literaturnaya gazeta* he referred to the leader of the Revolution: 'More than once Lenin used Balalaykin as an image for the blather, lying, fraud and self-interest of bourgeois liberalism.'[27] And at a discussion in the Sovremennik he came out with a classic formulation that was promptly repeated all over Moscow: 'It is a long time since tsarism received such a slap in the face!'

It certainly was a slap in the face. Neither before nor after did Tovstonogov have the nerve to comment so frankly on the nature of the regime. There was no pure satire in it. In a sense the production was a confession. It was about how an intellectual colluded with the regime and the consequences of his collusion.

The designer Iosif Sumbatashvili had enclosed the stage of the Sovremennik in grey canvas. Behind it could be discerned silhouettes of Russian autocrats and generals. On it in bright colours and various sizes were medals of the Russian Empire. Above the stage, picked out in gold letters, was an epigraph intended to protect the production: 'One cannot understand Russia in the second half of the nineteenth century without Shchedrin. MAXIM GORKY.'

Dostoyevsky once said of Shchedrin: 'The object of his satire is the secret policeman who is lurking somewhere to eavesdrop on him and denounce him: this gives Mr Shchedrin no rest.' The author of *A Modern Idyll* accepted the jibe, but with one qualification: 'The policeman I am afraid of is the one who has ensconced himself inside every Russian. This is what I'm afraid of.' Tovstonogov's production was about the latter. He investigated the mind of an intellectual in which this policeman has taken up residence. With anatomical accuracy he laid bare the mechanisms by which the thought reflex in people is killed.

It all began with a new approach to the tongue. Being used to chatter and even to a certain audacity leading (after a few glasses of vodka) to a desire to say 'Surely, gentlemen, isn't it about time that –', the tongue was of course a dangerous organ during a period of 'waiting'. So it was left with only one function: the preliminary processing of food. In such a context, the theme of food, gluttony and drink took on an ideological significance. 'We eat, therefore we exist.'

But reducing life to food is not so easy. When you are eating, you also feel like having a chat, and sometimes you are even overcome by the atavistic desire to 'get to the bottom of things'. With deadly irony, Tovstonogov revealed the triviality of the liberals' waffle. The two main characters of the play were eating ham and one of them, the Narrator, started down a dangerous track: he speculated on how the ham had become ham, who had reared it, and why he had parted with it. 'And now we, who've reared nothing, are eating the ham from this pig!' At this point they were seized with horror at the audacity of their own thoughts. Immediately, a certain person materialized with feline stealth from the fear-impregnated air. He purred an invitation to come and see Ivan Timofeyevich at the police station. The wearisome 'waiting' in the intellectuals' apartment, eating ham, moved up a gear: they were invited for a 'cup of tea' at police headquarters.

The Narrator was played by Igor Kvasha and Glumov by Valentin Gaft. It was a brilliant double act, modelled on the white-faced clown with droopy eyes who is always expecting the worst, and the ginger clown who is always enthusiastic about things.

Ivan Timofeyevich (Pyotr Shcherbakov) put them through a kind of philosophy exam. With a neck as thick as a hippopotamus, and a whole train of big Party roles behind him, Shcherbakov asked our intellectuals two questions: is the soul immortal, and which education system did they prefer, classical or technical?[28] The white clown was so terrified that all he could do was um and er, but the ginger clown excelled himself. If the orders are that the soul is immortal, then it is immortal. If the orders are the opposite, then it is not. 'And if the law is unclear, then we must await further instructions on the matter.' Ivan Timofeyevich looked at Glumov: obviously, he would go far. Glumov answered the second question even more easily:

> I do not know of two education systems, I only know one. And it may be expressed in the following words: we must not burden people with excessive knowledge, we must do everything we can to show them that it is the duty of the householder promptly and unquestioningly to carry out the authorities' instructions! If these instructions are classic ones, then the execution thereof must be classical, and if they are technical, then the execution will be technical.

Here Glumov triumphantly picked up a chair and declaimed: 'And that is all. Other than that, I do not recognise any systems – classical or technical!' Everyone in the police station applauded and Ivan Timofeyevich added: 'Bravo!' But Glumov/Gaft picked up his diminutive partner and used him to conceal his own face, which was laughing beneath the mask.

The follow-up to this proved not so pleasant. Sitting out the times, 'waiting' under Ivan Timofeyevich's supervision 'without modifying one's inner convictions', proved impossible. The police headquarters sucked our friends into its monstrous belly. Tovstonogov lifted a corner on the psychology of people who can always find a private excuse for any betrayal. One of the most biting scenes in the production was when the Narrator and Glumov, who were now totally at home at police headquarters, helped Ivan Timofeyevich compose 'Rules for the Proper Conduct by Citizens of their Lives.' Ivan Timofeyevich would have composed them himself, but his style was extremely clumsy and what would foreigners think? 'We don't have flowing pens,' the officer sighed. So this was a superb opportunity for Glumov's genius and an alliance was forged between the police brain and the self-prostituting pen.

Glumov worked on the manuscript and what he sent back to headquarters was a pearl even by Shchedrin's standards. Even in this madness, however, Tovstonogov looked for method. The more ridiculous and fantastic Glumov's suggestions were (for instance, that every person should have two keys – one for himself and one at police head-quarters, so that the loyalty of subjects could be checked at any time of the day and night), the more subtly they were motivated. Glumov thought he could hoodwink Ivan Timofeyevich. His idea was to betray himself but retain his 'image' and avoid being spied on directly. But here the ginger clown was totally defenceless: when Ivan Timofeyevich summoned him on his own, he was ready to lick the officer's hand and go down on his knees, if only the officer would not ask him to do the most shameful thing. Inna Solovyova wrote that all through the performance you heard teeth chattering 'N-n-no!' at the thought of crossing the final boundary, which was when Ivan Timofeyevich would quite casually introduce our heroes to the editor of *The Muck-Rakers' Paper* with the words: 'Meet some of our colleagues – they're from the aristocracy.'[29]

The production told the story of how people had betrayed themselves; how betrayal had become the norm. 'It's difficult at first, but you soon get used to it,' commented the Narrator/Kvasha mournfully, stepping out of his part. The director studied this awakening sense of shame with particular interest. In the Narrator's case it was coloured with wistfulness and not accompanied by any explosion of emotion. He simply came on to the forestage and proposed to the audience that they think hard about what his, and our, 'excruciating self-abasement' was meant to achieve: 'At the end of the day it is not even in order to feel wanted, it is merely in order to be told condescendingly: "All right, you can live!" '

Tovstonogov's production was an exercise in open contempt. It was about fear, time, a dead period in Russia's history, and the repulsiveness of the middle-rank intellectual. We looked at ourselves in Shchedrin's glass, laughed, and . . . carried on waiting.

It was not surprising that *Balalaykin and Co.* was derived from a novel. In the 1970s Tovstonogov's art was oriented towards prose fiction. It was not just that there were no modern plays. People were looking in prose for new theatrical ideas. It was precisely the 'non-play' – a strange hydrid of prose, drama, film scenario, songs and so forth – that released the energy of directors. The further from the traditional play, they thought, the better. *The Story of a Horse*, staged by Tovstonogov at the BDT in 1975, was the very epitome of this.

The Frosts (1968–1985)

Lev Tolstoy was totally opposed to stage adaptations and even prayed for the souls of the 'botchers' who made them. Fortunately, his prayers were not heard. His long short story *Strider*, which is the autobiography of an old piebald gelding as told by him to the young horses in the stable, became the crowning achievement of the Russian stage in the seventies. Ideas that had been tested on various kinds of material by generations of Russian directors coalesced completely freely in Tovstonogov's production. The idea for the stage version of *Strider*, and its literary treatment, belonged to Mark Rozovsky, one of those dilettantes who Meyerhold predicted would be the salvation of the theatre. Tovstonogov took Rozovsky's idea, which was intended for a small experimental stage, and made it really breathe.

The impression one came away with from *The Story of a Horse* was of Tolstoy's awesome, unrelentless thought drilling to the very bedrock of human nature. Are compassion and the desire to do good natural human qualities, and if so how can they be reconciled with the law of the herd – animal and human – which bullies a horse to death simply because he is of a different colour? In the happy moments of Strider's birth, when he got up on to his trembling legs and looked with surprise around his stable, in the dance of the herd, in the wordless lament/groan that issued from the castrated horse's chest, in its death, and even in what happened after its death, the theatre disclosed the tragically beautiful nature of God's world. In the centre of the world-cum-stable designed by Eduard Kochergin, stood Strider, played by Yevgeny Lebedev, a centaur in a canvas smock, and began to tell the biblical story of the horse's life.

The biblical tone called for an absolute simplicity of staging. The songs, which were recordings of Rozovsky himself singing, were more like the kind of Russian songs sung round a party table than the traditional musical. Even acting at being horses was done transparently, with a kind of childish zest. The director used the most simple techniques of fairground theatre and parable to hurl at the audience Tolstoy's thoughts concerning the death of dead souls and the immortality of living ones.

Tolstoy distinguished two types of singing: from the throat and from the chest. These also symbolize two ways of life. Strider's voice came from his chest, whereas the herd's wild gypsy-style songs came

Plate 14   Yevgeny Lebedev as the horse in Georgy Tovstonogov's production
The Story of a Horse at the BDT, 1975.

from the throat. The sweetness of this chorus, its boundless, infectious
mirth, the triumph of the strong and identical over the 'piebalds' of
the world, was understood by Tovstonogov as the cruellest law of life.
'Only those who have everything still ahead of them, those whose every

muscle trembles with unnecessary tenseness and whose tails stick up, are always right!' sang the herd. The split vocal score of the production displayed this, one of life's deepest contradictions discovered by Tolstoy.

The history of the combined lament, howl and groan that Lebedev invented for his horse deserves a special mention. Stanislavsky once espoused the idea of the so-called affective memory, that is, the deepest emotional experiences of an actor, which he stores away in order to release them into a role at the right moment and give it a unique personal resonance. Lee Strasberg subsequently built the most influential acting school in America on this idea. In Russia this technique was forgotten for decades, as no one much wanted to share the secrets of their 'affective memory'. But there had to be a personal source for what Lebedev achieved with this sound. You cannot get something as spiritual as that from books. Several years after the opening of *The Story of a Horse* I asked Lebedev where he had found this keening groan of Strider's, since I thought there was nothing like it in the original. The actor recalled the year 1930. He told me what it meant to be 'piebald' in the human herd then (Lebedev was the son of a priest, which was enough for him to be ostracized). He recalled collectivization and watching his peasant neighbours' last cow being led away. A woman followed the people leading out the cow and shrieked/howled in the voice that burst from the chest of Tolstoy's horse several decades later. A good example of a Russian actor's 'affective memory'.

Tolstoy had 'made strange' the world through a horse's eyes. Tovstonogov tried to find a stage equivalent to this. At the beginning, for instance, he had Strider stand centre stage before his water trough, with Vyazopurikha's voice, her high, voluptuous neighing, ringing in his ears. Then the triumphant roar of the stallion Mily overlaid it rhythmically. Love and betrayal were described here as fearlessly as Strider's death.

Tovstonogov juxtaposed the gelding's old age with that of its one-time master. He had them lay their heads on each other's shoulder as though they were both horses, and Prince Serpukhovskoy complained to the animal: 'I am so tired of living.' The first to die was the horse. He was tied to a post and slashed with a knife by the same drunk stableman he had played with as a foal. A child's scarlet ribbon spurted from his throat, shutters were torn back in the rough grey hessian of the pen, exposing blood-red flowers, and these and the butterfly fluttering above his body were Strider's last earthly vision. Yevgeny Lebedev enacted the horse's death, the final convulsions of his body and the last glimmer of consciousness, absolutely naturalistically. A spotlight lay on Strider, then got narrower and narrower, creating a highly charged ending.

However, Tovstonogov went further than such effects. As the audience burst into applause, he brought the house lights up, thus destroying the theatrical illusion. Lebedev (Strider) stopped the applause with a gesture, then with a quick movement of his hands made as though removing the exhausted animal's mask from his face (actually he was only made up). In complete silence, and speaking as themselves, Lebedev and Basilashvili (who had just played the Prince) delivered Tolstoy's final words about how the hide, flesh and bones of the horse had been of use to people and wolves, but the remains of the Prince had been of no use to anyone.

Stepping out of the role like this was a hallmark of the new theatrical culture. All the artistic experience of the twentieth century, from Brecht's brash intolerance to the Western tragical musical humanized by the age-old Russian emphasis on psychology, together with children's make believe, reminiscences of the ancient chorus and Russian fairground theatre, and the techniques of pop songs – all of these were brought together in the production. Tovstonogov took his riches where he found them, oblivious of the very relative boundaries in art between 'mine' and 'other people's'. He flung all kinds of ideas, forms and techniques onto his palette and through the powerful metaphorical set created by Kochergin, a designer of the new generation, he refreshed a space that he had grown over-used to. So his mission as mediator was accomplished.

The Tolstoy production was the high point of Tovstonogov's art. After this a slow, steady decline set in. He still had the best company in Russia, and he navigated confidently through the putrid waters of stagnation. He directed Gorky, Chekhov, Sholokhov, Dickens, Vs. Vishnevsky, and Sukhovo-Kobylin.[30] In the latter production he once again attempted to encapsulate an historical period – not of fear or stagnation this time, but of collapse, of the regime's death throes. The BDT put on an 'opera-farce' based on the most vicious play in the Russian classical repertoire. The bureaucrats and policemen of Russia danced and sang around the 'death' of Tarelkin. The production opened in

1983, strangely in time for the death of Russia's own chief policeman, Yury Andropov. Quite unexpectedly, it marked and as it were recorded Andropov's brief reign and secretive death.[31]

I last saw Tovstonogov in a small town in southern Italy in 1988, the third year of the Gorbachev thaw. He was receiving a prize for his contribution to world theatre. He had lost a lot of weight, had difficulty walking, but still smoked like a chimney. The opportunities offered by the new life did not inspire him. He did not want to change his habits or his lifestyle. He had a constant feeling that the denouement was close. He spoke about it with the same calmness and objectivity that startled one in his best productions. On 8 May 1989 he left the theatre in his Mercedes as usual, drove a short distance through the city, and stopped at the traffic lights. He died at the wheel without breaking the highway code.

His funeral was held in St Petersburg's old cathedral, which was unheard-of for a Soviet theatre director.[32] It was a ritual performance in which he was playing a non-speaking part for the first time. The service was solemn, it lasted exactly an hour, and it observed strict rhythmic laws just like his best productions. Now and then it seemed as though the words had been written specially for this funeral the way Tolstoy's and Dostoyevsky's texts had sounded in his productions. 'By His death trampling death' – the coda of the Orthodox funeral service was completing his path in life and reminding us of what had been the main theme of his art.

He was a man of his times and his country. For decades he had walked an outrageous tightrope. At the end, when the air changed and it was easier to breathe and to walk, his legs gave way beneath him.

The whole of Leningrad came to his theatre. Around the coffin on the BDT's stage flickered clusters of candles stuck on vertical poles. These candle-stands had come from a production based on Bulgakov's *Molière* and directed by Sergey Yursky on this very stage. In telling the story of the cunning, flattering Gaul, they had wanted at the time to 'set the air alight'. Georgy Tovstonogov was one of those who set alight the air of our art. He kept the flame alive in his home for nearly thirty years. With his passing the mission of the Soviet stage was brought to a symbolic close.

'Lord, now lettest thou thy servant depart in peace.'

3 The Black Box (1985–1997)

The paradoxes of freedom

In December 1995 free elections were held to the Russian Parliament. For those times this was no trivial event, and it involved the theatre. As a bait to catch voters, most of the forty-three parties put up actors, pop singers and television gameshow presenters as candidates. Actors were as sought after as generals. Each party, according to its taste, had video shorts made which were then run on all the television channels every day for two months. Only one party produced no video shorts and did not flash across our screens. This was the Russian Communist Party. It won.

This unexpected comeback crowned an historic decade for which there is as yet no stable definition. For the first five years the new age was called *perestroika*, but this slid smoothly into 'the criminal revolution'.[1] Another name for it, which is very popular with post-Soviet intellectuals, is '*nomenklatura* capitalism'.[2] Whilst history is still looking for a name, the Russian theatre and Russian art in general are carrying on their age-old job. This could be compared with the black box in an aircraft, working away quite independently, recording the flight. One cannot object to flight recorders (especially if there is an accident). They just keep recording away, and often it is impossible to distinguish the important data from the rest. But time will pass and these readings will be used to reconstruct a critical period that changed the world.

Sometimes people compare the 'readings' of the art produced in the post-revolutionary years with the artistic results of ten years of freedom. The comparison proves baffling. The great Utopia certainly provoked some phenomenal theatrical ideas. So far, the period since 1985 has not produced anything remotely comparable in importance to the theatre of the twenties. This is the first paradox of freedom that needs decoding.

It cannot be understood without recalling the conditions in which Russia's free 'flight' took place. The period of euphoria triggered by Gorbachev's *glasnost* was very quickly followed by a bad hangover. Freedom fell on the country 'from above' and the ground was completely unprepared for it. The power of 'democratic' bureaucrats instantly fused with that of the mafia. The police state had fallen apart, but what began to rise from its ruins was a very strange social phenomenon with no parallels in world history (just as there are no precedents for the process of moving from socialism to capitalism). When *perestroika* started, people assumed that Russia would take the Swedish path, but it actually became more reminiscent of Colombia. The Mexican soap operas that filled the television screens only accentuated the impression.

The writer Vasily Rozanov was shocked when in October 1917 Christian Russia dissolved in literally three days. This was precisely how long it took in August 1991 for Soviet Russia to fade. The rejoicing was universal. The square outside the White House was immediately renamed Free Russia Square. The hated statues were toppled from their pedestals, several towns and streets were renamed, and work began on rebuilding the Cathedral of Christ the Saviour in Moscow; the necessary ritual motions were gone through. However, the political will was lacking to carry out the most important ritual of all, namely burying Lenin's body according to Christian custom.

In times of upheaval life usually becomes highly theatricalized. So it was with us. In the autumn of 1993 tanks rolled on to Free Russia Square and started pounding the very building that was supposed to symbolize democracy. The country watched the revolt on CNN. The cameras showed what was happening dispassionately. The country became the audience at an awesome performance. The day was unusually sunny and clear, and sometimes it all looked more like a computer game than the beginning of a civil war, with different coloured soldiers, guns, shots and puffs of smoke. The theatricality of it was increased by the presence of spectators, as thousands of people came to watch the carnage. Many had brought their children with them.

The black box of the theatre would record in its language both the euphoria of freedom and the terrible disappointment felt by those who saw themselves as the 'engineers of *perestroika*'. The old ideology had been demolished, but the ideal of the free market – especially in its Russian form – inspired hardly anyone.

Symbolic of the break with the past was the return of Solzhenitsyn. He came like the mystical Inspector in Gogol's comedy. His every action was semiotic, starting with his journey from Vladivostok to Moscow. It was a conscious act of role playing that was intended to reinforce the image of a Russian writer/preacher with something to say to his lost sheep. At first the 'sheep' listened. He was given a programme on television and began to address the nation. The blazing eyes, the beard and the torrent of words reminded you of Dostoyevsky, whilst the views reminded you of Don Quixote. The author of *The Gulag Archipelago* was tilting at windmills. He called the nascent regime an oligarchy and despised the American-style pop culture that went with it. His programme was soon closed down and no one missed it. Society had become as indifferent to television sermons as it was to theatrical ones. To celebrate the Inspector/Classic's return, MKhAT put on his play *The Love-Girl and the Innocent*, which had been banned since the sixties. It played to half-houses.

Time fracture-tested the very idea of the 'theatre-church'. The deaths of Anatoly Efros and Georgy Tovstonogov coincided with crises at MKhAT and the Taganka, the two most important theatrical institutions of the previous period. In May 1987 the huge company of the Art Theatre divided into two. Oleg Yefremov stayed at the helm of MKhAT 1 and Tatyana Doronina became head of MKhAT 2. The division of MKhAT immediately acquired an ideological flavour. MKhAT 1 called itself after Chekhov, MKhAT 2 kept the name Gorky. Whilst Yefremov – for the umpteenth time! – endeavoured to recreate a 'partnership of belief', Tatyana Doronina looked for political support and turned her stage over to Sergey Kurginyan, who decided to sing the praises of Stalin. At the end of *Batum*, based on the play by Bulgakov,[3] the generalissimo in his white jacket gazed thoughtfully into the distance and the whole audience stood up as the old Soviet national anthem thundered forth.

The two MKhATs, one on either side of Tverskaya Street, were the pefect image of the divided country. The same could be said of the Taganka. Lyubimov's return was a great occasion; he was mobbed like

Plate 15   Lyubimov's study at the Taganka Theatre, 1988. From left to right: David Borovsky, designer; Nikolay Gubenko, actor and subsequently last Minister of Culture of the USSR; Yury Lyubimov.

a hero, with the audience chanting 'Stay! Stay!' Some people wept even – in early 1988 Moscow was still in euphoric mood. He did stay, he revived his banned productions, and staged several new ones, including Nikolay Erdman's *The Suicide*.[4] They had no success, because the 'wall' had gone. Lyubimov had no one to fight: he had returned to a different country and at first did not realize it. When he did realize, it was too late. His own actor and disciple Nikolay Gubenko became his main opponent. The trouble at the Taganka came in the market form of a division of property. As in the case of the Art Theatre, the division had ideological overtones: Gubenko favoured the communists.

In a situation of freedom and spiritual vacuum, the Russian theatre lost its special significance. You could say that the 'super-theatre' became just 'theatre'. Actually, all forms of spiritual activity lost their status. The readership of the 'super-newspapers' and 'super-magazines' shrank several hundredfold. Playwrights, directors and writers who had regarded themselves as the spiritual leaders of the people, were bewildered. Freedom of artistic expression ceased to be looked upon as something exceptional and beneficial; people soon got as used to it as air. State subsidies no longer covered half of a theatre's expenses. In order to survive, Moscow's theatres set up casinos and nightclubs in their buildings. The word *Exchange* often decorated their entrances. But it was not exactly clear what was being exchanged for what, and at what rate, so to speak. One of the most important results of the 'exchange' was the loss of social status and of the special feeling of 'leading' which had been taken for granted by everyone engaged in art in Russia.

Since *Homo sovieticus* was being superseded by the 'new Russian', the theatre began to describe a new human type.[5] Dealing with the new life on the stage was difficult, but it easily fitted into the classical framework. Aleksandr Ostrovsky, who had described the rise of the Russian bourgeoisie in the last century, became one of the most popular playwrights in the new Moscow. The titles of his comedies and dramas sparkled again and filled with topical meaning: *Easy Money, Wolves and Sheep, More Sinned Against Than Sinning.* The classics played to full houses, because they dealt with topical subjects.

This new Time of Troubles has not yet destroyed the system of state-subsidized theatres that was set up in the Soviet era. The new Russia has retained this system, and even expanded it. During the years of economic collapse about 100 new theatres sprang up financed by the state. The Soviet ideology is dead, but the idea of the theatre-home, the theatre-church, on which the Art Theatre had been founded and which in a different form had continued to bear fruit under the Soviet regime, has proved remarkably resilient.

The crisis in the Russian theatre during the age of freedom is a necessary crisis. A 100-year-long cycle has come to an end. We need a new Slavyansky Bazar (the 1897 meeting in the Moscow restaurant of that name at which Stanislavsky and Nemirovich-Danchenko conceived MKhT) in order to discuss the main question, which is: now that we have our freedom, are we prepared to create a genuinely free theatre that is capable of combining (1) supreme artistic standards plus the ethics of long-term creative collaboration (without which there can be no theatre-church), with (2) the ruthless laws of natural selection that are synonymous with the 'free market'?

Russian theatre directors have different answers to this crucial question.

The splitting of the Moscow Arts

So much mythology surrounds this subject that it is as well to start with the question of whose idea it was.

I think the copyright belongs to Oleg Yefremov. Some years later Tatyana Doronina began to state publicly that Yefremov was not the author of the split but had been the victim of a conspiracy. The present writer has often been offered the laurels as 'MKhAT's grave-digger'. Tempting though the honour is (after all, history only remembers those who start and finish a thing), I must decline it.

The copyright on the idea is Yefremov's, but I agree with Doronina that it is doubtful whether Yefremov himself was responsible for the actual process of division. He did not draw up any lists of which actors he wanted and which not. (This happened almost spontaneously when at one of our stormy meetings Oleg Tabakov asked the actors who supported Yefremov's idea to go into another room; those that did then formed the core of the new company.) Moreover, Yefremov had no clear idea of how the two companies would coexist. Even in his worst dreams he could not have imagined that eventually another MKhAT would spring up in Moscow which would be a symbol of Soviet Russia. Looking back on it, we can see that it was not Yefremov, or Doronina, or a conspiracy of grave-diggers that split MKhAT, but the times. It went into meltdown along with the country it had represented for fifty years.

The division of MKhAT anticipated the collapse of the USSR. The Chekhov MKhAT and the Gorky MKhAT ended up on different sides of the renamed Tverskaya and do not even have diplomatic relations. The split should be viewed not politically, but in terms of a theme that has recurred all through MKhAT's history, namely that 'MKhAT's finished'. On numerous occasions in the past the company has felt this, but each time a new cycle in its work has started up, with new concerns that have bound it together again.

In 1923 Stanislavsky wrote in a 'most confidential letter' to Nemirovich-Danchenko from America, where the company was on tour:

We must get used to the idea that the Art Theatre no longer exists. You seem to have realized this before I did; I have been flattering myself all these years and salvaging the mouldy remains of it. During this trip everything has become blindingly clear to me. No one has any *thought*, or *idea*, or big *aim* any longer. And without that no intellectual enterprise can exist.[6]

Stanislavsky's premonition was right. After they returned from America, the period of the Soviet Art Theatre began. The resuscitation of MKhAT that Yefremov undertook in the 1970s and 1980s was the final phase in the Soviet history of the Art Theatre. It was this MKhAT that collapsed in 1987. The difference between 1924 and 1987 is one of frankness. Yefremov did not use a confidential letter to discuss the fact that yet again MKhAT was 'finished' – he informed the whole world of it. By going public he put an end to MKhAT's 'eventless' existence, which had gone on for far too long. In a certain sense he was also condemning himself. Parting was easy. Becoming the Moscow Art Theatre again proved unbelievably difficult.

The first production that the new MKhAT staged in the autumn of 1987 to mark its return to the renovated theatre in Kamergersky pereulok was Mikhail Roshchin's *Mother O'Pearl Zinaida*. It had been banned for many years and Yefremov and Roshchin had revised it endlessly. It was a comedy written in the early eighties and it reached audiences in the period of *glasnost* when people were laughing at other things and in a different way. Yefremov imagined a light, elegant, paradoxical tale with a fantastical element to it, rather like the stage version of *The Master and Margarita*. He himself took the main part of the writer Aladin, who was poised between two worlds – his cockroach-infested communal flat and the divine visions he had of the past and the future, Russia, the West, and the mad world that was coming into being beyond the theatre walls.

Yefremov may be very close to the author of *Mother O'Pearl Zinaida*, but he is made of different artistic stuff. He has a different temperament and sense of humour, and makes different demands upon life. Yefremov 'talked Roshchin round' to altering the play completely (I have never met an author whom Yefremov could not talk round). However, Yefremov could not change the original authorial intonation of the play. He was out of place in it both as a director and as an actor. Unfortunately, the new stage machinery did not work very well either and slowed everything down. The 'light fantasy' turned into a rather plodding MKhAT musical which when it opened was not appreciated.

The imperfections of the production detonated a kind of land-slide in-house. It was as though the split in MKhAT was carrying on via a chain reaction within the new group. The end of the eighties was marked by the break-up of the small company that Yefremov had formed over almost two decades. For various reasons, Anastasiya Vertinskaya, Aleksandr Kalyagin, Yekaterina Vasilyeva and Oleg Borisov left the new MKhAT (or at least distanced themselves from it), and Yevgeny Yevstigneyev retired. It was a blow which Yefremov accepted with his usual fatalism. If someone left, it must be necessary, and it was a good thing they went. He had to create a new theatre, without stars, or at least without those whose demands were destroying the basis of the theatre as a collective enterprise.

This theme was particularly audible in MKhAT's 1988 production of Bulgakov's *Cabal of Hypocrites (Molière)*. Adolf Shapiro was invited to direct it, but the whole point about it was that the artistic director of MKhAT would play the director of the Palais Royal. Bulgakov's play was returning to MKhAT's stage after fifty years, weighed down with all its stage history. Everyone knew that the previous *Molière* had been ruined by the authorities, but what stuck in the theatre's memory most was the unseemly haste with which MKhAT had fallen in with the leading article in *Pravda* and strangled the production at birth. In 1988 MKhAT had no need to defend Bulgakov. It was more a question of the theatre clearing its conscience (if one accepts that a collective artist like a theatre can have such a thing).

No great fuss was made of the fact that Bulgakov's play was returning to MKhAT, but the fact that the cream of the theatre were appearing in it was, of course, significant. Yefremov played Molière; Smoktunovsky, the King; and Tabakov, Bouton. The director refocused many of the play's main themes, including that of the artist and polit-ical power, which came across quite differently in 1988 from how it had in the mid-thirties. Yefremov and Smoktunovsky did not even discuss the possibility of refurbishing the theme of the reciprocal seduction of stage and throne, which had been extremely topical for Bulgakov. In the old MKhAT they would have said that they did not have the reserves of affective memory for it. Whence, indeed, could Yefremov have drawn the rapture to exclaim to the King 'I love you!'? And whence could Smoktunovsky have acquired the belief that this tough old comedian was flattering him from the heart?

Yefremov acted not the beginning of the road but the end. Behind this Molière (or so it seemed to me) stood the recent division of MKhAT, which like the *Tartuffe* affair had occurred with the active participation of the highest authorities. Yefremov's Molière was broken; even his outbursts of anger, which usually refresh a director, lasted only fractions of a second. The 'builder of the theatre' was tired. His life hung on the fate of *Tartuffe*. The fact that the King could destroy the play, the theatre, and the actor himself, was simply in the nature of things. Why bellow about it? Yefremov/Molière did not bellow. The 'militant' phrase 'I hate autocratic tyranny' (which had once been expunged by the censor) was delivered by the head of MKhAT extremely simply, as though to himself, as a long-standing belief that needed no italics.

The nerve of the production lay in the duet between Actor and King. The two dissemblers played up to each other, once even sitting down next to each other on the palace's staircase: a touching picture of Utopian harmony. The King always seemed to be looking at himself in the mirror of history and giving object lessons: for the benefit of his whole *état*, he would share a chicken bone with Molière or play some music. Molière and the King understood each other as one performer understands another, one carpenter another.

In 1936 *Molière* was performed seven times before it was taken off. *The Cabal of Hypocrites* has now been running for ten years. In 1995 Innokenty Smoktunovsky died and some parts are now being played by a second or even third cast. Oleg Yefremov as Molière, however, remains permanent.

The loss of Smoktunovsky was one of those blows from which you do not recover. He occupied an absolutely unique position in the Art Theatre: all the time he was there, there was a feeling of order, of an acting hierarchy if you like. Everyone knew where they stood, because he provided a yardstick. I had the impression that when he was acting opposite Smoktunovsky, Yefremov experienced the kind of simple joy that has been so rare for him in recent years. For once there was no burden of duty, just the happiness of theatrical play with a great partner and friend. He would not have been Yefremov if he had not occasionally sounded off: 'He's impossible to act with, he doesn't understand the collective nature of theatre, he hogs the stage!' But then a glowing Smoktunovsky would come into the dressing-room, say something funny, and Yefremov would forgive him everything, just as Molière 'grew wise' and forgave his actors everything.

The new Russia did not just change the way key lines sounded in Bulgakov's play about Molière; it affected Yefremov's whole life and creative outlook. The 'battering-ram' lost the target which to a great extent had concentrated all his efforts for decades. The 'wall' had gone; there was no need to destroy anything, to fight the regime or to indulge it in regal games. As with many of his contemporaries, Yefremov's artistic vision retuned itself. He purposely kept out of the post-Soviet theatrical élite that was being courted by the new government. He preserved his own identity and did not join in what became known as 'political *tusovkas*' (endless jamborees). He openly distanced himself from all the forces that were establishing themselves on Russia's political stage. When Gorbachev left this stage, Yefremov took it as a personal loss. The creation of a new, free MKhT became his *raison d'être*, an ongoing drama that he had to live with.

Open social protest ceased to inspire him as a director. In 1988 he turned down a play by Shatrov after it had actually been announced for MKhAT's next season, because it debunked Stalin but did not tackle Lenin. Instead he staged Lyudmila Petrushevskaya's *Moscow Choir*. Petrushevskaya was not interested in ideology and the bosses, she was interested in ordinary people. She rejected the Soviet problem play and parodied it with her own themes and heroes. She did not advocate anything directly, she basically used language to reinstate the very fabric of everyday life. This 'fabric' was the one from which Yefremov had once formed the Sovremennik and himself as an artist. Petrushevskaya was taking him back thirty years.

Petrushevskaya was MKhAT's new author. The alliance promised much, but did not become a firm one. For many years Yefremov waited for a 'big play' from Petrushevskaya and all his other authors, but it never came. During the years of freedom, everyone had the opportunity to do what he wanted. Aleksandr Gelman (co-author of *Misha's Party*) returned to journalism. Shatrov stopped writing plays and took off as a businessman. Yefremov turned to the classics. He directed four productions that had difficult, not to say agonizing births: *The Cherry Orchard* (1989), *Woe from Wit* (1992), *Boris Godunov* (1994), and *Three Sisters* (1997).

Since I was working at the Art Theatre in these years, it is difficult for me to judge Yefremov's productions from outside. I am writing not a critical study but a sketch of the theatrical career of one of the leading figures of the post-Stalin stage. For this purpose it is not so important which production won acclaim and which did not. What Yefremov asks of MKhAT today and from his own productions is far deeper than anything demanded by his critics. If he had the resources, he would direct Griboyedov's play all over again in order to achieve the perfect lightness that would bring out the idea of 'woe from love'. He would restage *Boris Godunov* (he dreams of doing so), in order to get rid of the cumbersome battle scenes and lay bare the throbbing nerve of a play that is about Russia's first Time of Troubles. Basically, *Godunov* is carried along now by Yefremov's own acting achievement as Boris; he has very little support from the ensemble. His loneliness in the theatre, his relations with his actors, and his unattainable perfectionism, have all gone straight into this play.

Yefremov's production of *Three Sisters* also came out of the air that we breathe. It received the kind of rave reviews that Yefremov had not had for a long time. The culmination of a Chekhov cycle that stretched back almost thirty years, it summed up one of the central themes of this cycle – that of the house and the garden. In *Ivanov* (1976) the hero could find no home. Both his house and his garden seemed doomed. In *The Seagull* (1980) people lived in a house with no walls and were constantly dissolving into the garden. In *Uncle Vanya* (1985) the house was metaphorically disintegrating and only the one in the distance, with its light, seemed to offer a real home. In *The Cherry Orchard* the director and designer again split the perception of the house. The estate was represented life-size, but on the forestage it also existed as a set of models – a toy house, orchard, and even church.

Returning to Chekhov after eight years, for *Three Sisters* Yefremov and Levental put the house on a revolve. Here human habitation is spiritualized. It breathes, turns, and even changes its colours as it responds to the changes in the space around it, in this instance a park or enormous garden that projects the principal colours of a dying or reviving Nature. The seasons and their movement are not an outdoor phenomenon here, but an indoor one of light and colour. The inside walls of the Prozorovs' house are the white of spring or the crimson of autumn; they soak up the dense dark blue colour of winter and the rusty red of the languid, arid Russian summer. Never before had Yefremov laid such emphasis on the link between human destiny and the natural cycle. Never before in his art had the theme of tiredness and parting been sounded so clearly. The three sisters' hysterics at the end, set amidst an indifferent Nature, when they cling to each other but a powerful force tears them apart – this theme was familiar from Yefremov's other Chekhov productions, but here it was given a much stricter, more concentrated form.

In order to attain the tragic simplicity of the 'flow of life', Yefremov had to overcome the Chekhovian clichés that had cramped more than one generation of MKhAT actors. He tried to get rid of the lumbering rhythm associated with Chekhov, to prevent his actors from playing 'characters', from *imitating* the real/pretended communication between Chekhov's people, and their isolation. He overcame the temptation of the 'poetic Chekhov' created by Nemirovich-Danchenko in his pre-war *Three Sisters*, which had been the most intense theatrical experience of Yefremov's youth. Not that he cut down the avenue of birches or rejected the 'yearning for a better life'. He simply heard in Chekhov's play a different diagnosis. There is no didacticism in the production, no obvious perspective, no little light in the distance as there was in *Uncle Vanya*. The house and the garden are caught in a circle out of which no one can tear themselves. The 'order of the acts' cannot be changed, but this does not rob us of courage or of the understanding that life is a gift which can be taken away from us at any time. And this is how Masha (Yelena Mayorova), Irina (Polina Medvedeva) and Olga (Olga Barnet) existed in the production (Mayorova died tragically in August 1997). Viktor Gvozditsky (Tuzenbakh) projects a similar sense of disembodiment. He is 'as light as a sheet of paper which if you blew on it would fly away'.[7] In fact they are all such stuff as dreams are made of, from the dashing Colonel Vershinin (Stanislav Lyubshin) to the pathetic, infinitely touching schoolmaster Kulygin (Andrey Myagkov).

As an ensemble production *Three Sisters* is sustained by its director's extreme objectivity, which accepts the tragic basis of life.

It may be the most pitiless production in Yefremov's Chekhov cycle, but strangely it is also the most hopeful. The hope appears to reside in the very circularity of the play's movement, which is here enacted with absolute consistency. It is not just the spring and summer that will pass; this winter, and this autumn in which the baron was killed, will also pass. May will return and the garden will flower again. At the end of the performance this garden completely crowds out and replaces the Chekhovian house/home. The latter recedes into the depths of the stage; dissolves among the trees, in the dying light of an autumn evening. Then music by Scriabin is heard. Its tragic depths drown the military march, Chebutykin's 'Ta-ra-ra boom-de-ay' and the prayer-like words of the women, hopelessly alone and turning into as much a part of Nature as the trees and clouds.

This new version of *Three Sisters* has compressed within it the experience of the generations whose possible happiness Chekhov's characters speculate about so much. As Petrushevskaya wrote soon after the production opened, Irina enthuses about being a workman who gets up at first light and breaks stones on a road, but what she and the others got was a pickaxe and wheelbarrow, permafrost, chains and a plank bed. But the fact that the characters' predictions were wildly wrong has not led the director to display blistering irony or aggressive despair. The dominant tone is one of shared experience and compassion, directed as much at ourselves as at the past. For many people the production is a very personal event. As Stanislavsky would have said, what they come away with from MKhAT is life.

Before he departs for Poland with his brigade, Vershinin philosophizes. For ages what he says has been delivered as an exercise in stage rhetoric; so it sounds meaningless. In the context of the new *Three Sisters*, however, it acquires fresh force. 'Previously', he says, 'mankind was preoccupied with wars, filling its existence with military campaigns, raids, victories, but now that's all had its day, leaving behind a vast empty space, and at the moment there is nothing to fill it with.'

As a nation, we have nothing to fill that 'vast empty space' in which we find ourselves. This is the time and space that the new *Three Sisters* exists in. This is the point at which the Chekhov Art Theatre is, following its split and in the year of its centenary. May I remind you that for almost one-third of this 100 years its fate has been inseparable from that of Oleg Yefremov.

Mark Zakharov and the King's games

With the deaths of Efros and Tovstonogov, the balance of forces in the Russian theatre changed. New stars rose and set, some became leaders, others became deputy leaders. Freedom of choice and the absence of a common enemy enabled Russian theatre directors to practise self-determination. Things began to take on their natural shapes, which were often radically different from what was expected. One of the most important transformations in the period of freedom was that of Mark Zakharov, the artistic director of Moscow's Lenkom.

Mark Anatolyevich Zakharov (born 1933) studied at GITIS, acted in the provinces, then made a name for himself in Moscow University's student theatre with Shvarts's *The Dragon* and Brecht's *Resistible Rise of Arturo Ui*. For several years he wrote humorous articles and sketches, which he performed himself on the popular Sunday radio programme *Good Morning*. In 1967 he staged Ostrovsky's *A Profitable Position* at Moscow's Satire Theatre. He became principal director of the Lenkom in 1974, where he remains to this day.

Fame as a director came to Zakharov with *A Profitable Position*. It was one of those productions that together with Efros's *Three Sisters* and Pyotr Fomenko's *The Death of Tarelkin* was suppressed in the 1960s. The ideological steam-roller flattened productions that had almost opposing messages. Efros's highly emotional tone and the 'devils' mayhem' woven by Fomenko were totally different from the theatrical prognosis offered at the time by Mark Zakharov.

On the stage of the Satire Theatre, Vasily Zhadov, a young man around in 1856 (the period immediately following the death of Nicholas I), was grappling with problems that faced young people of the post-Stalin generation. There was no need to draw any special attention to the parallels between the two periods: they were as alike as two pins. Mark Zakharov and his designer Valery Levental placed Ostrovsky's hero in a maze of doors, chairs and tables set on two circles, one inside the other. Sometimes the circles turned in different directions and the hero had to dodge around the stage looking for a way out. The maze had been created under the influence of Kafka's *The Trial*, which was a seminal text for our sixties men. The hero was attempting to live in Russia without degrading himself, without taking bribes and without having a 'profitable position'. For him, understanding life meant orienting himself in the stage space.

The director treated stage time just as daringly. He repeated important parts of the play several times at different tempi and in different settings. Zhadov might start a monologue in one room, then pick his way through the maze and repeat the text in a different space, which changed the tone and sense of what was said. This technique 'framed' each episode and broke up the unity of time.

The choice of Andrey Mironov to play Zhadov was inspired. Mironov was just beginning; soon he would become the darling of the nation. His popularity could be compared only with that of Vysotsky. They were performers of the same vintage and both died young, at the peak of their fame. But they responded to the challenge of their time quite differently. When Vysotsky joined Lyubimov's team he filled his voice with the power of protest, laughter and mockery of the pig-ugly system. After his meteoric rise in *A Profitable Position* and his performance in *The Marriage of Figaro* (1969), Andrey Mironov settled into a 'profitable position' at the Satire Theatre. He became the hero of a theatre which in the 1970s would be virtually the chief place of entertainment in the empire.[8] Vysotsky became the lead actor of the generation of angry young men, Mironov of the generation of people fate had treated kindly.

In *A Profitable Position* Mironov's hero was a herald and promise of victory. He charmed you the moment he came on. Whistling and full of bounce, the young man with his irresistible smile walked against the motion of the revolve, throwing open endless doors. He was walking against the tide of fate. Zhadov had decided to opt out of the life lined up for him that his seniors were accustomed to. The revolve bore him and his fiancée into various corners of the stage, including its most impecunious and cheerless ones. Tables, waiters and taverns whirled past them, but the two young people stuck together, attempting to resist the ghastly laws of social survival.

Of course, these laws won. Another 'Common Story' unfolded, like the one performed shortly before at the Sovremennik. The younger generation were tamed. In place of bureaucrats of the old school, along came young Belogubov, who was of Zhadov's own generation. He was a bloodsucker of the latest, extremely dangerous type. Having obtained a post, that is, a 'profitable position', the young scoundrel celebrated in a tavern. As the guests danced, they tore up and burned liberal newspapers that were writing 'God knows what'. The dominant colour of the clothes at this victory feast was brown: these characters of Ostrovsky's were fascists, and behind them loomed the shadows of those who would soon crush Prague and everything alive in Russia itself that had begun to emerge since the death of Stalin. Zhadov/Mironov left the tavern in terror, dragged a tablecloth with him, and wrapped himself up in it like a shroud. The revolve turned, the interior changed, and there was the company of triumphant yobs jeering and pointing at Zhadov. The staging reproduced that of Tovstonogov's *Woe from Wit*, where the rebellious hero was surrounded by a crowd in masks and fainted.

A final test awaited the hero when he got home. His fiancée Polinka positively did not want to think of higher things; all she wanted was to be well dressed and have a good time. She wanted to be like everyone else. So she gave the hero an ultimatum and for the first time he pronounced the weighty phrase 'Let me think about it.' He was borne off into another space, which got more desolate with each turn of the revolve. 'I must think about it,' the young man repeated to himself, to the audience, to all of us. 'I must. I must think about it,' he said over and over again, seeking the simple, irrefutable, well-worn arguments that we usually find to justify our self-betrayal. 'It's a good thing, isn't it, when a good wife is well dressed? And it's a good thing to go out with her in a good carriage.' The revolve bore him off to his influential uncle and he started muttering pitifully: 'Forgive me . . . it was the impulsiveness of youth, ignorance of life, I know now what it is to live without support . . . without patronage . . . Let me work again in your department . . . Uncle, provide for me! Give me a position . . . in which I – I could acquire something.'

The audience froze with fear and pity, because it had previously fallen in love with this radiant young man. Andrey Mironov himself, it seemed, blushed with shame as the uncle lectured him. A few seconds later, he sprang out of his stupor and landed on the forestage, in the precise spot that the creators of the production had christened among themselves the 'conscience point'.[9] He repeated several times and in various ways 'I am not a hero, I am an ordinary weak human being. Like most of us, I don't have much willpower. But one lesson is enough to resurrect me . . . I may waver, but I shall not commit a crime. I may stumble, but I won't fall.' The music that had accompanied the hero throughout now came in again: a grating mixture of sad and jaunty. Zhadov/Mironov suddenly smiled. He was reassuring us, giving us hope. It was all right, everything would sort itself out. This farewell smile was unforgettable. He went upstage, where by now there was nothing left: no doors, desks, walls or maze. Just a scary emptiness and the sad/jaunty tune. But high up, above it all, was a frame, and in it stood three ladies wearing costumes from another age. It was like something out of Madame Tussaud's.

The production was soon closed. Zakharov then put on Arkanov's and Gorin's comedy *The Banquet* at the Satire Theatre (1968). This experiment is worth mentioning as it was the beginning of Zakharov's collaboration with Grigory Gorin, who was to be the author with him of many of his future productions. However, even this totally censor-friendly satire, with which Zakharov wanted to fill a gap in his life, was banned, because it was suspected of absurdist tendencies. Having suffered two bans one after the other right at the beginning of his directing career, Zakharov paused to take stock. At this point he was invited by Andrey Goncharov, the artistic director of the Mayakovsky Theatre, to direct a stage adaptation of *The Rout*. He accepted, and it changed his life.

Fadeyev's novel written in the mid-twenties was one of the cornerstones of Socialist realism. Young theatre directors of the time of the Thaw avoided such things: no one was keen to experiment with Soviet mythology. However, after Tovstonogov's production of *An Optimistic Tragedy* and especially after *The Mother* at the Taganka, Zakharov scented the possibility of victory and decided to take the risk. *The Rout* was presented in the style of a revolutionary saga about an iron-willed Bolshevik, Levinson, who was the commander of a partisan detachment in the Far East and led his men through all the obstacles that the genre demanded, into the future. The detachment was decimated, but this merely accentuated the mythic nature of the plot. The unflinching faith of the Bolshevik Jew Levinson was akin to the fanaticism of young Jewish partisans at the dawn of Christianity.

The critics were divided. Some savoured the allusions to Russian black shirts, others heard nothing in the production's music other than a sincere hymn to the Party's zealots. It contained both. Zakharov was doing what the Sovremennik did with its revolutionary trilogy: attempting to get back to basics. However, the tottering regime indulged in state anti-Semitism and did not like to be reminded of its past. The reminder that Levinson was a bearer of the Bolshevik faith was ambiguous, but in the end purely theatrical arguments prevailed. Levinson was superbly acted by Armen Dzhigarkhanyan, who in *The Rout* began to conquer Moscow. Vitality, irresistible masculine charm, the will to self-fulfilment – everything that was to become the trademark of this actor – was used by Zakharov to refurbish the revolutionary myth.

The success of *The Rout* encouraged Zakharov to continue his risky game. With the composer Grigory Gladkov he staged a musical at the Satire Theatre entitled *Tempo 1929*. It was based on a play by Nikolay Pogodin about the shock workers of the first five-year plan. The actors sang and postured all over the place and it was difficult to tell whether they were sending up Soviet clichés or trying to recreate their original élan. Those who decided the fates of directors in those years appreciated Zakharov's flexibility. In 1974 he was given the Lenkom – the theatre from which Efros had been removed with so much fuss in the mid-sixties. Zakharov took note of his predecessor's unhappy experience and felt his way carefully.

The Lenkom was never equated with the Sovremennik, the Taganka, or the Leningrad BDT. Zakharov had no pretensions to be top, he never fell greatly out of favour, and he did not wear a martyr's crown (without which it is difficult to become a 'shaper of minds' in Russia). Rather like Zhadov/Mironov, at critical moments in his life he was able to laugh things off wryly. He decided to create in his niche not a 'church' but a young theatrical subculture, and since there was no other the Lenkom became practically the most popular theatre in Moscow. It was here that the first Soviet musicals were born, and our first rock-opera *'Yunona' and 'Avos'*, with music by Aleksey Rybnikov to verse by Andrey Voznesensky (1981). The spirit of dissidence hung about the Lenkom, but it was not so much freedom of ideas as of theatrical technique. The music, the showy staging, the lighting and sound effects, and all the manifold ways of producing shock, were designed to rouse the audience from its lethargy and indifference.

To go to the Lenkom was like travelling abroad. Musically its young subculture was merely serving up what was already *passé* in the West, but theatrically the Lenkom was extending ideas first discovered by Moscow's top companies. The infectious energy of Zakharov's lead actor Nikolay Karachentsev, his throaty singing voice, and even his theatrical despair, immediately reminded you of Vysotsky, and the inventive metaphorical spaces designed by Oleg Sheyntsis harked back to discoveries made by David Borovsky at the Taganka. Literarily, things went no further than Shatrov's Leniniana and Arbuzov's *Cruel Games* (1979).

To be the principal director of a Soviet theatre-church meant agreeing to compromise. The question was, how far was one prepared to go in the haggling that this always involved? Mark Zakharov had an infallible feel for the limit. He would always go for an agreement without hysterics; he did not lower his horns like Lyubimov; he did not hit the bottle and blow his top like Yefremov. He would bluff elegantly, when necessary mount productions for Party anniversaries, and continue his games with the Soviet classics, not to mention plays about Lenin. All this was done with a light touch, a smile, and even some impudence. The words were not new, but the order he put them in, so to speak, was. This is how theatre politics (indeed life itself) were conducted in those days.

The only production that the authorities would not accept from Zakharov was *Three Girls in Blue* by Petrushevskaya. Our Grundies were right: this was the first time since *A Profitable Position* that Zakharov had risked staging a real play by a real writer. By its very nature the play excluded any moral and theatrical tightrope-walking. After fifteen years, Zakharov had 'stumbled'. He had bared his heart, without sheltering behind pop music or Lenin.

Petrushevskaya's play did not simply present a different aesthetic. You felt that she was opening up an unknown country, in which other laws operated, a different language was used, and there was a different scale of hell. The cat had gone missing – a disaster; the roof was leaking – a catastrophe; there was no lavatory in the dacha and you had to go in a henhouse – a nightmare. All of these were more important than a Party Congress. It was life under the microscope; events in a microworld.

Petrushevskaya's plays led to the slang word *chernukha* entering editors' and censors' vocabularies. This word is roughly the equivalent of 'kitchen sink' and was used to describe Petrushevskaya's extremely gloomy attitude to our radiant Soviet reality. In fact, reducing Petrushevskaya's plays to *chernukha* (or 'true life', as her defenders claimed) was merely a sign of aesthetic deafness. In her plays we enter 'not so much the prose of life as the poetry of language'.[10] As I said earlier, Petrushevskaya turned all the usual themes and plot lines of our drama on their heads and juggled brilliantly with verbal clichés. She created her theatre from the murky element of the Russian/Soviet sublanguage in which characters expressed themselves. Her favourite characters are old people, children and alcoholics; people of dislocated and voluble speech. 'I put on my tan shoes my teeth my blue mac the daughter-in-law gave me once in my life', the Lenkom's wonderful old actress Tatyana Pelttser said in a single breath with no changes of intonation, and the audience collapsed with laughter.

Zakharov's production was certainly not *chernukha*. Although directing a 'domestic' play, he shaped it towards a catharsis that exploded unexpectedly. The beautiful, down-trodden heroine Ira (played by the Lenkom's star Inna Churikova) had rushed to the Crimea to be with her man, leaving her little boy in the care of her mother, who decided to teach her daughter a lesson and go into hospital precisely when the child was on his own in her flat. After being ditched by her lover, Ira attempted to catch a plane from Simferopol. There were no tickets, so she began to rush about among the airport crowds, and it was at this moment that the theatrical climax came. Churikova electrified the audience with a monologue consisting of five words: 'I might be too late.' This was not a sentimental moan, she was not begging, it was not even a scream. It was a soul-rending, hoarse sob worthy of Antigone or Medea. Ordinary life was deafeningly tragic. With this production (and the ban on it!) the Lenkom joined the ranks of the country's most important theatres.

The production was finally released when *glasnost* arrived. The new era made Mark Zakharov into a central figure. He was the first to sense that the boundaries of the forbidden zone in which he had made himself at home could be pushed outwards. He began to destroy this 'zone' from within, first as a journalist and then as a director. In *Literaturnaya gazeta* and other prestigious publications he fired off a series of witty articles about theatrical reform and the mad way that the Soviet theatre operated.[11] He demanded the right to choose and stage plays freely (without preliminary censorship), he sang the praises of a theatre that was economically free, and so on. In dealing with a particular question – the way our theatres were run – he was inevitably talking about the whole political system, since the theatre was its spitting image. On the wave of criticism of the regime, Zakharov became a prominent publicist, secretary of the newly formed Union of Theatre Workers of the USSR,[12] and then a deputy in the last Soviet parliament (1989). Everyone criticized the regime in those days, but Zakharov was one of the few who did it without losing his sense of humour.

Sensing a demand, Zakharov swiftly adapted his young subculture for political theatre. In the years of *glasnost* this flower too, which had never been seen on our stage before, bloomed briefly. Lyubimov had not yet returned to Russia and the Lenkom had no serious competitors. At MKhAT they marked *glasnost* with the inarticulate *Silver Wedding* by Misharin, at the Yermolova Theatre Valery Fokin put on a pop show called *Speak!*, and at the Theatre of the Soviet Army Yury Yeryomin attacked 'distortions of socialism' with a piece of propaganda by Roman Solntsev called *The Newspaper Article*. None of these was remotely comparable with what Zakharov allowed himself in Shatrov's *Dictatorship of Conscience* (1986).

The sense of impending social catastrophe was achieved by destroying theatrical illusion. In the prologue Zakharov and his designer Sheyntsis created a box-set in the style of the early fifties. There was a ceiling, chandeliers, and a view of Moscow's skyscrapers through painted windows. A meeting of the editors of a youth newspaper was in progress. They were discussing how to educate young people and someone, recalling the popular agitprop performances of the 1920s, suggested holding a 'Trial of Lenin'. The conservatives were aghast, the progressives over the moon, and at this point the paper box-set fell to pieces. Zakharov flung the stage wide open, blasted music in as loud as the theatre would take, brought back all his shock techniques, and the theatrical 'trial' began. Even the hero of Dostoyevsky's *Devils*, Pyotr

Plate 16   Mark Zakharov (centre) at a rehearsal, mid-1980s. Left: the actor Oleg Yankovsky. Right: director Yury Makhayev.

Verkhovensky (played by Aleksandr Abdulov), was called as a witness. For the first time on the Soviet stage he expounded his 'right to dishonourable actions', and the audience sat stunned by how accurately the modern 'devils' had fulfilled the novel's extraordinary prophecy.

All through the performance there were 'improvization spaces', when the actors said their own things, commented personally on events, or invited comments from the audience. A character called The Outsider (Oleg Yankovsky) went around the auditorium. The questions had not been approved beforehand, let alone the answers; often they were prompted by the morning 'papers or some sensational television programme. It was a kind of Speaker's Corner and in 1986 it shocked and delighted audiences by turns. There was always some celebrity in the audience (such as the then Secretary of the Moscow Party Committee, Boris Yeltsin) and the emboldened actors interviewed him too. They were as happy as puppies let off their leads to play in the street, without knowing for how long.

Naturally, in the 'Trial of Lenin' the accused was acquitted. The senior actress of the theatre, Tatyana Pelttser, came forward at the end and addressed the audience with the words of Nadezhda Krupskaya, Lenin's widow: 'If you want to honour Vladimir Ilich's memory, put into practice his precepts in all things.' In 1986, apparently, that was as far as Mark Zakharov would go. Who could have guessed that five years later the country created by Lenin would collapse in three days and the Lenkom's director would publicly, before millions of television viewers, burn his Party card? No one else in Russia could have thought up such a stunt.

The performer of the stunt was invited to the victors' feast. Extremely interesting changes now began to occur at the Lenkom. This theatre was the first to open a foreign currency exchange and a nightclub. Evening life and nightlife began to merge. In the first part of the evening Treplev would be standing on the stage raving about the new theatre, then immediately after *The Seagull*, if you hung back as you collected your coat, you could watch this new theatre in action. Security men would quietly fill the foyer and set up special gates like metal detectors at an airport. The 'new Russians' would hand in their weapons, be given a tag for them, and go off to 'relax' in the Lenkom.

The *tusovka*s of the new bourgeoisie, politicians and theatre people needed a place to be held in. Mark Zakharov began to give form to the artistic ideology of the era, the 'free market'. The Brezhnev leadership went *en masse* to MKhAT, the Yeltsin leadership went to see *The Marriage of Figaro* at the Lenkom. After the Beaumarchais had opened, a sympathetic critic gave the following unpretentious definition of the Lenkom's 'message': 'The audience at Zakharov's production probably feel like addressing the *narod* (people) along these lines: "Gentlemen comrades, counts and the third estate! If you have a head on your shoulders like Figaro, you will get yourselves a fortune and a fine lifestyle by peaceful means. If not, then you can drink yourselves silly like the gardener Antonio. What you don't want to get involved with is rifles, cannons and revolutions, especially ones of the Great variety!" '[13]

However, knowing our hero as well as I do, I am convinced that this was not the only thing that moved him to his new version of *The Marriage of Figaro*. There was another calculation, another temptation, behind it, which Zakharov could not resist. For the first time in our lives, a government had come into being which professed the same ideas as had been held for decades by the Russian liberal intelligentsia. The director decided to serve the 'democratic Utopia' in the same way that Meyerhold went off to serve the communist one in 1917. The government, apparently, had changed its spots, and Mark Zakharov decisively crossed the line which people in Russia tried in the past not to cross. In 1993 the artistic director of the Lenkom joined the Presidential Council, which his critics regarded as just another form of 'profitable position'.

In Russia, to 'go to the government' is to break one of the intelligentsia's biggest taboos. It did not pass unnoticed. In April 1992 Zakharov published an article in *Izvestiya* entitled 'A Visit to the President'.[14] Realizing the riskiness of his position, Zakharov tried to bring things down to earth by the use of irony. However, the previous history of the genre asserted itself. A journalist on *Literaturnaya gazeta* immediately identified the hidden source of Zakharov's inspiration: H. G. Wells's chat with the 'Dreamer in the Kremlin' and Leon Feuchtwanger's meeting with the 'Kremlin's Mountain-dweller'.[15] The parallel was obvious: the director and the president had been discussing the 'democratic Utopia' that they were going to create in Russia under the command of the former Secretary of Sverdlovsk Regional Committee. At the end of his article, Zakharov lost his sense of humour and distance – he 'stumbled' – and described the boss of the Kremlin office as 'simple and enigmatic'.[16]

At this point all of the past was thrown in his face. He was reminded, for instance, that 'the masters of culture probably contributed more to the creation of the previous cults than anyone else. And afterwards they probably suffered more from them, wept more, and cursed them more, than anyone else. Often it all started with a single newspaper article'.[17] Zakharov replied in an open letter in which he defended his right if not to love at least to respect the president. He brushed things aside and laughed things off, but even his jokes showed that he understood what a taboo had been broken: 'If you consider yourself an intellectual, you must not betray the traditions of the Russian intelligentsia . . . If someone you respect becomes a boss, then make sure you keep him at arm's length and adopt an expression appropriate to the Opposition. Because in our long-suffering country a boss is always an Enemy.'[18]

Eighteen months later, on 13 October 1993, a party was held at the Lenkom to celebrate Zakharov's sixtieth birthday. As it happened, it was the ninth day after the carnage at the White House – the day on which a wake is traditionally held for the souls of the departed. Despite the fact that a state of emergency had been declared and there was a curfew, the 'whole of Moscow' came to the party. The showman's birthday suddenly turned into a state occasion demonstrating the informal solidarity that existed between the government and the Russian artistic élite. Actors, prima ballerinas, pop stars, bankers, the mayors of Moscow and St Petersburg, all performed their party pieces, and the climax came when Yeltsin arrived back from Japan and his first words from the tarmac were reported as: 'And how is our Mark today?' No one had ever been accorded this kind of honour before in the history of the Russian theatre. In 1997, at the Lenkom's seventieth birthday celebrations, the president even addressed the company on their new freedoms and presented each of the stars with a Zhiguli car. Zakharov replied expansively that 'all Russian theatre people rejoice at your visiting us'. From the stalls, Zakharov's old friend the actor Aleksandr Shirvindt shouted 'Not all, Mark!', but the president did not hear him.

These two 'jubilees' were a blatant departure from the established ritual in Russia whereby the government is one thing, the artist another, and never the twain shall meet.

Or can they? Are people who think and feel in Russia always doomed to oppose the government? *Every* government? And who then is going to help such a government, who is going to make it more civilized?! Mark Zakharov answered these questions by doing something. He was not afraid of public opinion and he established contact with the government at the highest level. He even did not abandon his president when, shaken by the blood-bath in Chechnya, one after another of his most famous lieutenants deserted him. Only future generations, it seems, will be able to make sense of these readings from Russia's 'black box'.

Having been elevated to top theatre director in the country and had every thinkable and unthinkable award and prize showered on him, Mark Zakharov is probably rather worried. He still has not lost his sense of humour and is trying to survive as an artist. He directs fewer and fewer shows, and for all their up-beat tone it is difficult to feel the pulse of his productions. It is difficult to see what really engages his mind. He has put on *The King's Games*, which is an opera for a theatre company by Grigory Gorin and Shandor Kallash based on a play by Maxwell Anderson. It is about Henry VIII and Anne Boleyn. The times are bloody, religion is changing, but a new country is being born. The parallels are fairly obvious, but the production has no theatrical content whatsoever. It has been directed on autopilot. The Zakharov hallmarks are there, but the 'attractions' do not surprise you and the blaring music is instantly forgettable.

In Soviet times the film director Andrey Tarkovsky, who was immolated every time he produced a new film, said of other film directors, his colleagues, that they thought you could live life one way and art another, but in Russia you cannot. This is presumably why Mark Zakharov is trying to discover in art an inner vindication of his present lifestyle. It would seem to be the source of his 1997 production *Barbarian and Heretic*, an adaptation of Dostoyevsky's *The Gambler*.

We are presented with a symbolic town called Roulettenburg and a handful of Russians feverishly gambling in the hope of changing their fortunes overnight. Stage left is a huge, bizarre piece of machinery, rather like a working model of a roulette wheel, with all kinds of turning parts (the work of designer Oleg Sheyntsis). The light show is brilliant, amplified music cuts in and out, and all the techniques introduced at the Lenkom twenty-five years ago are used to full effect. And suddenly (Dostoyevsky's favourite word) something happens . . .

I shall not remind you how the game ends in the novel. All games of chance end the same way. The accursed wheel spins, the deafening music blasts out, people clown around and are destroyed. Right at the end of the Lenkom's show the hero comes on to the forestage in a white nightshirt, barefooted, ready for his final monologue. There is nothing, it seems, to warn you of the extraordinary human display, a kind of confession, in which Zakharov's protagonist sums up his gambling. The actor's face is suddenly distorted by an expression of ineluctable

Plate 17   Kama Ginkas, Geta Yanovskaya and Daniel Ginkas, 1990s.

sorrow, a spasm of shame or some feeling close to it. Whether he is
crying or laughing it is difficult to discern, but what is happening to him
at this moment is real. It lasts for two seconds, no more. But even these
seconds are enough to remind you of the ending of *A Profitable Position*
and the farewell smile of Zhadov, the character with whom Zakharov
began his 'King's games' thirty years ago.

Family portrait (Kama Ginkas and Geta Yanovskaya)

The way Mark Zakharov developed had sociopolitical implications.
Kama Ginkas and his wife Geta Yanovskaya are the exact opposite. In
their best years this couple had no theatrical home and no pretensions
to a 'profitable position'. They were regarded as hopelessly fringe figures
with no relation to either the Soviet or post-Soviet political jamboree.
Both directors have made their names in the years of freedom and under-
gone an evolution that is as telling as Zakharov's.

Kama Ginkas was born in Kaunas (Lithuania) in 1941, a month
before war broke out. He spent his childhood in the ghetto. A few children survived, of whom a high proportion later turned to the arts. For
adults the ghetto was a death factory; for children it was their 'homeland
in Time'. A ludic approach to death entered the very genes of Ginkas's

art, determining the sources and the brio of his theatre. After the war he attended a Jewish school, then he learned Lithuanian, and later Russian. The Talmud and the New Testament rubbed shoulders in his life. He came to directing from the Vilnius Conservatory, where he graduated from the acting school. Lithuania was at that time the Soviet 'West' and when he arrived in Leningrad at the start of the sixties and joined Tovstonogov's workshop he already knew about the Theatre of the Absurd.

He met Geta Yanovskaya in Tovstonogov's group in 1962. Whether she knew anything about the Absurdists by then, I do not know. She certainly knew a lot about radar, because before training as a director she had worked in various top-secret research institutes. After that she worked in a bookshop, which increased her intellectual qualifications. A unique phenomenon then came about: two Directors in one family. I use the capital letter to convey this couple's attitude towards the directing profession. Tovstonogov instilled in them the belief that there is nothing higher in the world than a Director. The actor, the designer, the manager, are nothing – there is just the Director, in whom the others die and are dissolved. The Director has no right to complain about an actor: if you chose him, then he must act well. Either replace him or make him *look* as though he is acting well. The Director is all-powerful. Everything that is born in his imagination must be implemented, at whatever cost. Neither Soviet power nor objective circumstances can absolve the Director of his responsibility for what happens in the Theatre. The Director, in fact, is a personification of Theatre that is always with you.

This all-or-nothing attitude doomed Kama and Geta to two decades of struggling to survive. They worked together for two seasons in Siberia, at Krasnoyarsk, then they brought their theatre to Leningrad and played several productions including an unexpected *Hamlet* that Ginkas mounted with his designer Eduard Kochergin. This was so successful that the doors of all the Leningrad theatres were promptly slammed in their faces: no one needed competitors, even their own teacher Tovstonogov, who was not at all sentimental in such matters.

Having been ousted from Leningrad, they attempted to win over Moscow. The first to break through there was Kama. In the early eighties he put on a theatre creation entitled *Pushkin and Nathalie.*

This had been premiered in Leningrad, where I saw it in a small room at the Palace of Arts. It opened with an act of sacrilege. A tall young man did a parody of Pushkin: he tried a false whisker for size, then tried to walk 'like Pushkin', dragging one foot up to the next. Then he immersed himself in Pushkin's letters, his contemporaries' memoirs, and began to read out old documents with different intonations, as though studying them or providing a commentary on them. Some phrases he rendered sarcastically, inviting us to test the legend. Then some young women from a folk ensemble, who had been sitting in the audience, started to sing traditional Russian songs, laments and incantations. They did not simply sing, they keened and wailed the way peasant women do in Rus'. Within ten minutes you had stopped noticing the ironic intonations and could not take your eyes off the brilliant young man, who was played by Viktor Gvozditsky, or the a cappella choir that strangely blended with Pushkin's texts.

The new 'word order' here was achieved by Ginkas refusing to express truth on the stage by 'truthful' means. He had evoked the spirit of the national poet through irony and parody. Play as the dimension into which he plunges a harsh and bitter naturalism is the formula for Ginkas's directing style. He uses this indirect route to pose the 'final questions'. In the production *The Execution of the Decembrists*, the audience were led to the acting area by arrows saying 'To the execution' – a typical piece of ambiguity for this director, of the kind that sustains his theatre. Suffering, a man's last minutes before execution, and execution itself, become the object of play. Everything that threatens us with death unleashes a surge of theatrical energy in the director. He works in the mythological realm and believes that only myth can convey the truth about human existence: 'in myth one does not hear the icy tones of some high priest, but the stupid, living breath of man.'[19]

He has discovered this 'breath' in Dostoyevsky. He may be far from Dostoyevsky's ideas, but the 'order of their words' is similar. The author of *The Idiot*, condemned to death, prepared for death, and then pardoned seconds before death, spent the rest of his literary career wrestling with one question: 'What goes on in a man's soul at that moment?' Kama Ginkas, the boy from the ghetto, has his gaze fixed in the same direction. In an interview at the time of his production of *The Execution of the Decembrists* he recounted an interesting biographical fact:

The Black Box (1985–1997)

> When I was a student I put on a production of Dürrenmatt's
> *Conversation at Night with a Despised Person*. An executioner
> comes to a writer's flat at night to kill him. For the wise writer
> the executioner is just an illiterate brute, a machine that does
> the state's dirty work for it. The writer insults him – literally
> spits in his face. But the executioner unexpectedly turns out to
> be more experienced in the rather important business of dying.
> Sadly and patiently he teaches the writer how to do it.[20]

This production was the beginning of Ginkas's road. Death is for him a
'rather important business' for which one must prepare. This is especially clear in his cycle of work on Dostoyevsky. Its centrepiece was his
adaptation of *Crime and Punishment*, and its very title expresses
Ginkas's directorial idea: *We Play 'The Crime'*.

Ginkas staged *We Play 'The Crime'* in 1990 at the Moscow Young
People's Theatre (TYuZ), which has been run since 1986 by his wife (her
appointment was one of the first auspicious omens of the period of freedom). He rented an outbuilding stuck on to the theatre. It had recently
been whitewashed, so the smell followed the protagonist wherever he
went – a felicitous stage image from the novel! Raskolnikov had a crew
cut, wore a long black coat that was obviously too big for him, and boots
that could have belonged to a clown or a convict. He either mumbled
or spoke in a sort of double-Dutch. Sometimes, with enormous effort
and a syllable at a time, he tried to explain himself in Russian. This is
how Ginkas saw the hero of the novel. To play the part he had invited
Markus Grott, a Swedish actor from Helsinki.

This eccentric idea was very soon vindicated. Having a Raskolnikov
like this meant that all one's automatic responses to a classic text were
laid aside. The actor's difficulties with the language exposed the difficulties of getting to the real meaning of the book. Deconstruction of the
text is usually an element in the theatrical game that Ginkas sets up.
Raskolnikov's bilingualism thrust the searing meaning of the book in
our faces.

The performance developed as an absurd linguistic duel. A
young man possessed by an idea was trying to explain himself; for him
it was a matter of life and death to be understood. He was in Russia, the
home of the Great Revolution, so they must surely understand him

Plate 18   Markus Grott (centre) as Raskolnikov in Kama Ginkas's production
We Play 'The Crime', Moscow TYuZ, 1990.

here?! He just had to find the right words to explain to them his idea
about Napoleon, the ants, and ends and means. But he could not get it
across. On the contrary, he realized that the 'red' country had not had in
it for ages the people he was looking for. The close-cropped maniac in
the ridiculous boots had come looking for the home of the Revolution

and found himself in a land of Philistines who could not understand him without an interpreter. All the 'reds' were long since dead and there was only one person left, called Porfiry Petrovich, who understood Raskolnikov implicitly.

Viktor Gvozditsky played the famous investigator as an extremely skilled dissembler. He tried on dozens of masks, and played with words as masterfully as he did with Raskolnikov's soul. And suddenly through all these cat-and-mouse games there broke a moment of naked truth stripped of all ludic masks. He said: 'Who am I? I am someone who's been done in!' This was no longer the dissembler, a devil, an investigator speaking, but the author of the novel – Raskolnikov's double who had passed through the temptation of the idea of revolution, served ten years' hard labour, and come to understand the most important thing about life.

Ginkas tries to find a way to 'the most important thing' through a new physiology of the theatre. Often – especially with new audiences – his productions hurt. He goads his audience and is not afraid to throw the sordid and the divine together. He drills away until you are writhing; whereupon almost always a chorale or other heavenly music breaks in. He knows how to influence indirectly the modern member of the audience who no longer trusts the 'straight words'. In his productions truth comes through non-verbal means, such as the keening of women or the extraordinary incoherence of Raskolnikov. Ginkas has to use theatrical provocation to make old truths glow with new meaning. In *Notes from Underground* (with Gvozditsky playing the lead) he used shock tactics to convey what Dostoyevsky's 'underground' really is. He wanted to respond to the fearlessness of the writer with a fearlessness of theatrical play, but it was not understood or accepted. The hero with the 'underground consciousness' was a sophisticated hypocrite in an old dressing-gown and with a beret over one ear, who regurgitated his 'underground' at us the way someone might sick-up bad food. Crude naturalism and extreme theatricality were combined within a single production. Gvozditsky played an exhausting game with God and himself which for sheer complexity probably had no equal on the contemporary stage.

The production played to small houses despite the fact that the TYuZ auditorium was halved by installing a screen. It was Ginkas's first and last production on the main stage of the theatre run by his wife.

For years afterwards he withdrew into the 'underground' of the small space and Yanovskaya remained alone with her theatre and its large stage. After all, she was responsible not only for putting on productions but for creating a theatrical family, which for so many years she had not had. Geta was building another theatrical 'church'; Kama was only interested in his next production. This was how they divided the roles in their double-act.

Yanovskaya took Moscow by storm with Bulgakov's *Heart of a Dog*. The opening of the production in June 1987 coincided with the magazine publication of the original story, which had been banned since 1925. The flower of *perestroika* Moscow could be seen in TYuZ's auditorium at that time. As was often the case during the Gorbachev euphoria, people were more interested in the 'forbidden fruit' than in the production itself. But in fact it was the production that was new, and its content could certainly not be reduced to any political metaphor extractable from the text.

The designer Sergey Barkhin brought together two worlds within the play's space. The first was the gilded world of opera, where extras performed a parody of *Aida* (the hero's and author's favourite) amongst pillars shaped like lotuses. This confronted and as it were overflowed into, a space that was charred and stripped. The stage was carpeted with what looked like charcoal or ash. It produced an image of scorched earth, of the 'black snow' that Bulgakov had once seen in a dream.

Although the original story predicted in detail all the consequences of the revolution's experiment in creating a new person, Yanovskaya removed its satirical sting. She began the show with the plaintive howl of the blizzard, merging with the howling of people. All the actors sat on the forestage and set up a heart-rending wail, or moan, a collective complaint directed into the theatrical heavens. Then the noise gradually subsided and all that remained was the howl of the mongrel Sharik, whom Professor Preobrazhensky was going to stroke, feed up, and place on the operating table. Having arrogated to himself the rights of the creator, the Professor would produce a homunculus with a human face and a dog's heart.

Like Ginkas, Yanovskaya recognizes only one law in the theatre – the law of play, outside which no idea can be expressed. She made a theatrical celebration out of the way that Poligraf Sharikov hatched from the likeable mongrel. For the first time on our stage, *Homo sovieticus* stood there in all his revolting glory. A tall youth with a bandage on his head stepped out of the dog's skin and stretched his arms out towards his 'father', who, tearful with emotion, fought to remain vertical. Gales of laughter greeted his first words as the human Sharikov, words which he had acquired, of course, when still a dog: 'bugroff, pest' and 'stop shoving, sodyer'. Then the 'new man', whose hypophysis had been transplanted from the drunkard Klim Chugunkin, grabbed a bottle of cheap port and plugged on to it. The tune from *Aida* struck up again . . .

This production at a children's theatre presented the audience not with a political metaphor but with a vital question concerning the limits of human knowledge and man's right to interfere in the very nature of life, its holy of holies. The great experiment advertised as creating a 'new man' proved catastrophic both for Sharikov and those who created him. It was as difficult to change Sharikov back as it was to encase the Chernobyl reactor in a 'sarcophagus'. The Professor and his assistant jumped on their laboratory-made monster and murdered him (which is not in Bulgakov's original). They strangled Sharikov quickly, efficiently and silently, against all their enlightened principles and theories.

The great professor got his likeable mongrel back and was left alone with him centre stage. The black snow fell and the light slowly faded. No *Aida*, or any other theatrical sounds. Complete quiet.

Heart of a Dog was a huge success. Sharikov travelled round Europe and from one festival to another. The actors were able to buy some decent clothes and put on weight. The future seemed cloudless. Few realized at the time how dangerous the air of freedom would prove for a theatre used to existing in an enclosed space. The tours and festivals took over from working together creatively every day. New productions were few and far between and did not enjoy much success. The company began to grumble, there were uprisings, and these were put down. The idea of the theatre-home was clearly in trouble. In such a situation every production might be the last.

Geta Yanovskaya overcame the crisis, but she lost the gift of lightness. Whatever she put on subsequently, whether it was Chekhov's *Ivanov* or Offenbach's *Bluebeard*, the super-objective was to prove that she was a Director, still a Director; and this extra burden made her productions top-heavy. A simple fact became clear: the mood of a theatre-home was not determined by the Direction and the productions alone. A *gift for building a theatrical family* was also needed – that human gift which Geta's and Kama's common teacher had possessed. But when Tovstonogov began the new BDT, he made sure he obtained the right to break up the company (an extremely rare instance in Soviet circumstances) and invite in his own actors. Yanovskaya was not given this right. The era of freedom had not overcome the impossibility or extreme difficulty of obtaining a divorce from a Soviet theatrical family. Theatrical serfdom had not yet been abolished in Russia.

This makes Ginkas's case all the more interesting. Whilst Geta was trying to sort out her theatre, Kama made himself at home in one room. He was free to choose his own actors; his only commitments were to his own imagination and ideas. Every season some small project came to fruition which increased his fame as a director. When he lost his out-building, he moved into the foyer. Here he again started to play with Dostoyevsky, and put on *K. I. from 'Crime and Punishment'* (1994). This was an hour and a half monologue by K. I., that is, Katerina Ivanovna, the widow of Marmeladov and mother of Sonya. It was performed by Oksana Mysina, one of that rare breed of actresses who are clowns with deep feelings. She had three children with her, who played up to her. The acting was built around changes of masks and moods. She looked like a beanpole, wore a black unfastened coat and outsize circus-like boots, and played – frequently with no perceptible transition – a tipsy trouble-making baggage, a caring and affectionate mother, or an ecstatic Christian. At the end, in a trademark metaphor of Ginkas's, she grabbed a rope, climbed up towards the ceiling, and beat on it hysterically, praying to be let in, above, where all who suffer find comfort. This was accompanied by a surge of music.

The reviewers called this the best production of the Moscow season. I saw it myself a year later, when it was past its prime. There were no critics in the audience, just a few dozen normal-looking people, and the actress had great difficulty getting through to them. She picked arguments with them, she addressed them, she tried to draw a reaction out of them. It did not work. Her attempts at goading the audience into an area of risk did not bring them closer to K. I., they pushed them further away. The small space, which had seemed a salvation for the theatre in a time of trouble, was revealing hidden drawbacks. The theatre was losing out not in terms of numbers but in terms of theatrical experience.

Nemirovich-Danchenko once tried to convince Stanislavsky that a small studio space is dangerous for the actor's art. He felt that when the art of the stage is bottled up in a studio theatre it may be the object of an experiment which reveals qualities that are valuable for the stage generally, but it can never be as bold and exciting as in a full-scale theatre:

> There is something in the actor that expands, that develops and comes across more powerfully as a result of having to overcome the resonance of a big space; something that not only infects the auditorium but is infected by it. Something starts happening to the actor that enables him to become bigger, broader and clearer in proportion to the breadth and clarity of the auditorium's acoustic.[21]

This discussion occurred on 31 December 1917 at a turning point in Russian life and MKhT's art.

For several years Kama Ginkas and other major Russian directors deserted the big theatres for the small space. They withdrew into this ecological niche to discover a new 'performing culture'. But a number of shallower and cannier directors also went that way, because they were taken by the idea of a chamber theatre that would bring quick success and the opportunity of foreign tours. Mark Zakharov used to frighten his colleagues by saying that he would stage his next production in a lift. I have not yet seen a production in a lift, but seating the audience in the foyer, a corridor, or on the stage itself, and amputating the auditorium like a useless appendix, has certainly become the norm.

For *The Execution of the Decembrists* (1996) Ginkas had just a handful of audience on the stage of TYuZ. The play was of his own manufacture. He began rehearsing it at MKhAT in the early eighties: we thought that a documentary drama about the execution of Russia's best people, and how we cannot even hang people properly, would create a strong impression. Moreover, the subject contained all the requisite ingredients for Ginkas's theatre: fact and myth, humour and the absurd, and playing with death. But people in MKhAT regarded the play as ideologically dubious and the rehearsals soon stalled.

The years passed and Ginkas's old idea emerged in a new context – one in which death was subject to as much inflation as the rouble. When you see charred faces and dismembered bodies on your television screen from morning to night, theatrical games with death do not quite come off. The theatre of the ludic 'fact' showed us samples of the nooses and hooks with which they executed people in Old Russia, and the characters discussed in detail who stood where and the fact that the ropes broke (by the time the Decembrists were executed in 1826 the executioners had forgotten their trade as no one had been hanged in Russia for fifty years). The actors wore on their chests the names of the characters they were playing. But there was no one you could sympathize with or hate, any more than there was any of the 'stupid, living breath of man' that Ginkas is a master at showing. Not being rooted in people, the Brechtian ploys were counterproductive. The more the actors 'stepped out of' their non-existent parts and the more they 'made strange' an emptiness, the more embarrassed the audience felt, sitting up there where it had no call to be.

The central role of the Author or Historian was 'made strange' by Geta Yanovskaya. The idea was that the Author would give a dry, factual commentary on what was happening. The play relied on the fact that people actually participating in history cannot recreate the truth. Even as it is happening, history is transformed into myth, and no one can say precisely how many ropes broke, who stood where during the execution, and what he did before dying. The Historian sat in the first row with her back to the audience and gave the cues. But Yanovskaya was unable to remain dry and factual. Her civic passion got the better of her. In the end she joined the actors. She tried to raise their spirits, she showed sympathy with them, she even smoked a cigarette with them and commiserated with them over Russia's unhappy fate.

I am afraid to say that the more she suffered, the more alienated I became. My feelings, which had been blunted by the daily spectacle of slaughter, did not go out to meet the theatre. 'Straight words' delivered with a tear in the eye were rebuffed by the secret defence mechanisms with which the human psyche is equipped. Ginkas's virtuoso montage techniques had come up against something that a director must always take into account, namely not only where the 'game threshold' is today, but the 'pain threshold' as well, because in the theatre the final 'montage' is made not by the director or even the actor. It is made in the hearts and minds of the audience, who bring the street in with them. I must admit that on that evening I was a bad audience. The montage constructed in my head from the execution of the Decembrists included frames from the war in Chechnya. Theatre games were powerless before such a montage.

In 1997 Ginkas staged *Macbeth* in Helsinki with Finnish actors. Again he was attempting to extract energy from the collision between death and game. He plunged the play into a kind of primeval tribal environment not yet touched by Christian civilization. Imagine an African desert with stunted, gnarled vegetation, and a panel of scorched cloth that is suddenly pulled upwards, twists and turns like a flame, inches towards the sky, and sets there as a rock. Lady Macbeth is clinging to a bump on this crag, curled up on it like a foetus. Then imagine tents, people with bloated heads and bodies covered in bandages, carts, chariots, and dummy corpses being dragged from one end of the stage to the other and beaten with sticks. Finally, imagine a Hamlet who has decided at the very beginning of the play to kill Claudius, and you have *Macbeth* at Helsinki's City Theatre.

In Russia, Ginkas is regarded as a director of the intellectual variety. This is probably wrong. Geta is the one with brains in this family, Kama the one with intuition. He starts with an impression, he is hooked by a bright colour or a chance theme, which he works on until he has got to the bottom of it, where he occasionally discovers a powerful source (in this he probably has a lot in common with his designer Sergey Barkhin, who can respond to or back up his director's surrealistic visions). The dominant image in this *Macbeth* is the biblical one of a desert. Counterpointing it is the image of the hole. All over Ginkas's and Barkhin's world there are gaps, perforations, slits from which people appear and into which they fall. From some of these holes/wells beautiful young witches appear. From others, warriors are brought into the world. This ritual is repeated several times. The disturbing combination of barren desert and a life that continues to play and to writhe in labour, is about the most lasting impression that one comes away with from the Helsinki *Macbeth*. Ginkas has done wonders with his actors, but he has not 'died' in them. It is the extraordinary overall picture, the agility and resourcefulness of his imagination, that satisfies one's eye – and what greater pleasure is there in the theatre?

Having a body to be resurrected (Lev Dodin and Anatoly Vasilyev)

The 'lost' generation (to which the heroes of the previous chapter also belong) are those who entered our theatre at the end of the sixties and were stuck for almost two decades in a dead period of our history. Strictly speaking they were 'sixties men', but they were rejected by the bureaucrats and their own teachers alike. There was no organic changeover of generations: the feudal system in the Soviet theatre meant that only someone who possessed or could create their own theatrical home, their actor-family, their circle of playwrights and critics, and their own audience, was valid. The theatres were apportioned by bureaucrats, so it was impossible for people outside the establishment, people from the theatrical fringe, to get their hands on a 'home' of their own. There was practically no counter-culture in the Soviet theatre that could act as a source of new ideas. Neither Tovstonogov, Lyubimov or Yefremov (let alone the homeless Efros) could help their own pupils. Nor did they want to. Tovstonogov was quite open about the impossibility of letting someone into his home who had a different view of theatre from his. The more talented the pupil, the bigger the threat he posed. No one wanted to destroy their own home and abet their own 'grave-diggers'.

Nevertheless, the grave-diggers arrived and did their job. Painfully, and with an enormous delay, the necessary revision of sixties ideas was effected. The central figures in this 'revision' were Lev Dodin and Anatoly Vasilyev. They had a common historical task and the circumstances they were working in were similar, but there are no two more different directors in our theatre. Basically, they represent the two poles of the Russian stage today – the 'epic' and the 'lyrical'.

Anatoly Vasilyev was a pupil of Mariya Knebel and Andrey Popov, two faithful MKhAT-ists. Lev Dodin was a student of Boris Zon, who was a direct disciple of Stanislavsky and one of his most intelligent interpreters.[22] It is important to note their common root, and the fact that their generation grew up in the war and early post-war years.

Vasilyev is a provincial, a southerner from Rostov-on-Don. After graduating in chemistry, he joined a research vessel which plied the Pacific Ocean. What pushed the seafaring chemist into directing, I do not know. In 1968, however, just before the Soviet tanks entered Prague, he joined GITIS. In 1972 he had a studentship at MKhAT, where he began to rehearse *Solo for a Chiming Clock* with MKhAT's 'old-timers'. He was not allowed to complete the production (thanks partly to the illustrious old-timers). His expulsion from MKhAT became a seminal event in his life. Ever since then he has detested our star actors and always refers to them as 'the portraits'.

Dodin comes from an academic family. He has spent all his life in Petersburg, plied no oceans, and has no other interests than the theatre. He graduated from a theatre institute and in 1967 became apprenticed to Zinovy Korogodsky at the children's theatre, which in those days had a high profile. Like the artistic director of the BDT, the boss of the Leningrad TYuZ needed apprentices. Dodin stayed there for quite a few years in that capacity. As soon as he demonstrated that he was an independent director (this happened in 1972 and the play was Ostrovsky's *The Bankrupt*), the clouds gathered above his head. He had to leave the TYuZ and take up the life of a wandering theatre director.

Both Vasilyev and Dodin are perfectionists, but in different ways. Dodin's fanaticism is concealed beneath an outward *bonhomie*. He looks like a successful academic. Or a rabbi. He has a well-trimmed prematurely greying beard and wears a leather jacket, horn-rimmed glasses and a black jumper – he always wears black. His tone is gently authoritarian. He speaks unhurriedly, circles a subject for ages like a bird of prey, then swoops on it and reveals a completely unexpected side to it. He also directs with an endless attention to detail, to creating the pattern of life. His mind is novelistic. He 'excavates' plays from prose. A normal play does not give him room to expand; he does not feel he is author enough. He needs something that is a composition made up of several patterns, with a perspective opening into infinity. You prepare for some of his productions as if you are going on a long journey. *Brothers and Sisters* lasts two evenings, *The Devils* ten hours with two intervals in which to change planes. People bring their own food and drink with them, knowing that what they are going to is both entertaining and an ordeal. This is what our theatrical 'epics' these days are like.

Vasilyev looks like a strange mixture of Dostoyevsky and Rasputin. He has wide-set eyes, a grey apparently unkempt beard, long hair tied in a pigtail, and wears a neckerchief, a casual jacket, or a long shirt with a belt *à la* Tolstoy. He is artist, quack, holy man and wizard rolled into one. Everything about him, however, is stylish, picturesque and theatrical in a way that is neither monk-like nor very Russian. Faith and Play form part of his conception of theatre, yet his Orthodox mysticism is relieved by flashes of provocative humour. His main authors are Dostoyevsky and Pirandello. He works at the interface between religion and knowledge. He always has to find the method that lies at the bottom of any form of madness. He talks as he writes – in aphoristic agglomerations of words. He dampens critics' initiative by explaining himself in detail and with taste. He publishes his diaries before their time, taking readers into his own psychiatric laboratory. He idolizes and mythologizes the Russian 'Silver Age' of literature. Hence his particular ideals, his inner turmoil and his aversion to the box-set, which he invariably subverts. Theatre for him exists on the plane of dream. He compares it with the childhood experience of being in a cool, dark barn and watching motes of dust milling in the sunlight coming through chinks in the walls. This 'milling' is what he tries to tell us about.

It was not easy for either Vasilyev or Dodin to find their theatre. Dodin tried his luck in various places, on one occasion even staging Dostoyevsky's *The Meek One* at Tovstonogov's theatre. However, as soon as success loomed it became obvious he would not be able to stay there. In the early eighties he offered MKhAT the adaptation of Fyodor Abramov's *The House* which he had recently directed at Leningrad's Maly Dramatic Theatre. At his request, I read the play to the actors of Stanislavsky's home. The bemedalled 'realists' turned up their noses at the stench of life in a modern Soviet village. Dodin was not at that time allowed into MKhAT. And when we succeeded in giving him a production of *The Golovlyovs* (Saltykov-Shchedrin's novel adapted by Dodin himself), the process by which the production was created became a theatrical legend. For eighteen months Dodin wove a vast stage canvas a millimetre at a time, inviting the actors to co-author the script with him and attempting to inject some enthusiasm into them for this kind of cobbling together. The hopelessly out of condition body of the national theatre was strained to its limits. The first run-through lasted eight hours. Towards the end, the great ones were acting with expressions that suggested the first thing they were going to do when they got off stage was throttle this rabbi who was tormenting them with his obsessions.

Unlike Vasilyev, Dodin passed his test at MKhAT, and this may have been one of the Art Theatre's most important productions before the sunset of empire.

The director and his designer Eduard Kochergin saw Golovlyovo as a microcosm of Russia, with its boundless yet claustrophobic and paralyzing spaciousness. Kochergin shaped an acting area on MKhAT's stage from the folds of an enormous fur coat, which hung wide open around the stage perimeter. Everything in *The Golovlyovs* was contained and debrained in the embrace of this coat. At the end the fur coat fell to the stage, revealing nothing behind it. The treatment of the space was reinforced by light and sound. A mystical semi-darkness reigned throughout the production, in which icon lamps twinkled. The amplified beating of a human heart gave the spectacle a rhythm reminiscent of the liturgy.

It was appropriate that the beating of the human heart should be part of the music, as the production's dominant tone was one not of satire but of ritual and rite. These have become virtually the main element in Dodin's directorial compositions. In *The Golovlyovs* people played cards ritually, chin-wagged ritually around the samovar, drank and sinned ritually, came into and departed from the world ritually. Moreover, it was the kind of ritual that drained human psychology of all content: the form was there, but its meaning had been sucked out. The embodiment of this pure form devoid of content was Porfiry Golovlyov (Iudushka), who must count as one of Smoktunovsky's greatest acting achievements.

'Somehow the features of his face dissolved, became mealy and colourless', a critic wrote of Iudushka/Smoktunovsky in 1984. Although he was not made up, 'something mind-boggling happens to the actor's familiar face'.[23] This happened because of the recesses of the human mind that the actor was probing. Smoktunovsky touched on the mysterious interaction between word and soul, which occasionally come together and blossom but sometimes fail to terribly and are locked in enmity. In the card-game scene, Innokenty Smoktunovsky and Anastasiya Georgiyevskaya produced a masterpiece of domestic verbiage. The virtuosity of each tiny verbal gesture was matched by its physical counterpart. There was something deeply tribal, ancestral, in all this, something stretching back into the chaos of the nation's history.

'Darling mamma' and her little son, who had not yet sent her to her grave, were enjoying life as a verbal ritual.

This was one pole of speech in the production. Smoktunovsky revealed the other pole gradually and as it were independently of his character, or of his consciousness at least. Speech-making was steeped in Iudushka's subconscious and became an instrument of slow torture. He gradually wound his interlocutor in the treacly thread of his slow, deliberate speech and the victim suffocated. Smoktunovsky would say something and then check whether it had worked – whether it had thrown another loop around his victim. The rhythm was exhausting, the intonation vibrant, babbling, penetrating. He produced a stream of Russian diminutives that seemed to caress and lick the very wounds he was inflicting. With these diminutives he reduced his victim to a state of zombification. Every other word was 'God'. The actor succeeded in creating the very image and essence of *Pustosloviye* (Blather), which Shchedrin identified as a monster of Russian life whose tentacles would stretch far into the future. (In 1985, a year after the production opened, I heard the last GenSec, Mikhail Gorbachev, denouncing *Pustosloviye* from the top of Lenin's mausoleum!)

One side effect of Dodin's discussions with MKhAT was that the Leningrad authorities decided to give him the run-down Maly Drama Theatre (MDT), which was supposed to serve workers from the agricultural districts of Leningrad province. Once he had acquired his own theatre, Dodin began to 'serve' the whole world. His change in status began with the theatrical fresco *Brothers and Sisters*, which he created from Fyodor Abramov's novel. It was as though he was putting an historical foundation beneath his production *The House*, since the action of *Brothers and Sisters* lay not in the 1970s but in the first years after World War II.

The production was mainly performed by young actors who had been students of Dodin's. They were well trained and Dodin had the advantage of Lyubimov's experience of directing *The Wooden Horses*. The leader of the Taganka had been ostracized and Dodin obviously intended to pick up his baton. What was actually daring was that the saga of collective-farm life was to be acted by urban intellectuals – boys and girls just out of drama school.

They began not with invention, but with an act of memory. They recalled that once upon a time in its early years MKhT's actors had gone to Khitrov market to 'study life' for their production of Gorky's *The Lower Depths*. In exactly the same way Dodin and his actors decamped to Archangel province in the north, much to the derision of our theatrical Philistines. They spent the summer in Abramov's home village, which had not changed since the war. They studied and assimilated the people's speech there; that special northern accent and intonation in which the soul of a person is indelibly imprinted. They discovered dozens of nuances in this accent, which were subsequently used to brilliant effect on the stage. It is always embarrassing when actors imitate the way the people speak. Dodin's actors did not do this. They mastered the *intonations* of the people's life, and this was enough to portray it totally convincingly.

Right across the middle of the stage was a large panel like the wall of a peasant hut, made up of old, undressed logs. To either side of the proscenium arch was a long curved wooden pole. These poles were fixed at the bottom and could be swung downwards to shut off the stage, or up again to open it for those who wanted to go in. Then a wartime newsreel was projected on to the log 'screen' and you heard the voice with the Georgian accent over the radio. Stalin addressed the Soviet people not as 'comrades', but as 'brothers and sisters'. At the critical moment the one-time seminarist had remembered his Bible and ignored the term that he himself had made law. Then the wooden screen rose and revealed behind it a group of people peering tensely into the distance. Freeze. It was a kind of epigraph. Those very 'brothers and sisters' were looking out at us from a bygone age, from the past.

Kochergin's wooden curtain behaved rather like Borovsky's woollen curtain in *Hamlet*. It too could transform itself endlessly, releasing reserves of metaphorical energy: one moment it was the ceiling of a hut, the next the canopy of the sky, then it was the earth, then a love nest, then the oppressive image of all-levelling death.

The two evenings distilled by Dodin from Abramov's rather limp prose recreated a whole period of Russian post-war life. He used almost fifty actors in the production and managed to unite them in a single artistic will. The collective image of the dying village was recreated with a spiritual commitment that reminded one of the early MKhT or young Sovremennik.

The concept of 'people's theatre' that had been vulgarized by decades of ersatz now had its original meaning restored to it. The actor was learning a new theatrical grammar, a new sculptural and musical feeling of space. Using this rural material, Dodin created a visual theatre akin to that of Tadeusz Kantor or Bob Wilson. Only, in Dodin's case 'literature' did not take second place. The audience were taught not only how to see, but how to live. In Russia the theatrical epic cannot exist without this element of didacticism.

The post-war Soviet village, like the pre-revolutionary one of Golovlyovy, existed on the stage through its canonical rituals and myths. The spectacle cohered around biblical ritualistic symbols. For instance, during the first post-war sowing the women 'swam' towards us in spots of light, giving fresh life to the earth with each sweep of their arms. Then there was a resurrection scene in which everyone who had been killed turned up in the village at once and rushed into the arms of their wives, old people and children. And in an image of unfertilized nature, the women of the village who had survived the war lay on their backs and suddenly formed a single huge body or sunflower begging for energy from heaven. Without parents or husbands, warmed by the sparse northern sun, they lay quite still beneath it like the spring earth waiting for the life-giving seed.

The moral and material life of the people was recreated with a meticulous poetic eye. The quilted jackets and tarpaulin boots, which made both sexes look alike; the patent leather shoes brought back from the war, which they threw off their foot cloths to try on; the smell of meat, of which they ate their fill during a public holiday for the first time in years; the fragrance of the birch twigs with which they resurrected their bodies in the steam bath; the loaf of bread that is not cut but broken into many pieces in biblical fashion, to remember a dead father – it all found its place in this mythopoeic reworking of Soviet life.

The production was totally free of any patriarchal illusions. It told the story of the collective self-destruction of the nation. There was something satanic about this in itself. These people had defeated fascism in someone else's country, but after the war they set about destroying themselves even more ruthlessly.

In the self-destruction of the people, art played a special role. Dodin began the second part of *Brothers and Sisters* by projecting on to the log screen clips from the model Stalinist screen comedy *The Kuban Cossacks*, which had been made in the early fifties at a time of faminine in order to provide a 'parallel reality'. A sea of grain poured over the screen, the rural beauty queens flashed their smiles, a chorus of triumphant voices celebrated the record harvest, then the 'screen' rose imperceptibly and beneath it stood the same people as before: the poverty-stricken, dying village was watching a masterpiece of the Russian cinema. The song about the harvest continued to roar out, whilst the stream of grain now beat down not on the wooden screen but over the villagers, over their prison jackets, over their sorrowful, dear, wary, joyful faces. Yes, joyful. In their collective portrait of the village, the director and his actors also captured this extremely important point: the nation carried on destroying itself whilst believing in an imminent communist paradise that was to compensate for all its sacrifices ('we are starving, but look at the Kuban – it's already a land flowing with milk and honey').

This theatre was offering a new level of existence for literature in the theatre and a new level of existence for the actor on the stage. The young actors were united not in hatred, but in love. They loved those they were telling the story about and were clearly proud of their ability to express on the stage those extremely difficult things known collectively as 'the structure of the people's life'. Dodin had produced a company of artists possessed of a common faith and capable of staying together for a long time. With *Brothers and Sisters* Leningrad was clearly acquiring another theatre-home; one of those theatres where a production is more than a production, where the biography of the theatre takes shape with that of the audience, who look at themselves in the mirror of their theatre and make the kind of demands of it which by definition are never made of 'theatres for acting's sake'.

The birth of a theatre-home in Russia is an extremely rare occurrence (I should think there have been only ten this century). Essentially it is an event of national cultural significance. It happened in March 1985 in the still unrenamed city of Leningrad. After showing the local authorities their eight-hour production, the actors of the MDT, the new 'brothers and sisters', spilled out on to the empty streets in the early hours of the morning. They did not know the fate of their baby yet, although one of the bosses had even burst into tears at the end of the marathon, either from fright or from appreciation. It was one of those special cases when the production could not be mutilated in the usual way by cutting a few lines and retouching others. The work was so powerful and large that it had either to be cut off at the root or left entirely alone.

The actors were in no hurry to split up, and wandered through the night streets. As dawn approached, they noticed that people were beginning to hang black banners on the buildings. The actors were scared by the strange coincidence: perhaps the mourning was for their production? At that time in the day no one knew why the 'cradle of the Revolution' was being decked in crêpe. A few hours later the secret was out. During the night of 11 March 1985, the birth-day of the production, Konstantin Chernenko had died. The era of the great Blather was over, and with it the theatre it had engendered. The new 'brothers and sisters' would have to demonstrate the viability of their 'home' in quite different historical circumstances.

For Vasilyev, getting his own theatre together was a much more painful experience. In the mid-seventies, having been driven out of MKhAT, he went to various Moscow theatres with ideas that seemed barmy. He was avoided like the plague. He suggested to the Theatre of the Soviet Army, for instance, where I then worked, that he direct for them the famous musical comedy from Stalinist times *Wedding at Malinovka*, and tried to work up some enthusiasm in our military men for his idea of having plywood tractors ploughing plywood fields. Even then he looked upon socialist realism as a particular style that he was prepared to master theatrically.

He got his first 'home' at the end of the seventies. The Moscow bureaucrats decided to give the Stanislavsky Drama Theatre to Andrey Popov and three of his students. There Vasilyev managed to put on the original version of Gorky's *Vassa Zheleznova* (1978) and Viktor Slavkin's *The Grown-Up Daughter of a Young Man* (1979) – two productions that rocketed him into the ranks of the country's best directors.

The fact that it was the first (pre-revolutionary) version of Gorky's play that Vasilyev chose was not just an attempt to shock literary scholars. To reject the 'second version' (made in 1935) was to reject the Soviet ideology that Gorky succumbed to towards the end of his life. Vasilyev returned to the original and began a 'slow reading' of what had happened in the house of the rich Volga merchant's wife Vassa Zheleznova. This analytical method was undoubtedly derived from Stanislavsky and his ability to create a novel about human life from a play. The emphasis on narration, however, concealed a tightly coiled spring. The audience were being asked to follow something different from what they were used to. Vasilyev had essentially begun an experiment in saving 'psychological realism' and the acting technique that the founder of MKhT had been looking for. In classic Method terms, the plot was driven not so much by its destination/purpose (which was extremely vague) as by the weight of the past, the hidden force of an original event.

Life in Vassa Petrovna's house began at dawn. Some anxious doves were walking up and down in a cage high above the stage. Their cooing was strangely interwoven with the sound of blues. A maid was tittering over a cheap novel. She read for a long time, then got up, came downstage, and performed an intricate *pas* as she stretched her numb limbs. The members of the household started to come in. Vassa (Yelizaveta Nikishchikhina), a short woman, the 'boss of the Volga', went over to the mirror and untied her hair. In shuffled her brother Prokhor (Georgy Burkov), exhausted by a night of debauchery, in his socks and white nightshirt with a fur coat thrown over the top. The samovar was brought in and they sat down ritually round it. Vassa's son Pavel (Vasily Bochkaryov) appeared. He was a hunchback and it was his wife that his uncle had spent the night with. Pavel stared fiercely at everyone present, then ran upstage, beneath the doves, flung open the door on to the street, and informed the world with a blood-curdling whoop: 'Zheleznov's wife's a whore!'

You could have retold the story of the production as a detective novel, but the tension was not verbal, it was theatrical. It seemed to come from the very air that Vasilyev had managed to conjure up on stage. He had a very strong ally in the designer and architect Igor Popov, who from then on became his permanent co-author. He divided the space of Zheleznova's house into two unequal halves along a diagonal (this low wall or curtain, setting up two worlds that mirror each other, became for many years the trademark of Vasilyev's productions). Behind the off-white wall Zheleznov senior was dying; there, so to speak, was the realm of death, whereas on this side a weird life went on which the production was to investigate. The wall was decorated with a pattern used by Frants Shekhtel in his design of the Art Theatre. This quotation reminded us of the era of the Russian *moderne* in which the first version of the play was performed, but also of Vasilyev's recent past. The nervous cooing of the doves filled the pauses in the performance, suggesting that this world was going to come to a bad end.

Zheleznova's family was trying to 'break free'. The whoremonger and rapist Zheleznov senior, whose death everyone was waiting for; his sons, riddled with syphilis and impotence; the profligate Prokhor, who had violently seduced his dotty nephew's wife; the maidservant, who strangled the baby she had by Vassa's son; and, finally, Vassa herself – they all wanted to 'be free'. In this production, the traditional social themes associated with a fight over an inheritance, which Gorky had writ large, were transformed out of all recognition. It was not about inheritance. Under Vasilyev's microscope it became about the nature of Russia's so-called 'liberation' in the Revolution.

Each of the three acts was a section through this 'freedom'. In the first, when Zheleznov senior was dying behind the wall, the craving for release took the form merely of wild, lawless explosions of sensuality. The household was beginning to go on the rampage. The 'social' was reflected in the carnal with a frankness not seen on our stage before. The second act was all confessions, admissions and hysterics. This tale of human life was revealing what might be called the 'underground' of 'freedom'. The pernicious hatred among these people led to the first earth tremors: the maidservant was killed and the hunchbacked Pashka tried to kill his uncle. In the third act a bacchanalia of 'freedom' broke out.

The old man died. There was no one in charge any longer. Vassa, pursuing some secret vision of her own, let go of the reins. In a similar way, some enlightened capitalists at the turn of the century had invested money in the Russian Revolution and later committed suicide (for example, Savva Morozov, one of MKhT's first backers). The intoxicating poison of so-called freedom produced an orgy of bestial passions. In a fit of impotent rage, and screaming threats of murder, the hunchback grabbed a basket full of dove's feathers and sprang monkey-like through space scattering them all over the stage. The house began to whirl in a white dance of death. As the family went for each other, you saw the extent of that other catastrophe, which Vasilyev had 'read into' the pauses in Gorky's play written a year before the outbreak of World War I and four years before the Russian Revolution.

Moscow was astonished by the production. Twenty years after the Sovremennik and fourteen years after the appearance of the Taganka, a new theatre company was being born. Famous actors and ones whom nobody knew were becoming 'brothers and sisters' in another family. They were becoming master craftsmen who in addition to their individual traits bore the unique imprint of their 'home' and of Vasilyev's lyrical gift. Many years later Vasilyev was to borrow his friend Grotowski's terminology and talk of 'vertical' theatre, of the religious, spiritual basis of an actor's profession. He began his quest for such a theatre in *Vassa*. The actor's flesh and spirit existed here in a new unity. What interested the director was not the problem of 'sex' as it confronted the hypocrisy of sexless socialist realism, or even the contradictory wholeness of man that Efros's directing was concerned with and from which Vasilyev had learned. The behaviour of man in *Vassa* was so unpredictable that you had to think not so much in terms of his 'contradictory wholeness' as of his genetic ability to 'throw up varieties'. The new psychology revealed man not as a tight unity but as a set of possibilities; and this alluring idea began to be 'read' on the stage for the first time. Although in the case of *Vassa* the theatrical structure was rough, the idea sprang from deep lyrical sources. Vasilyev was using the theatre to explore his relationship with himself.

Moscow did not realize at first what had happened. The critics had grown used to the idea that nothing could ever happen in our cosy swamp, so they were wary. It was Vasilyev's second production, *The Grown-Up Daughter of a Young Man*, which made them reassess *Vassa*. The new production put forward similar theatrical ideas, but used more accessible material. Slavkin's play was about the 'sixties men', a generation with whom Vasilyev had his own score to settle. There was the same diagonal wall, but it cut across the space of a standard Soviet flat. Details ruled here, too: the actors prepared a salad in the kitchen, cut up cold potatoes, shelled eggs, etc., but it was all a theatrical game in which the real-life minutiae were necessary in order to recall time past 'in detail'. And people did remember it! From the swamp of stagnation, from the disgrace of submission and mental impoverishment, Vasilyev transported us back to the era of the Thaw. By musical and three-dimensional means he recreated the pitiful yet beautiful image of our 'homeland in Time'. Drainpipe trousers, crêpe-soled shoes and jackets with massive shoulder pads were rescued from attics, ties were knotted in unbelievable fashions, and records of underground boogy-woogies were played that had been made by our virtuosi using old X-ray plates (this was known as 'jazz on the bones'). Vasilyev was calling the dance of a whole generation – a dance of liberation, of despair, of failed hopes.

The director was tapping one of the most powerful sources of energy in the theatre: the energy of recreated time. Our 'homeland in Time' may be terrible, but it is the only one we have got. This is why in this production 40-year-old people danced their hearts out to the cha-cha and a Muscovite saxophonist produced improvizations that set your soul on fire.

But Vasilyev's luck did not hold. The new theatre spoilt the picture of a controlled process. Like the saxophonist, Vasilyev might come up with some unexpected improvization. His theatre had to be destroyed. It was done very cleverly: the easy-going Andrey Popov was removed and shunted back to MKhAT to play Chekhovian intellectuals, and a new artistic director appointed who was as colourless as the times themselves. The reckoning was that Vasilyev would not put up with this, and would walk away. Which is what he did. Lyubimov gave him refuge on the second stage of the Taganka. Here Vasilyev revived *Vassa Zheleznova*, and later, when Efros took over, rehearsed another play by Slavkin, *Hoopla*, but without having any contact with Efros.

Again the play was about Vasilyev's own generation – those who lacked the courage to step out of the flow of time and say 'no'. Some sixties friends arrived at a dacha to spend the weekend together, 'unpacked' the house after its hibernation, unboarded the windows, warmed themselves up, reminisced about their past life together, and attempted to pick up the threads. It proved impossible. They boarded up the house again and parted. In this simple story Vasilyev endeavoured to hear the voice of other worlds. He constructed a house, around which he seated the audience, and created a space unmarked-off from them by footlights (as a rule, from now on he would do anything to get rid of the footlights in his productions). After two years of rehearsals the performers could dance and sing songs fantastically. Albert Filozov, who played the lead, even learnt to play the piano (in all of Vasilyev's productions people sing, dance and play a piano). The director was creating what Michael Chekhov used to call a 'musical score of atmospheres'. With the aid of this score the audience were to glimpse some other reality. Vasilyev created a particularly clear-cut, translucent style of acting. As Meyerhold once dreamed, the people and their characters became not an end, but a means to creating a mystical and lyrical mood.

Vasilyev achieved this idea of Russian theatrical symbolism with visual means that bordered on literalism. He seated his contemporaries around a table with a starched white cloth on it, put the texts of people from the 'Silver Age' into their hands, and gave them impossibly beautiful glasses containing wine of a fabulous garnet colour. You heard works from a bygone age and voices came together and parted in a complex musical composition. It was not a reading but a spellbinding mixture of theatre and spiritualist seance. The actors tuned themselves like supersensitive antennae, so as to step out of themselves and let the past 'sing *them*', as Grotowski would put it. In *The Golovlyovs* the 'epic' Dodin told a tale about the blighting of the national language. Simultaneously, the 'lyrical' Vasilyev was attempting to penetrate to the unsullied sources of this national language.

He was not allowed to complete the experiment. Efros, naturally, had no time for *Hoopla*. Vasilyev packed his production like a suitcase and went out into the night. When *glasnost* arrived, he put *Hoopla* on at numerous festivals in Europe and America and discovered what real fame is. On the crest of this wave, in 1987 he finally set up his own theatre in a cellar on Vorovsky Street and called it 'The School of Dramatic Art'. This theatre soon folded and the actors to whom Vasilyev had brought fame and foreign travel left him. He started again from scratch and turned his cellar into an aesthetic retreat, a small monastery if you like, from which the 'uninitiated' would be barred. The history of this little monastery in the 1990s is another response to the question-mark hanging over the future of the Russian theatrical idea. Vasilyev's response can only really be understood against the background of the respectable European theatre company that Dodin was setting up in the same years.

Dodin's theatrical strategy during the period of freedom has been little studied. Since the end of the eighties he and his actors have consciously existed in two worlds: six months in Russia and six outside. This way of theatrical life needs to be seen in a wider context, however.

Freedom confronted the artists of theatrical Russia with problems that have been well known for ages. They can be summed up in a single word: money. For the first time in decades artists had to think of the box-office and learn how to pronounce the new foreign words *sponsor* and *producer*. The concepts of *commercial* and *non-commercial* theatre simply had not existed in the USSR; everyone was under the state's thumb and was paid from one purse. The thumb was no longer there, but the purse had gone too. Dodin had to think of himself and his theatre in a new set of circumstances, ones in which an entertainment industry had sprung up overnight, television was purveying *chernukha* daily, and the congresses of people's deputies were competing with the circus. Directors who had previously been deeply in the shade shot to the fore. It was at this time, for instance, that Roman Viktyuk's star began to ascend above Moscow. Viktyuk shocked our pious city with the brashness of his 'gay theatre'. Some directors were cashing in on previously forbidden themes, others acquired a 'profitable position' working with the new government, others were skulking in outbuildings, cellars and attics, having cut themselves off from so-called mass audiences. The biggest test awaited those who wanted to keep their audience but did not want to kowtow to the new masters. The challenge was, how to develop the traditional idea of the theatre-home in a situation where everyone was buying or selling?

Dodin and Vasilyev were probably the first to overcome the 'prisoner mentality' and offer Russian theatre on the world's touring and festival markets. Others rushed to join them. Russia was in fashion and not much was expected of Russians at that time: something about Chekhov and Stanislavsky, and a bit about how we had suffered and been persecuted. What had become a commodity for theatre businessmen to buy and sell was for people like Vasilyev a source of agony turning to disgust for the whole current theatrical scene. When I met him at the Avignon Festival in 1988 (where they were playing Pirandello), the founder of the 'School of Dramatic Art' tossed off the enigmatic statement: 'A month's touring in the West and Russian theatre is finished.' I was very soon able to appreciate how far-sighted this diagnosis was.

At the MDT they were well aware of the perils of going out into the capitalist cosmos without spacesuits. Dodin has said that at first he had to *force* his actors not to try and save their daily allowance but to eat well in order to conserve their strength for the evening's performance. These master-actors accustomed to eating out of tins had to give Europe and America the kind of Russian theatre that since the times of Stanislavsky had only been a legend there. Dodin presented *Brothers and Sisters* followed by the student production *Gaudeamus* and Dostoyevsky's *Devils*, that is, fundamentally different things deriving from different traditions of the Russian and European stage. For many serious theatre people in the West it was a revelation. Peter Brook, having seen the Petersburg ensemble in Paris, came to Russia for a few days to see their other productions and understand the Russian miracle which for want of other words we call the *theatre-home*. In spring 1994 he told me that Dodin's ensemble occupied in European art the place that for many years had been held by Strehler and his theatre in Milan. He was referring to the feeling of a golden mean, the ability to stand above both the so-called tradition and the so-called avant-garde; to transcend these extremes in an art of *'grand style'*.

The fact that the theatre from Petersburg took off in the West certainly did not mean that it would have an easier time in Russia. On the contrary, the more successful Dodin's company was abroad, the more difficult it got for him at home. Critics shaped by the idea of the theatre-church could not get used to the idea of the MDT 'church' being empty for half of the year at a time. A 'service' that was held principally abroad did not suit the Russian theatrical congregation. Natalya Krymova, the most authoritative critic of the sixties generation and incidentally Efros's widow, commented thus on Dodin's fame in an article about the MDT's autumn 1995 Moscow season (the first time it had played there for eight years):

> One might merely have rejoiced at the sensational news that the MDT is 'Russia's best theatre' and Lev Dodin 'the world's number one director', but it raises some questions. Which of the newspapermen *knows* the whole of theatrical Russia? Which directors' names are on the list in which Dodin is number one?

And she concluded characteristically: 'The MDT's reputation today was made somewhere where we aren't. That's why there are all these questions.'[24]

Dodin began to be written off in Russia almost as soon as he had his big successes in the West.[25] He tries not to react to this, and does not read the newspapers (or so he says). He is busy with other things. Basically, he is trying to save the ideology and practice of the theatre-home in a country that has not yet heard of income tax and national insurance. He has not let a square inch of theatrical space to the 'new Russians', despite the fact that he has a theatrical family of fifty actors and seventeen students to feed. His worries are profoundly traditional for this type of theatre. How to combine the 'old-timers' who began the theatre with the generation that has grown up with *Gaudeamus* and *Claustrophobia*? How to curb actors' egos and solve the hundreds of everyday problems inherent in the way that a group of artistic people live?

To create a theatre-home is very difficult, to keep it together almost impossible. It used to be thought in MKhT that the life of such a theatre is eighteen to twenty years, and Dodin is nearing that mark. He does not put on many new productions, and can rehearse for months or even years if necessary. In Paris or London the company continue with their daily exercises as though they were in Petersburg. They take teachers with them for their exercises, rather as Russian families used to take tutors abroad with them. Building up the family from within has become part of the daily routine. Nothing is too small to matter. Disaster threatens on every side (this obsession is also very reminiscent of Stanislavsky). They are therefore always on the alert and turn theatrical routine into a matter of conscious service. They still all assemble before each performance to 'centre' themselves, to 'get away from the street' and attune themselves for acting. The mood backstage communicates itself instantly to the stage, so it has to be kept in its place, has to be quelled every day by means of small and large rituals, friendly gatherings, games and celebrations. Just like his mentors, Dodin is afraid of the home being destroyed and hardly allows any other directors into his theatre. So, warily and defending itself on all fronts, one of our last theatrical 'homes' survives in market conditions.

Its latest productions have opened not in Petersburg but in Paris or Weimar. *The Cherry Orchard* and *Claustrophobia* were first played as part of a Russian season in France. They are two theatrical faces of Russia, past and present, linked by a feeling of catastrophe hanging over the country. In *Claustrophobia*, moreover, Dodin's theatre moved into the 'new Russian prose', which has been completely ignored by the theatre and most of Russian society. In Paris people reacted to the 'sweet-smelling mixture of blood and excrement' differently from in Russia.[26] Having no common language with the actors, or common memory, the Parisians simply enjoyed the vividness of the metaphors running through the show and the energy of young actors presenting a ghastly image of an unknown country. In Russia itself the 'blood and excrement' of the show were indistinguishable from the colour and stench of life outside it, and people reacted badly to Dodin's new aesthetic that attempted to combine the absolutely beautiful with the absolutely ugly.

The cacophonous Russian press concluded that Dodin was moving towards a new theatrical palette. They interpreted the fact that in *Claustrophobia* the blinding white space of the dancing class was transformed into a cosmic rubbish dump, as a philosophical statement. 'The white begins to colour, to crumple up, to wrinkle, to tear, to froth. What was pure becomes spotted. What was untouched has by the end been soiled by handling, become bedraggled, dog-eared, beaten senseless. It pongs, it stinks.' The text and the action were interpreted as being in counterpoint to the sculptural/painterly aspect, and again received a different explanation in Moscow from Paris: 'There are three leitmotivs: *mat* (swearing), excrement, and sex (copulation in public). They are supposed to corroborate the sense of universal madness that the sophistic-ated Petersburg theatre wants to wail about *urbi et orbi*.'[27]

In Russia people did not restrict themselves to an aesthetic appraisal of Dodin's new still lifes. They reproached him with making money out of the nation's misery. Productions created for export were suspected of being 'committed' to one thing. It looked as though willy-nilly Dodin was giving foreigners what they wanted to see. Basically, our old phobias were coming out again: in Russia people do not want to believe in reputations made 'where we are not'.

At one pole a home, at the other a monastery into which Russia's 'the-atrical lyricism' has retreated. You will recall that Vasilyev's theatre opened in the basement of an old house in Moscow on Vorovsky Street (which has now been renamed Povarskaya). For a theatrical heretic it is a very symbolic street. It was here that in 1905 Stanislavsky and Meyerhold founded their famous studio. It lasted only a few months, tore its founders apart for ever, and thereby determined the fate of twentieth-century Russian theatre.

Vasilyev's theatre also promised much. Its first production, *Six Characters in Search of an Author*, began a new and apparently happy cycle in Vasilyev's quest. But the honeymoon was soon over. The group of actors with whom he had begun the school, created the Pirandello and toured the world, fell apart. It is difficult to say why. Maybe Vasilyev does not have the 'familial' gene in his theatrical blood and is physiologically incapable of being a diplomat, nanny and psychoanalyst all at once, as the part of 'father of a theatrical family' demands in addition to directing. He does not keep a constant eye on what makes an actor tick, on what he is acting today and what he will be acting tomorrow. Vasilyev's theatre is, above all, him. He is all for actors as co-authors, but can only tolerate pupils and followers. As soon as an actor becomes a 'portrait', as soon as he starts to look at his watch during rehearsals, he is wasting his time working with Vasilyev.

Vasilyev often reminds me of the old women in Erdman's *The Suicide* who are worried by the fact that corpses are being cremated rather than buried. They are afraid that on the great day people will have 'no body to be resurrected'. For Vasilyev this is not a joke. His actors hardly ever work in films or television. He knows how quickly actors' muscles deteriorate there; that once their faces are known to millions they lose their individuality. 'What will we have left to be resurrected with?' becomes for him 'what will we have left to act with?'

Whilst Dodin was conquering the world, Vasilyev withdrew into laboratory research. He stopped directing work that was accessible to the public. He stopped staging productions and lost interest in audiences. From the early nineties onwards the School on Povarskaya virtually closed its doors to 'laymen'. He created a theatre not for audiences but for those making this theatre. The basement turned into an experimental workshop in which he studied Plato, Homer, Thomas Mann, Pushkin, Molière and Dostoyevsky. Vasilyev severed all links with the 'open praxis' of the new Russian stage.

I shall not attempt to describe the five years up to 1995 that Vasilyev spent in his retreat on Povarskaya. I hardly ever went there and the videos of his main experiments do not convey the theatre's essence at all. I did not see *The Devils*, Molière's *Amphitryon*, the Pushkin programmes, or the 'visible Homeric hexameters'. But I did see the production about Plato's *Republic*, in which five performers juggled with abstract ideas. The actors attempted to understand how human thought works and how these workings can be expressed theatrically. Socrates conducted a dialogue about the perpetual problems of organizing a state. What is power and do people derive pleasure from it, how should people be ruled, and what should be regarded as just? The object of the theatre was not character, but language, the way the brain is actually organized. The latter operated here rather like a computer. Socrates asked his interlocutors questions that could only be answered 'yes' or 'no'. They were given no other alternatives. 'Perhaps' is no good for a computer. So we were drawn into a bizarre theatrical game in which the philosopher wore his interlocutors out. He channelled the flow of thought on the stage and his opponents' brains could not withstand this extraordinary intellectual drill driving into them. 'Yes or no, yes or no!' he kept repeating, and in the end his interlocutor collapsed lifeless. Then the philosopher would stand over his defeated rival and go on asking him questions and tormenting him with his 'yes or no?'. There was no 'psychology', or even the dregs of psychology. The performing artist perched upon the person he was playing like a statue on a plinth. He did not just play a part, he played with the part, and this genuinely rejuvenated the very terms of theatrical existence.

Plato's *Republic* was acted in a tiny space surrounded by scaffolding and builder's rubbish. In the early 1990s work began on redesigning the basement. The philosophers in white (Vasilyev cannot imagine his theatre outside this colour) conducted their dialogues walking over rubble. Thus although the director was cut off from Russia's problems, having retired into his monastery to do only theatre, the air of the times seemed to penetrate even here.

By the winter of 1996 Vasilyev's basement had been transformed. The floor of the room above had been taken out, revealing the painted ceilings of a sumptuous property built in 1913. A stunningly beautiful little two-tiered theatre had been produced. It has no footlights, of course,

Plate 19   Anatoly Vasilyev in the 1990s.

but a single white space that can be soaked with light and colour as though it were canvas. The theatre machinery is not just exposed, it has been made part of Igor Popov's architectural design. He and Vasilyev returned from their stay at the Comédie Française with the idea for a huge wooden wheel like the ones used in Molière's time to move scenery. This now stands on the second level, where inquisitive members of the audience can inspect it and touch it. The actors' dressing-rooms are also open to look around.

That winter, the 'School of Dramatic Art' opened its first production in the new theatre and for the first time in five years invited in the public. The new house was consecrated with *The Lamentations of Jeremiah*, set to music by Vladimir Martynov and sung not by actors but by a church choir, the Ensemble of Ancient Russian Ecclesiastical Music. The poster told us that the 'scenography and *mise-en-scène*' were by Vasilyev.

This production is a theatrical prayer on the theme of the 'solitary, comfortless and despised Jerusalem', whose fame is fled. The 'Lord is righteous' and has destroyed the land that trampled on his commandments; its children are starving, the rod of the Lord's wrath has brought the prophet into darkness, and he has become a 'mark for arrows'. 'My soul is humbled in me', Jeremiah cries out, and tries to comfort his people beset by enemies. These are the themes of the church singing, which is in several sections with pauses to let the production breathe. This is 'vertical' theatre, operating through sound, setting and atmosphere. The parquet floor has been polished until it shines, and the choir changes its robes from black to white and from white to sky-blue. In the decorative white wall that as always in Vasilyev bisects the acting area, arches and windows have been cut. These immediately give you the feeling of a Russian cathedral and the square in front of it. The choir raise their lamentation and ritually light hundreds of candles fixed to the wall. White doves, which Vasilyev first used two decades ago, wander all over the parquet, then noisily fly upwards and settle on the wall. And suddenly this 'cathedral' wall starts to tip forwards. It is as though the doves had set the massive object in motion with their infinitesimal weight. It covers us with its shadow. For a few seconds the choir disappear from sight and all you can hear is their ascending voices. We are left alone with a spirit-filled space. It is theatre without actors, space without people, but you are incredibly moved by the soul of the art being created before you. 'Remember O Lord, what is come upon us', the last lamentation goes up, the choir put on blue cloaks with hoods, and the bearded singers, all looking like Vasilyev, process along the white wall. The burning wax crackles and the doves coo loudly and anxiously, mingling with the prayer. As usual in Vasilyev, the theatre starts on a light breath, seems to rise out of nothing, then shimmers off into purity and the void. At the end, there are only the still-burning candles and the doves walking boldly all over the deserted square, which is lit by a fading evening light.

Your soul is left in a state of peace and tranquillity. This is a rare, indeed virtually unique feeling in today's theatre. Evidently it was in order to preserve the sources of this tranquillity that Vasilyev had to retreat into his theatrical monastery.

Vasilyev and Dodin have not met for many years and their paths as directors do not cross. They do not see each other's productions and do not know what 'projects' are being hatched in the basement on Moscow's Povarskaya Street or on Rubinstein Street in St Petersburg. The Russian theatrical community has fallen apart; it is every man for himself. When I tell Dodin about Vasilyev or vice versa, they tense up. Even a description of someone else's work is viewed as an assault on the territory they have staked out. Nevertheless, each is extremely interested in the other's experience and fate. They are inseparable but not joined, rather like the poles on a magnet. This is why I wanted to put them side by side. 'Comparative biography' is one of the surest ways of conveying the spirit of an age: in this case what may be termed the 'epic' and the 'lyrical' in Russian theatre today.

Pyotr Fomenko's 'three cards'

Pyotr Naumovich Fomenko was born in 1932, did a teacher-training course in Moscow, then graduated from the directors' faculty of GITIS. He started work at the Moscow Theatre of Drama and Comedy (MTDK) in 1963. Chronologically he is a sixties man, but there can be no doubt that theatrically he belongs to another period. He concentrated and transfigured all the achievements of his generation, including the social ones, into his own sense of theatre – a theatre that was patently doomed.

He is fascinated by the evil that is diffused throughout life, he gives an eccentric reading of the basic human passions taken to their limits (from the joy of love to the automatism of lust), and has produced mischievous political slapstick combined with mystical guignol. These differences of opinion with the 'grand style' of post-Stalin theatre were enough for him to become an outcast from it, or more accurately, a rolling stone.

Fomenko left the MTDK and went to Moscow's Mayakovsky Theatre, where in 1966 he directed Sukhovo-Kobylin's *Tarelkin's Death*. This was one of the most sensational and promising débuts of the Thaw. Fomenko's talent was ideal for this play, which is unique even in the Russian classical repertoire. It was written in 1869 and muzzled by the censor for over thirty years. Basically, it is the only work in Russian drama that tackles the holy of holies of the state system – the police torture chamber. The playwright himself spent many years in prison suspected of having murdered his mistress. Although he was an aristocrat *pur sang*, he came up against what many of our writers suffered later. He transformed the story of his ordeals into a new literature for the theatre, thus initiating a line in Russian drama which is usually termed 'fantastical realism' (after Dostoyevsky), but which should probably be called 'mystical realism'. Here the nineteenth-century writer hit it off with the new director just starting his career, Pyotr Fomenko.

Briefly, the plot of the play is this. Tarelkin, a petty criminal in the police, fakes his own death in order not only to escape his creditors but to 'nail' a much bigger and more successful crook in the police force, with the symbolic name Varravin (in English 'Barabbin'). It is a fight, then, between members of the same gang. The bigger crooks catch the smaller one and torture him. The play is not satire, it is a diaboliada whose protaginists are officials and policemen – 'vampires, werewolves and mafiosi', as Sukhovo-Kobylin called them. He portrayed a life in which the 'maw' of the police and bureaucracy had gone 'mad with greed'. Unusually for Russia, virtue was totally absent from the play and there was not a single 'humane passage' of the kind that even the Russian censorsip had come to expect.

The censor found a rather original reason for banning *Tarelkin's Death*. The play would, he feared, make the audience 'shudder' and this could be dangerous. The author was proud of this assessment and developed it by saying that to shudder at evil is the highest form of morality. In pre-revolutionary Russian theatre the aesthetics of the 'shudder' were virtually undeveloped, and in Soviet theatre even more so. After the Revolution, Meyerhold staged the play as *Rasplyuyev's Happy Days*, but the play very soon fell into disfavour again. The 'happy days' of the Revolution came to an end, the state bounced back, and this 'police diaboliada' disappeared from the theatre for decades. Just before the curtain came down on our Thaw, the young Fomenko decided to risk it. In his interpretation, the play presented an image of the country as a torture chamber. It was a theatrical underworld in which the 'vampires, werewolves and mafiosi' had an uproarious time but their merriment was suffused with the gloomiest mysticism.

Before they decided to transfer it to the main stage, the production was performed in a small room hung with grey army cloth. Right in front of the audience was a coffin with its lid open, like a grand piano (a typical Fomenko ambiguity). From behind a screen emerged the hero of the piece, Tarelkin, played by Nikolay Eybozhenko. His face and hair were completely colourless, as though they had lost their pigment. The bestial grin of the fake suicide and the albino's mask that he was wearing portended extraordinary events. An atmosphere of spine-chilling fear was created, well described decades later by Yevgeny Lazarev, who played Rasplyuyev in the production: 'Out of these dark depths anything could materialize and instantly disappear again: rooms, taverns, the police station, cells, torture chambers . . . Spies – police ones and civil service ones – suddenly appeared from nowhere and whisked someone off. It was amazing how in such a small room something very Russian was conjured up: spacious and dark, not lit by electricity, a bit drunk, and dangerous.' Amongst the music accompanying the diaboliada, you would suddenly hear snatches of rousing Soviet marches, and to this music 'searches were being carried out everywhere, everyone was being trailed, and there were informers, informers, informers . . . That one there, did he turn into something? Yes he did: he turned into a wall!'[28]

This was not the European absurd, or even the Soviet variety, it was the pan-Russian absurd that grew out of the depths of our Tatar–Mongol slavery, our feudal servitude and our utter contempt for the human being. 'Spacious and dark, a bit drunk, and dangerous' also described the perspective of 'mystical realism' that had not been employed in the Russian theatre since the times of Meyerhold and Michael Chekhov. Fomenko pointed his production in the direction of the 'shudder at evil' and it got there. The Varravins of the time said 'Goodness no' and it was removed from the repertoire.

The banning of this production was a turning-point in Fomenko's life. His company was dispersed between the two capitals and he spent a lot of time shuttling between them. But whatever theatre he moved into, he had no difficulty in tempting his 'birds' to act for him. He hears the music of 'mystical realism' but is equally at home with lyrical farce. His versatility comes from his being a *skomorokh*, that is, one of Russia's medieval wandering actor-minstrels. However, he is one of those *skomorokh*s who remember their past – the time when they used to have their tongues torn out and were not allowed to be buried in a graveyard with ordinary people.

Interestingly, Fomenko is a trained violinist. Musical principles inform his directing, but quite often they leave it high and dry with an effect that is melancholy, cloying, and says nothing. In the mid-seventies, for instance, he directed a play by Gennady Nikitin called *The Muse* which was subtitled 'My Friend Mozart'. The reason Mozart came into it was that the hero, a drunk called Marasanov, had learned to play the violin when he was a boy and decided along with two of his drinking partners to be reborn through Music. The action was set in a factory workshop. Rolls of paper littered the stage, and thick lagged pipes writhed weirdly up through the floor. But suddenly the whole socialist realist collage was rent asunder by a piece of staging that flung open the director's soul.

The three dipsomaniacs went to their local House of Culture to visit an old acquaintance, Muza Appolonovna, who ran a children's choir. Children appeared on the rafters in their black and white uniforms. The ethereal Muza in the shape of Olga Volkova (definitely a Fomenko actress) asked the choir to think of something really happy – 'a field, your childhood, a sea of dandelions'. And suddenly this angelic Soviet children's choir swamped us, the drunks and the whole filth-steeped world, with 'Ave, Maria'. The musical blow was sustained visually. Light was projected through the factory walls, revealing frescoes in them; the plumbing became organ pipes; and a scrap of blue sky right at the top (the hallmark of Fomenko's world) completed the composition. The drunks were bowled over. For a second the divine fire was rekindled in their souls. It was probably for the sake of this one second that the whole production was conjured out of an otherwise non-existent play.

What Fomenko finds absorbing is the moment when 'reality' is transfigured into art. In the 1970s he directed Mayakovsky's *A Buffo Mystery Play* in an adaptation by Mark Rozovsky at the Lensoviet theatre. He tried to combine political slapstick with the art of the mystery play. He 'made strange' Mayakovsky's agitprop with touches of biblical sublimity, and even ended with the Sermon on the Mount. Naturally, the production was banned.

For Fomenko 'buffo mystery' is not just the name of a play, it is the best definition of his kind of theatre. 'Buffo mystery' is for him life at breaking-point. It is precisely this breaking-point that interests him. Acting is a part of this worldwide buffo mystery and is more than a 'profession'. Anyone who has penetrated the mystery of transfiguration and communion, who has fallen and got up again, sinned and repented, anyone who has heard his 'Ave, Maria' at least once, is no longer hopeless. Whether Sukhovo-Kobylin's vampires or Ostrovsky's wolves, sheep and 'more sinned against than sinning', in Fomenko's composition they are all immersed in a world that is constantly play-acting. They all play the fool and feign ignorance. The brotherliness of actors and their depravity are indissolubly linked.

For Fomenko, man wears no labels. He is in flux, he is light and dark, and he is capable of *actes gratuits* which the director revels in recording. Fomenko's heroes play various games. They play with love, power, life beyond the grave, and in fact with death, which preoccupies Fomenko enormously – to the very depths of his comedian's soul. He sometimes treats it with awe and respect, sometimes rudely as in fairground theatre. He teases death and hurls theatrical curses at it. The hero of his production of Eduardo de Filippo's *Exams Are Never Over* (1978), a pathetic character by the name of Guglielmo Speranza (which means 'Hope'), even rose from the grave to deliver a phallic gesture at death meaning roughly 'up yours!'

'Up yours!' the director himself might say, after all the 'reverses of fortune' he has experienced. His present theatrical language, despite its apparent piety, is pagan, and his best actors are aware of it. Behind his cheeky behaviour lies the tradition of the Russian *skomorokh*s, or the marketplaces of the European towns, where according to Bakhtin people delighted in despatching each other to the 'material-corporeal lower depths'. Like Zakharov, Fomenko has an instinctive understanding of 'Russian roulette', but he plays a different game. For years he incubated a production of *The Queen of Spades*, and in the end he staged it. He did not get to the bottom of the 'secret of the three cards', but he did discover something important for himself, which was that in the art of the theatre there are things that it is impossible to get to the bottom of – you just have to live with them. And that is how he has lived in recent years.

Fomenko loves enclosed space. A scrap of light blue high up, curtains jerked back to reveal 'another life', anything mysterious and dazzlingly beautiful that is hidden behind a screen: this is his theme, his image, his directorial secret. In Arbuzov's melodrama *Dear Old House* (1973), Fomenko turned the stage into an eyrie for strange bird-people. They sat on various levels like birds perched in a tree and musical instruments hung around them. The people did not so much speak as sing, twitter, exchange calls. The walls of the house merged smoothly into trees, nature, and the cosmos with its inevitable blue open space high up.

The break in the clouds of Fomenko's own directorial career came in the early eighties, when he vanished from the Soviet repertory theatre system and went to ground in GITIS. Instead of 'portraits', he acquired pupils with whom he eventually founded his Workshop. He equipped them for the period of freedom. He developed in them a special theatrical ear and an understanding of the musical nature of any verbal text. His pupils perform Ostrovsky and Tsvetayeva, Faulkner and Blok, side by side without feeling that there is any chasm between them. In the past ten years he has composed a 'pedagogic saga' of his own that replicates Lyubimov's. But his own path has been in the opposite direction from that of the Taganka. Fomenko is building not a political but a poetic theatre, and in conditions of primary accumulation of capital this has turned out to be incredibly difficult.

Having lost its principal 'homes', the Russian theatrical idea seems to have chosen Fomenko as its next victim/hero called upon to occupy the vacant seat. He was not ready to play a hero, but is attempting to do justice to the part. For several years now he has been working with his pupils on a production of *War and Peace*, which apart from anything else he regards as a very consoling book. Fomenko is quite open about the 'consolatory' function of theatre.

He keeps having heart attacks. He knows that his days are numbered, so he does not indulge in any 'King's games'. He speaks in a rather high-flown manner, often as though his listeners were not there. It is not so much speaking as casting a spell; it is as though he is obeying something within him, hearing something of his own – the music I referred to earlier, for example. And you follow not so much what he is saying as the man himself, his wonderfully sculpted head, his deep-set eyes, and his voice driving him along. This voice gets fainter every year; it is as though he is running out of breath and wants to articulate a final thought. At rehearsals he is fanatically determined to catch the rhythm of a scene, its slippery melody. Once he has found it, he does not fix it and fuss over it. His imagination is always overtaking his ability to fix something; he is always re-solving, re-positioning, re-scoring. His productions are busy crossroads. They live by their impulses, and sometimes die by them without having found their tone. But a production in which he is in tune with himself and the time is truly amazing.

Such a production was Ostrovsky's melodrama about provincial actors in the last century, *More Sinned Against Than Sinning*, which Fomenko directed at the Vakhtangov Theatre in 1993. He had returned to working with stars, but came to them rejuvenated from working with students and charged with happy energy. The critics rushed to the production like people who have caught sight of a patch of green grass after a long winter.

It was one of those occasions when, because of the context it finds itself in, a fairly ordinary play acquires a significance beyond its creator's wildest dreams. The theatre, it transpired, marked what may be called 'the end of ideology' with this melodrama. It was a vibrant fusion of spectacle, parody, songs, tears, and all the other pranks peculiar to the theatre – and it was all done without forcing, with an irresistible freedom and naturalness.

Fomenko staged this celebration in the foyer bar of the theatre before a few dozen people (the reason for this eccentric choice is given in the play, when the comic actor Shmaga remarks that an actor's place is in the bar). Utterly stereotypic Vakhtangov actors (definitely

Plate 20   Yevgeny Knyazev (left) as Neznamov and Yury Volyntsev as Shmaga in Pyotr Fomenko's production of *More Sinned Against Than Sinning*, Vakhtangov Theatre foyer, 1993.

'portraits' in Vasilyev's sense) submitted themselves to the laws of a different space and aesthetic. It was as though they had all drunk a magic potion. The stars, it seemed, were in the same conjunction as when Vakhtangov's production of *Turandot* had been born in this theatre in 1922. Fomenko not only 'remembered' *Turandot*, he had taken the idea of a new *Turandot* to its ultimate conclusion. His production was full of pure theatrical joy and its carnival spirit was also an indirect quotation from *Turandot*.

At turning-points in history the theatre talks to us about what it knows best – itself. In the play, the rich landowner who adores actresses tells us that performers are people with no security. He gives two versions of the concept of being an actor: in Europe they are proletarians, 'but in Russia they are birds of the air, who peck when grain has been put out for them, and starve when it hasn't'. In Fomenko's production these 'birds of the air' became a motley but integrated bunch of favourite folk 'types', from the philosophizing drunkard and lady's man to the 'selfless heroine'.

The director and his designer Tatyana Selvinskaya decided to ignore Ostrovsky's stage description of bleak dressing-rooms with peeling wallpaper, etc., and separate the bar from 'life' with shutters of various colours, which exposed us to or cut us off from the light of the street outside (the performances were in daytime). The big world and the theatrical microcosm reached out to each other but did not meet. The same light-play occurred throughout the space: the chandeliers were masked with coloured material, and the provincial characters themselves – both actors and non-actors – reminded one in their bright cloaks of characters from the *commedia dell'arte*. The clash of 'art' and 'life' produced carnival; but it was a very Russian carnival, a Muscovite carnival with all our passions, drunken moaning and songs in which people poured out their soul. A provincial performer, a 'bird of the air', would pluck a few strings of his guitar and his fans would melt in anticipation of the blissful melancholy that would flow from his fingers.

Almost everyone recalled *Turandot* when they saw Fomenko's production, but they recalled it in different ways. Some restricted themselves to performance ('it's the pure joy of theatre'), others tried to understand the foyer masterpiece's wider resonance. The resonance was indeed the point – the atmosphere in which it was created and which it responded to in its own way. Like Vakhtangov's, Fomenko's production appeared at a critical time for Russia. In the spring of 1922 theatrical Moscow celebrated with Gozzi's fairytale the end of the Civil War. In spring 1993 Fomenko, with a similar celebration of theatricality, marked the fact that Russia had avoided civil war and emerged from its seventy-year ordeal without, apparently, spilling blood. But this paradoxical claim cannot be proved or disproved, since the 'resonance' of a production is the air of theatre, its energy, which is everywhere and nowhere at once. It comes about on the stage and in the auditorium simultaneously; it unites the theatre and the street. Here, too, the final montage was made not by the director but by the audience. You must take my word for it, therefore, that when these provincial tragedians and comedians joined hands at the end of Fomenko's production and skipped round in a circle, breathless with delight, something quite special happened to the audience (and to me too!).

With Ostrovsky, Fomenko discovered new ways of surviving theatrically. He did not retire into a monastery, nor did he go out into the world's theatrical marketplace. For the time being he has dissolved himself in his students and kissed his native soil. Fomenko's Workshop 'home' still lacks a roof – literally and metaphorically – but the fate of this 'builder' strikes me as one of the most important in Russian art today.

He put his whole comedian's heart into Ostrovsky's melodrama. This is presumably why the carnival in the Vakhtangov foyer bar attained a significance far beyond the theatre. If you like, Fomenko's production was the long-awaited sign that we were gaining our freedom. Through Ostrovsky, he beckoned to us and made us feel that we were still alive, that the theatre was alive, that the plague had seemingly passed. These comedians, these buffoons, are amazingly, subconsciously sensitive to a change in the historical weather.

Why? Because they are 'birds of the air'.

Conclusion

It is difficult to write a concluding chapter to a book about the modern theatre. As soon as you have put the last full stop, another production comes along which demands to be taken into account or simply over-turns all your pet theories. The 'black box' of the Russian theatre is still recording, and to attempt to decipher its readings while still in flight is a thankless task. Fortunately, however, life itself has provided us with an appropriate place to end.

On 22 June 1997 the Moscow Art Theatre celebrated the centenary of Slavyansky Bazar, Stanislavsky's and Nemirovich-Danchenko's eighteen-hour meeting in the Moscow restaurant of that name at which they resolved to found a new theatrical enterprise. Two people put forward a plan for the ideal theatre. What were the results of this plan, one of whose side effects was to turn theatre directing into a super-profession of the twentieth century? This is what we were meeting to discuss.

We invited the main *dramatis personae* of the Russian stage today, as well as many of the world's major directors. The response was extraordinary, and for me very fortunate. All of the living heroes of this book (with one exception) came together and looked each other in the face for the first time since the period of freedom began. Some of them were more nervous as they came onstage than they are on their own first nights. Lev Dodin had flown in for the day from Milan, and Pyotr Fomenko had discharged himself from hospital to be there. I did not have to persuade anyone to come: it seemed to be taken for granted that if you called yourself a Russian theatre director you had to be at the Moscow Art Theatre that day.

Conclusion

The proceedings were opened by Oleg Yefremov as the host. Then Lyubimov spoke in his capacity as 'patriarch'. This must have been the first time the creator of the Taganka had appeared before theatrical Moscow since returning from his enforced emigration. He instantly reminded us of the latter with a breathtaking admission: 'I had to survive and I learnt some very hard lessons. We have forgotten how to work seriously – the way that many European actors do, for instance. Let's put an end to our stupid romanticism and self-indulgence. For seventy-five years we were taught to believe in some idiotic myths, and now we cannot get a proper grip on ourselves.'[1] He proposed starting the new millennium by completely reforming the theatre schools. He spoke of training actors as professionals who could create a theatre based on spectacle not words. Although aged eighty, he was on top form – a form seeking new content.

Lyubimov was adamant that every director is entitled to his own 'home'. The splitting of the Taganka cast a melancholy light over what he had to say. However, the idea of the theatre-home subject to a single artistic will was also questioned from a totally different quarter.

Sergey Yursky, who began his acting career in Tovstonogov's company in Petersburg, then left the theatre-home and went freelance, took issue with Lyubimov. He had come to the new Slavyansky Bazar prepared. He had written a pamphlet which he now performed on the Chekhovian boards. He astonished his audience with a series of brilliant paradoxes on the subject of 'director's theatre', which in his view indulged the director's ego and trampled on the freedom of those who from time immemorial had decided things in the theatre, that is, actors. 'Two men attempted to define the laws of theatrical creativity. They formulated these laws and it looked as though these laws would last forever, like the laws of nature. But the twentieth century became the age of lawlessness, it became as much a fight for freedom as it was an age of freedom trampled upon. We are witnessing the end of directorial dictatorship in the theatre.'

Yursky was protesting not against directing as such, but against what he called the 'wilfulness of the "boss" – the attitude not of a leader or a manager, but of a "boss" '. The director thinks he is the only artist involved and that the actors are merely paints which he squeezes out more or less skilfully onto the canvas of the stage. Yursky also had something to say about the actors:

> Actors occasionally realize how humiliating their position under a director is. They respond by trying to become stars. This is not difficult – real acting is much more difficult. Even if an actor joins the stars, he/she remains a tube of paint for the director, although this tube now costs a lot of money and above all has the right to flounce about and wind everyone up, including the great creator-director. This is the petty revenge of people who were once artists.

For his peroration the actor went over to the founders' armchairs, which we had placed on stage with a table and lamp from Stanislavsky's dressing-room, and addressed them ironically:

> Dear, sincerely respected Konstantin Sergeyevich and Vladimir Ivanovich! This season, 200 new shows have opened in Moscow. Almost every actor with a name has acquired his own theatre, or one named after him – now, even that is possible. We now have capitalism and people even boast of how much a production costs. They actually write: 'This is the most expensive show of the season, or the year, or the century, or of all times and countries.'[2] ... The most fashionable word in the theatre now is *sponsor*. The word existed in your time, but it was not bandied about so often, nor did people bow down to it so much.

Yursky's speech exasperated his audience and was immediately rebuffed. Another pupil of Tovstonogov's, Kama Ginkas, who has never attended large theatrical gatherings, ascribed the familiar attacks on directorial bossiness to our age-old malady. In his view, former Soviet citizens were still not free, still felt humiliated, and were defending their freedom against all comers. The people who invented the Art Theatre, Ginkas maintained, invented a system that prevented the actor from doing whatever he fancied on the stage, and made him bring his freedom into alignment with the wills of other artists who possessed equal rights to him. The creators of MKhT instilled in us the idea of freedom within a definite pattern, style, design, where everyone plays within definite limits and derives pleasure from the very laws of acting.

Conclusion

For Lev Dodin there was a mystery at the heart of the 'Artistic Theatre Open to All', as MKhT was first called. Dodin acknowledged the power of Stanislavsky's and Nemirovich-Danchenko's invention and endeavoured to comprehend the sources of it. He spoke of the fantastic power of idealism which in MKhT's best years was combined with an amazingly down-to-earth, businesslike attitude:

> This combination of extreme level-headedness and extreme idealism was the mighty engine produced by the nineteenth century and bequeathed to the twentieth. Our century distorted and betrayed idealism, not just theatrically but in universal human terms. It was distorted idealism that produced such cancers as communism and fascism, whilst level-headedness has degenerated into rationalism, materialism and the crude capitalization of art.

The founders' message, he said, had in many ways not been understood. Hence the survival (in Stanislavsky's name) of 'lifelike' theatre, and the fatal split between high culture and the avant-garde, which in the early MKhT coexisted productively. Dodin continued: 'I have been brought here by a yearning for all that was not achieved, that was modified, that was blown up.' Dodin did not sit in one of the museum armchairs. He offered them to the directors of another generation who still had to hold a really new Slavyansky Bazar, that is, not only in memory of the past one, but in order to start a new century which might change something, because the present one was colossally depressing and disillusioning. 'But, of course, nothing lasts for ever and even if you feel depressed, you also want to feel hope.'

Anatoly Vasilyev spoke about the same idealistic premises of the Russian theatrical idea, although *spoke* is not the word. He read the runes, he played the shaman, he made a public confession. He recalled those who had taught him, and in the slow, solemn enunciation of their names – from Mariya Knebel, Yury Lyubimov and Anatoly Efros to Oleg Yefremov and Jerzy Grotowski – there was something almost ritualistic. As Vasilyev sees it, the path of the Russian actor and the Russian theatre is one of sublime play, celebration and sacrifice. He did not elaborate on what he meant by *sacrifice*. He did not need to for this audience.

Vasilyev's sermon will go down in the history of the Russian stage, as will the immediate rebuke to him delivered in Pyotr Fomenko's confused, passionate and unpredictable speech. For Fomenko, theatre is least of all profundity of thought, or sacrifice, or crucifixion. He longs for 'light breathing', as Bunin called his famous short story; for a secret that does not have to be shrouded in mystery. For Fomenko, the experience of MKhT is also the experience of a tragic defeat, of a loss of faith, the loss of that very 'light breathing' without which the stage cannot live. The people who created the ideal theatre ended up not speaking to each other and would use any excuse not to see each other. This too should be remembered by anyone starting a life in the theatre. Fomenko believes in those who are just starting; he is keen to give his blessing to those breathing down his neck. He has heard their voices and seen their faces, which we as yet have not (neither at the 'Bazar' nor in this book).

It was my task to steward this marathon. Next to me sat Oleg Yefremov, who had fired the starting pistol. You should have seen the tenseness of the man who has managed the home called MKhAT for twenty-seven years – his reaction to every word uttered, to every gesture made by those who came on to address the armchairs! Each director was invited to sit down and say something to the founding fathers, but they all stood. Some delivered dithyrambs that merged into toasts, but most laughed things off nervously. And when it was all over, for some reason I remembered how Stanislavsky had once attempted after the Revolution to summarize in a few words the art of the theatre that he would like to be engaged in. He used four: 'lighter, higher, simpler, happier'.

He might have said the same at today's Slavyansky Bazar, three years before the close of the twentieth century.

Notes

FOREWORD

1 Vladislav Ivanov, 'Ot sostavitelya' (Foreword), *Mnemozina: dokumenty i fakty iz istorii russkogo teatra XX veka* (Mnemosyne: documents and facts from the history of the Russian theatre in the twentieth century) (Moscow: GITIS, 1996), pp. 4–5.
2 The altered photograph can be seen in *Anton Pavlovich Chekhov v teatre* (Anton Pavlovich Chekhov in the theatre) (Moscow: Iskusstvo, 1955), p. 26 and in almost every work on the Moscow Art Theatre published between 1940 and 1960. The ornamental chair in which Meyerhold was sitting was also removed, so that the actor in front of him, seated on a pouf, is suddenly promoted to a chair, its back filling the now available space.

PREFACE

1 'Energy of self-delusion' is a phrase of Lev Tolstoy's.
2 See, for example, Harold B. Segel's valuable book *Twentieth-Century Russian Drama from Gorky to the Present* (Baltimore: Johns Hopkins University Press, 1993). This is full of vital information about Russian plays, including those of the 1970s and 1980s, but for obvious reasons the author was not able to interpret the drama as part of a much wider and more complex process called the history of the Russian stage.
3 Between the fifties and the eighties plays in the USSR came about not so much through a theatre commissioning them as by agreement with special editorial boards dealing with repertoire, which were part of the Ministry of Culture of every Soviet republic. These boards sent the plays to Glavlit, that is, the censorship. Neither the theatre nor the playwright had any direct contact with Glavlit's board of censors. From the author's and the theatre's point of view the main 'censors' were the officials of the editorial/repertoire boards. The repertoire of all the theatres in the RSFSR was approved at so-called repertoire conferences held once a year, usually in the autumn. Plays were subject to double censorship in that approval was needed to publish them and special approval to perform them.

1 THE THAW (1953–1968)

1 Naum Berkovsky, *Literatura i teatr* (Literature and theatre) (Moscow: Iskusstvo, 1965), p. 538.

2 This term was introduced during the run-up to the First Congress of Soviet Writers in 1934. In his opening speech to the Congress, Zhdanov, the secretary of the Communist Party Central Committee, said that life must be depicted in its 'revolutionary development'. For decades this formula dictated the subject matter and methods of art in Russia.

3 V. Yerofeyev, 'Pominki po sovetskoy literature' (A funeral wake for Soviet literature), *Literaturnaya gazeta*, 4 July 1990.

4 See Mikhail Yampolsky, 'In the shadow of monuments: notes on iconoclasm and time', in Nancy Condee, ed., *Soviet Hieroglyphics: Visual Culture in Late Twentieth-Century Russia* (Bloomington: Indiana University Press, 1995), pp. 93–113.

5 When Brecht visited Moscow in 1955 he saw Mayakovsky's *The Bathhouse* at the Satire Theatre and was greatly impressed by the standard of the acting and the fact that there were 'alienation effects everywhere' (Bertolt Brecht, *Journals 1934–1955* (New York: Routledge, 1995), p. 460).

6 For an examination of the relationship between Shakespeare's *Hamlet* and Soviet culture after Stalin, see Maya Turovskaya, 'Gamlet i my' (Hamlet and us) in her *Pamyati tekushchego mgnoveniya* (In memory of the present moment) (Moscow: Sovetsky pisatel, 1987), pp. 8–32.

7 Iosif Yuzovsky, 'Gamlet i drugiye' (Hamlet and other people), *Teatr* 2 (1956), p. 145.

8 Boris Pasternak, 'Zamechaniya k perevodam iz Shekspira' (Notes on some translations of Shakespeare), in Boris Pasternak, *Izbrannoye v dvukh tomakh* (Selected works in two volumes) (Moscow: Khudozhestvennaya literatura, 1985), vol. II, p. 309.

9 *Ibid.*, p. 321.

10 Rozov said this in a programme about the Sovremennik theatre on Channel 2 of Russian television on 7 January 1996.

11 From Aleksandr Tvardovsky's poem 'Za dalyu dal' (On and On). Tvardovsky was destined to play a special part in the post-Stalin period of Russian literature.

12 'Ottepel' (The thaw) was the title of a story by Ilya Ehrenburg published in the magazine *Znamya* 5 (1954).

13 Igor Ilinsky, *Sam o sebe* (Myself about myself) (Moscow: Iskusstvo, 1984), p. 430.

14 Innokenty Annensky, *Kniga otrazheny* (A book of reflections) (St Petersburg: Izd. br. Bashmakovykh, 1906), p. 113.

15 Boris Zingerman, 'Klassika i sovremennost' (Classics and the world today), in *V tvorcheskom sorevnovanii* (Creative competition), ed. A. N. Anastasyev *et al.* (Moscow: Iskusstvo, 1958), p. 206.

16 Naum Berkovsky, 'Dostoyevsky na stsene' (Dostoyevsky on the stage), *Teatr* 2 (1958), p. 70.

17 All conversations with Oleg Yefremov are quoted from my diary or from my book *Oleg Yefremov: teatralny portret* (Oleg Yefremov, a theatrical portrait) (Moscow: VTO, 1987), which was based on my conversations with him.

18 See Natalya Krymova, *Imena* (First-names) (Moscow: Iskusstvo, 1971), p. 52.

19 *Two Colours*, by A. Zak and I. Kuznetsov, opened in 1959.

20 I. Solovyova, *Spektakl idyot segodnya* (Playing today) (Moscow: Iskusstvo, 1966), p. 98.

21 Nikolay Pogodin's best-known plays about Lenin are *The Man with the Gun* (1937), *The Kremlin Chimes* (1943), and *The Third, Pathétique* (1956).

22 Arkady Belinkov's *Yury Tynyanov* (Moscow: Iskusstvo, 1965), second edition, was one of the most exciting books passed by the censor in those years. He emigrated to the United States in the 1970s.

23 *Novy mir* was the leading literary magazine of the sixties. It was edited from 1960 to 1970 by Aleksandr Tvardovsky (1910–71) and it first published Solzhenitsyn's *A Day in the Life of Ivan Denisovich* (1962).

24 Described by Yury Trifonov in *Teatr* 9 (1977), pp. 52–3.

25 Yu. Yuzovsky. 'Na spektaklyakh "Berlinskogo ansamblya"' (At the Berliner Ensemble's performances), *Teatr* 8 (1957), p. 154.

26 Krymova, *Imena*, pp. 145–6.

27 V. Turbin, 'Ot nakhodok k otkrytiyam!' (Move from finding to discovering!), *Molodaya gvardiya* 5 (1964), p. 287.

28 Yury Lyubimov, production interview, 1963.

29 Konstantin Simonov, *Pravda*, 8 December 1963.

30 G. Smekhova, *Teatr na Taganke: 68-y i drugiye gody* (The Taganka Theatre: 1968 and other years) (Moscow: Ogonyok, 1991), pp. 25–6.

31 Conversation between myself and Yury Lyubimov broadcast on Channel 2 of Russian television, May 1989.

32 Tovstonogov's main articles are republished in his *Zerkalo stseny* (The mirror of the stage), 2 vols. (Leningrad: Iskusstvo, 1980). Shorthand records of his rehearsals are contained in Georgy Tovstonogov, *Besedy s kollegami* (Chats with colleagues) (Moscow: VTO, 1989).

33 Konstantin Rudnitsky, 'O rezhissyorskom iskusstve Tovstonogova' (Tovstonogov's art as a director), in Tovstonogov, *Zerkalo*, vol. I, p. 19.

34 The Gorky Bolshoy Drama Theatre was set up in February 1919 under the aegis of Aleksandr Blok and Maksim Gorky, who intended it to be a bastion of the heroic repertoire – of 'great tears and great laughter' (Blok).

35 V. I. Nemirovich-Danchenko, *Izbrannyye pisma* (Selected letters), 2 vols. (Moscow: Iskusstvo, 1979), vol. I, pp. 360–70.

36 B. Alpers, *Teatralnyye ocherki* (Theatrical sketches), 2 vols. (Moscow: Iskusstvo, 1977), vol. II, p. 434.

37 Efros's books *Repetitsiya – lyubov moya* (A love of rehearsals), *Professiya – rezhissyor* (Profession: director), and *Prodolzheniye teatralnogo rasskaza* (A theatrical tale continued) were republished in a four-volume edition by Panas (Moscow) in 1993. This also contains the posthumous *Kniga chetvyortaya* (Book four) assembled from his diaries and notebooks.

38 Efros staged Arbuzov's plays *Tales of Old Arbat*, *The Promise*, *The Happy Days of an Unhappy Man* and *A Memory*.

39 Anatoly Efros, 'Bedny Stanislavsky!' (Poor Stanislavsky!), *Teatr* 10 (1956), pp. 62–8.

40 Anatoly Efros, 'Kak bystro idyot vremya!' (How time flies!), *Teatr* 2 (1967), p. 68.

41 Mikhail Bulgakov wrote *Molière* (first entitled *The Cabal of Hypocrites*) in 1929. The play was rehearsed for five years, by amongst others

Stanislavsky. In 1935 Bulgakov and Stanislavsky disagreed about the interpretation and Nemirovich-Danchenko took over. The production opened on 5 February 1936 and was soon closed. Bulgakov, who had a job at MKhT, was forced to leave, and died in 1940. Efros was the first to stage *Molière* since the author's death. See Anatoly Smeliansky, *Is Comrade Bulgakov Dead? Mikhail Bulgakov at the Moscow Art Theatre* (London: Methuen, 1993), pp. 209–65.

42 Aleksandr Asarkan, 'Bulgakov. Molyer. 1966' (Bulgakov. Molière. 1966), *Teatralnaya zhizn* 24 (1988), p. 9.

43 Vadim Gayevsky, 'Priglasheniye k valsu' (Invitation to a waltz), in *Fleyta Gamleta* (Hamlet's recorder) (Moscow: Soyuzteatr, 1990), p. 54.

2 THE FROSTS (1968–1985)

1 From a conversation between Oleg Yefremov and Mikhail Shvydkoy, *Teatr* 10 (1983), pp. 110–28.

2 MKhAT's 'second generation' is the group of actors who joined it in 1924 immediately before the 'first group' returned from their American tour (1922–4). Basically they were from MKhAT's second studio.

3 Gelman's only play in this period was *Misha's Party*, about the August 1991 coup. However, this was written with American playwright Richard Nelson.

4 A. P. Chekhov, *Polnoye sobraniye sochineny i pisem v tridtsati tomakh* (Complete collected works in thirty volumes), vol. v, *Pisma* (Letters) (Moscow: Nauka, 1977), p. 133.

5 *Ibid.*, p. 134.

6 After a play had been passed for performance, the performance itself had to be 'accepted' by the censorship, since the authorities were well aware of the difference between a literary text and a theatre text. The people appointed to 'accept' MKhAT's productions were usually officials from the Ministry of Culture of the USSR and representatives of the Cultural Department of the Central Committee. The acceptance ceremony was shrouded in secrecy: the officials sat alone in the auditorium, and not even the actors' friends and relatives were allowed in.

7 Wagner, whose music featured several times in the production, was also suspect. Some kind soul told the authorities that Wagner was Hitler's favourite composer and MKhAT was suggesting a similarity between the two leaders.

8 For an account of Yefremov's Chekhov productions 1976–85 see Oleg Yefremov, 'A path to Chekhov', in Patrick Miles, ed., *Chekhov on the British Stage* (Cambridge: Cambridge University Press, 1993), pp. 126–35.

9 Sergey Eisenstein first proposed this term in an article in *Lef* 5 (1923). His idea was to get away from traditional play composition by using a 'montage' of frontal effects ('attractions'), including circus turns, placards and forms of light entertainment.

10 The production used three stories by Fyodor Abramov: *Wooden Horses*, *Pelageya* and *Alka*.

11 N. Potapov, 'Seans chorny magii na Taganke' (A black magic show at the Taganka), *Pravda*, 29 May 1977.

12 The idea of playing a 'whole author' originated with Meyerhold and was particularly strongly advocated by him at the time of his production of *The Government Inspector* (1926).

13 This lyrical theme from *Dead Souls* was heard throughout *Revizskaya skazka*.

14 N. V. Gogol, 'Vybrannyye mesta iz perepiski s druzyami' (Selected passages from correspondence with friends), in *Polnoye sobraniye sochineniy* (Complete collected works), vol. VIII (Leningrad: Izdatelstvo AN SSSR, 1952), p. 416.

15 Yury Karyakin, *Samoobman Raskolnikova: roman F. M. Dostoyevskogo 'Prestupleniye i nakazaniye'* (Raskolnikov's self-deception: Dostoyevsky's novel 'Crime and Punishment') (Moscow: Khudozhestvennaya literatura, 1976), pp. 158.

16 'The ears stick out' was a phrase used by Pushkin in a letter about *Boris Godunov* and the allusions it contains.

17 The scene in which Boris takes monastic vows was staged by Lyubimov with a liturgical simplicity and solemnity. This religious sacrament, with its induction into a different understanding of things, took the production beyond the 'theatre of allusions' that the Taganka had cultivated for so many years.

18 If we are to believe Lyubimov, his faith in Andropov derived from his once having advised Andropov's son against becoming an actor. Andropov junior became a diplomat and according to Lyubimov a grateful Andropov appointed himself the Taganka's unofficial patron.

19 During rehearsals I asked Efros: 'What about Lyubimov?' Efros answered: 'He's saying nothing. He sometimes looks in, but leaves very quickly. I understand. For him I'm an outsider coming into his home and messing around with his actors.'

20 In two seasons Efros staged Gorky's *Lower Depths*, Svetlana Alekseyevich's *War Has No Woman's Face*, Boris Mozhayev's *One Point Five Square Metres*, and Molière's *The Misanthrope*.

21 See *Sovetskaya kultura*, May 1972, p. 3.

22 N. Lordkipanidze, *Nedelya*, 28 May 1972.

23 *Sovetskaya kultura*, May 1972, p. 3.

24 Merezhkovsky's book was first published in 1906 and had a massive influence on how Gogol was interpreted in twentieth-century Russian art.

25 Yury Zubkov, 'Vysota kriteriyev' (Having high standards), *Pravda*, 15 August 1972.

26 Michael Chekhov acted Khlestakov in the 1921 MKhAT production directed by Stanislavsky. Dozens of books and articles have been written about his legendary performance. The best description is in Mariya Knebel, *Vsya zhizn* (The whole of life) (Moscow: VTO, 1967), pp. 51–139.

27 *Literaturnaya gazeta*, 19 September 1973.

28 A controversy was going on at the time over whether children should be taught 'classical' languages in school.

29 Inna Solovyova, *Nedelya*, 22–8 October 1973.

30 Tovstonogov's most important productions after *The Story of a Horse* were: Gorky's *Summerfolk* (1976), *Uncle Vanya* (1982), Ostrovsky's *Too Clever by Half* (1985), and Gorky's *Lower Depths* (1987). In 1983 he directed an opera-farce based on Sukhovo-Kobylin's *Tarelkin's Death*.

31 At that time I had a monthly theatre programme on Russian television's Channel 1 and in February 1983 I showed on it a few scenes from *Tarelkin's Death*. Immediately after transmission, the programme was axed. The reason became clear later, when *Andropov's* death was officially announced.

32 Stanislavsky, a believing Christian all his life, was buried in the Novo-Devichy monastery graveyard, but in 1938 it was not possible to erect a cross on his grave. This was done by the Moscow Art Theatre in 1994.

3 THE BLACK BOX (1985–1997)

1 Yury Burtin's term in *Literaturnaya gazeta*, 25 June 1997.

2 The title of Stanislav Govorukhin's film about Russia today.

3 *Batum* was commissioned from Bulgakov by MKhAT for Stalin's sixtieth birthday. For reasons that are still not entirely clear, it was immediately proscribed. See Smeliansky, *Is Comrade Bulgakov Dead?*, pp. 294–314.

4 After returning from his forced emigration, Lyubimov revived *Boris Godunov*, his production about Vysotsky, and *Alive* by Boris Mozhayev. As well as Erdman's play, he has directed Pushkin's *Little Tragedies*, Pasternak's *Doctor Zhivago*, *Electra*, *Medea*, and Dostoyevsky's *The Adolescent* (1996).

5 'The New Russians' was originally the title of a column in the newspaper *Kommersant*, but it is now universal. It is used mainly ironically to describe Russia's *nouveaux riches*.

6 K. S. Stanislavsky, *Sobraniye sochineny v vosmi tomakh* (Collected works in eight volumes) (Moscow: Iskusstvo, 1961), vol. VIII, p. 41.

7 Lyudmila Petrushevskaya, 'Tri li sestry?' (Just three sisters?), *Kommersant Daily*, 25 February 1997.

8 The main reason for this was that the theatre's principal actors also performed in a long-running television show, which brought them and the theatre's productions enormous popularity.

9 For a detailed description of the ideas behind *A Profitable Position* see Mark Zakharov's book *Kontakty na raznykh urovnyakh* (Contacts at various levels) (Moscow: Iskusstvo, 1988).

10 Roman Timenchik, 'Ty – chto? Ili vvedeniye v teatr Petrushevskoy' (Wha'dye mean? Or an introduction to Petrushevskaya's theatre), in L. Petrushevskaya, *Tri devushki v golubom* (Three girls in blue) (Moscow: Iskusstvo, 1989), p. 345.

11 Zakharov's first and most sensational article, entitled 'Applause can't be shared out', appeared in *Literaturnaya gazeta*, 31 July 1985.

12 In October 1986 the All-Russian Theatre Society became the Russian Union of Theatre Workers and in December of the same year the Union of Theatre Workers of the USSR was founded.

13 B. Lyubimov, 'Kak dobitsya krasivoy zhizni mirnym putyom' (How to acquire a fine lifestyle by peaceful means), *Argumenty i fakty* 4 (1993), p. 12.

14 Mark Zakharov, 'Vizit k prezidentu' (A visit to the President), *Izvestiya*, 22 April 1992.

15 Oleg Moroz, *Literaturnaya gazeta*, 7 May 1992.

16 These words were too reminiscent of the expression 'as simple as truth' in Gorky's famous sketch of Lenin.
17 Oleg Moroz, *Literaturnaya gazeta*, 7 May 1992.
18 Mark Zakharov, 'Spasibo publitsistu' (Thank you to a journalist), *Literaturnaya gazeta*, 13 May 1992.
19 Irina Glushenko, 'Zhivoye i myortvoye. Kama Ginkas priglashayet na kazn' (Alive and dead. Kama Ginkas invites us to an execution), *Nezavisimaya gazeta*, 17 January 1996.
20 *Ibid.*
21 The shorthand record of the meeting in MKhT on 31 December 1917 is preserved in MKhAT's museum.
22 In the mid–1930s Boris Zon attended Stanislavsky's classes at his opera/theatre studio and kept shorthand accounts of them, which he worked into an extremely interesting article called 'Encounters with Stanislavsky' published in *Teatralnoye nasledstvo. K. S. Stanislavsky. Materialy. Pisma. Issledovaniya* (The theatrical heritage. K. S. Stanislavsky. Documents. Letters. Research) (Moscow: Akademiya nauk, 1955).
23 Natalya Krymova, 'Golovlyovskiye prokazniki' (Golovlyov pranksters), *Literaturnaya gazeta*, 4 July 1984.
24 Natalya Krymova, 'Ochen razny MDT. Zametki o moskovskikh gastrolyakh Malogo dramaticheskogo' (A very different MDT. Comments on the Maly Drama's Moscow visit), *Nevskoye vremya*, 13 January 1996.
25 Dodin's fiercest opponent is Marina Dmitriyevskaya, who seems to have staked her critical reputation on 'exposing' the 'deception' foisted on the world by Dodin's company. Her main anti-Dodin articles have been published in *Peterburgsky teatralny zhurnal*, which was founded by her in 1992.
26 This phrase was first used by Stanislav Rassadin to describe the writing of Vladimir Sorokin, one of the leaders of the 'new wave' in Russian literature: see *Vek* 1 (1995), p. 3.
27 Lev Anninsky, 'Na voyne kak na voyne' (War is war), *Ekran i stsena* 46 (1995), p. 3.
28 Yevgeny Lazarev, 'Besovskoye deystviye' (Devilry), *Moskovsky nablyudatel* 3 (1991), pp. 9–10.

CONCLUSION

1 All unsourced extracts from speeches at the 'Slavyansky Bazar' are taken from a tape recording of the proceedings made by the Moscow Art Theatre.
2 Yursky was referring to the advertising for *The Threepenny Opera* at the Satirikon Theatre, which claimed that (contrary to its title!) it was the most 'expensive' show in Moscow's 1996/7 season.

Index

Index

Index

Index

Index

Index

Index